Lecture Notes in Computer Science

Vol. 270: E. Börger (Ed.), Computation Theory and Logic. IX, 442 pages. 1987.

Vol. 271: D. Snyers, A. Thayse, From Logic Design to Logic Programming. IV, 125 pages. 1987.

Vol. 272: P. Treleaven, M. Vanneschi (Eds.), Future Parallel Computers. Proceedings, 1986. V, 492 pages. 1987.

Vol. 273: J.S. Royer, A Connotational Theory of Program Structure. V, 186 pages. 1987.

Vol. 274: G. Kahn (Ed.), Functional Programming Languages and Computer Architecture. Proceedings. VI, 470 pages. 1987.

Vol. 275: A.N. Habermann, U. Montanari (Eds.), System Development and Ada. Proceedings, 1986. V, 305 pages. 1987.

Vol. 276: J. Bézivin, J.-M. Hullot, P. Cointe, H. Lieberman (Eds.), ECOOP '87. European Conference on Object-Oriented Programming. Proceedings. VI, 273 pages. 1987.

Vol. 277: B. Benninghofen, S. Kemmerich, M.M. Richter, Systems of Reductions. X, 265 pages. 1987.

Vol. 278: L. Budach, R.G. Bukharajev, O.B. Lupanov (Eds.), Fundamentals of Computation Theory. Proceedings, 1987. XIV, 505 pages. 1987.

Vol. 279: J.H. Fasel, R.M. Keller (Eds.), Graph Reduction. Proceedings, 1986. XVI, 450 pages. 1987.

Vol. 280: M. Venturini Zilli (Ed.), Mathematical Models for the Semantics of Parallelism. Proceedings, 1986. V, 231 pages. 1987.

Vol. 281: A. Kelemenová, J. Kelemen (Eds.), Trends, Techniques, and Problems in Theoretical Computer Science. Proceedings, 1986. VI, 213 pages. 1987.

Vol. 282: P. Gorny, M.J. Tauber (Eds.), Visualization in Programming. Proceedings, 1986. VII, 210 pages. 1987.

Vol. 283: D.H. Pitt, A. Poigné, D.E. Rydeheard (Eds.), Category Theory and Computer Science. Proceedings, 1987. V, 300 pages. 1987.

Vol. 284: A. Kündig, R.E. Bührer, J. Dähler (Eds.), Embedded Systems. Proceedings, 1986. V, 207 pages. 1987.

Vol. 285: C. Delgado Kloos, Semantics of Digital Circuits. IX, 124 pages. 1987.

Vol. 286: B. Bouchon, R.R. Yager (Eds.), Uncertainty in Knowledge-Based Systems. Proceedings, 1986. VII, 405 pages. 1987.

Vol. 287: K.V. Nori (Ed.), Foundations of Software Technology and Theoretical Computer Science. Proceedings, 1987. IX, 540 pages. 1987.

Vol. 288: A. Blikle, MetaSoft Primer. XIII, 140 pages. 1987.

Vol. 289: H.K. Nichols, D. Simpson (Eds.), ESEC '87. 1st European Software Engineering Conference. Proceedings, 1987. XII, 404 pages. 1987.

Vol. 290: T.X. Bui, Co-oP A Group Decision Support System for Cooperative Multiple Criteria Group Decision Making. XIII, 250 pages. 1987.

Vol. 291: H. Ehrig, M. Nagl, G. Rozenberg, A. Rosenfeld (Eds.), Graph-Grammars and Their Application to Computer Science. VIII, 609 pages. 1987.

Vol. 292: The Munich Project CIP. Volume II: The Program Transformation System CIP-S. By the CIP System Group. VIII, 522 pages. 1987.

Vol. 293: C. Pomerance (Ed.), Advances in Cryptology — CRYPTO '87. Proceedings. X, 463 pages. 1988.

Vol. 294: R. Cori, M. Wirsing (Eds.), STACS 88. Proceedings, 1988. IX, 404 pages. 1988.

Vol. 295: R. Dierstein, D. Müller-Wichards, H.-M. Wacker (Eds.), Parallel Computing in Science and Engineering. Proceedings, 1987. V, 185 pages. 1988.

Vol. 296: R. Janßen (Ed.), Trends in Computer Algebra. Proceedings, 1987. V, 197 pages. 1988.

Vol. 297: E.N. Houstis, T.S. Papatheodorou, C.D. Polychronopoulos (Eds.), Supercomputing. Proceedings, 1987. X, 1093 pages. 1988.

Vol. 298: M. Main, A. Melton, M. Mislove, D. Schmidt (Eds.), Mathematical Foundations of Programming Language Semantics. Proceedings, 1987. VIII, 637 pages. 1988.

Vol. 299: M. Dauchet, M. Nivat (Eds.), CAAP '88. Proceedings, 1988. VI, 304 pages. 1988.

Vol. 300: H. Ganzinger (Ed.), ESOP '88. Proceedings, 1988. VI, 381 pages. 1988.

Vol. 301: J. Kittler (Ed.), Pattern Recognition. Proceedings, 1988. VII, 668 pages. 1988.

Vol. 302: D.M. Yellin, Attribute Grammar Inversion and Source-to-source Translation. VIII, 176 pages. 1988.

Vol. 303: J.W. Schmidt, S. Ceri, M. Missikoff (Eds.), Advances in Database Technology – EDBT '88. X, 620 pages. 1988.

Vol. 304: W.L. Price, D. Chaum (Eds.), Advances in Cryptology – EUROCRYPT '87. Proceedings, 1987. VII, 314 pages. 1988.

Vol. 305: J. Biskup, J. Demetrovics, J. Paredaens, B. Thalheim (Eds.), MFDBS 87. Proceedings, 1987. V, 247 pages. 1988.

Vol. 306: M. Boscarol, L. Carlucci Aiello, G. Levi (Eds.), Foundations of Logic and Functional Programming. Proceedings, 1986. V, 218 pages. 1988.

Vol. 307: Th. Beth, M. Clausen (Eds.), Applicable Algebra, Error-Correcting Codes, Combinatorics and Computer Algebra. Proceedings, 1986. VI, 215 pages. 1988.

Vol. 308: S. Kaplan, J.-P. Jouannaud (Eds.), Conditional Term Rewriting Systems. Proceedings, 1987. VI, 278 pages. 1988.

Vol. 309: J. Nehmer (Ed.), Experiences with Distributed Systems. Proceedings, 1987. VI, 292 pages. 1988.

Vol. 310: E. Lusk, R. Overbeek (Eds.), 9th International Conference on Automated Deduction. Proceedings, 1988. X, 775 pages. 1988.

Vol. 311: G. Cohen, P. Godlewski (Eds.), Coding Theory and Applications 1986. Proceedings, 1986. XIV, 196 pages. 1988.

Vol. 312: J. van Leeuwen (Ed.), Distributed Algorithms 1987. Proceedings, 1987. VII, 430 pages. 1988.

Vol. 313: B. Bouchon, L. Saitta, R.R. Yager (Eds.), Uncertainty and Intelligent Systems. IPMU '88. Proceedings, 1988. VIII, 408 pages. 1988.

Vol. 314: H. Göttler, H.J. Schneider (Eds.), Graph-Theoretic Concepts in Computer Science. Proceedings, 1987. VI, 254 pages. 1988.

Vol. 315: K. Furukawa, H. Tanaka, T. Fujisaki (Eds.), Logic Programming '87. Proceedings, 1987. VI, 327 pages. 1988.

Vol. 316: C. Choffrut (Ed.), Automata Networks. Proceedings, 1986. VII, 125 pages. 1988.

Vol. 317: T. Lepistö, A. Salomaa (Eds.), Automata, Languages and Programming. Proceedings, 1988. XI, 741 pages. 1988.

Vol. 318: R. Karlsson, A. Lingas (Eds.), SWAT 88. Proceedings, 1988. VI, 262 pages. 1988.

Vol. 319: J.H. Reif (Ed.), VLSI Algorithms and Architectures – AWOC 88. Proceedings, 1988. X, 476 pages. 1988.

Vol. 320: A. Blaser (Ed.), Natural Language at the Computer. Proceedings, 1988. III, 176 pages. 1988.

Vol. 321: J. Zwiers, Compositionality, Concurrency and Partial Correctness. VI, 272 pages. 1989.

Vol. 322: S. Gjessing, K. Nygaard (Eds.), ECOOP '88. European Conference on Object-Oriented Programming. Proceedings, 1988. VI, 410 pages. 1988.

Vol. 323: P. Deransart, M. Jourdan, B. Lorho, Attribute Grammars. IX, 232 pages. 1988.

Lecture Notes in Computer Science

Edited by G. Goos and J. Hartmanis

376

Norman E. Gibbs (Ed.)

Software Engineering Education

SEI Conference 1989
Pittsburgh, Pennsylvania, USA, July 18–21, 1989
Proceedings

Springer-Verlag

Berlin Heidelberg New York London Paris Tokyo Hong Kong

Carnegie-Mellon University
Software Engineering Institute

CR Subject Classification (1987): D.2, K.3.2

ISBN 0-387-97090-8 Springer-Verlag New York Berlin Heidelberg
ISBN 3-540-97090-8 Springer-Verlag Berlin Heidelberg New York

Printing and binding: Druckhaus Beltz, Hemsbach/Bergstr.
2145/3140-543210 – Printed on acid-free paper

Preface

These proceedings are a record of two events held in Pittsburgh, Pennsylvania as part of the SEI Software Engineering Education and Training Week July 18–21, 1989. The first section includes the refereed papers presented at the *Third SEI Conference on Software Engineering Education* and the SEI Education Program's annual revised report on Master of Software Engineering curriculum recommendations. The second part contains unrefereed position papers submitted by participants in the *SEI Workshop on an Undergraduate Software Engineering Curriculum.*

The Software Engineering Institute (SEI) is a federally funded research and development center sponsored by the United States Department of Defense and operated by Carnegie Mellon University. Part of its mission is to increase the supply of qualified software engineers. The SEI Education Program addresses this need by encouraging the establishment of academic, industry, and government software engineering programs and by developing and promoting an infrastructure to support the exchange of information about software engineering education.

The annual *SEI Conference on Software Engineering Education*, which brings together educators from universities, industry, and government to discuss problems and issues of mutual interest, is an important part of this infrastructure. Its goals are to stimulate new educational approaches, to provide a forum for discussions of mutual problems, and to evaluate promising new ideas.

This year's conference is the third in the series. The Program Committee received more than forty papers, each of which was refereed by three or more committee members. Fifteen papers were accepted for presentation and publication in these proceedings. Five papers deal with industry issues and programs, three with teaching software maintenance, and three with undergraduate software engineering education. The remaining four address other related topics in software engineering education.

The Program Committee for the 1989 Conference included the following members:

Alan Adamson, *IBM*

Mark Ardis, *SEI*

Jon Bentley, *AT&T Bell Labs*

Daniel Berry, *Technion*

Alfs Berztiss, *University of Pittsburgh*

John Brackett, *Boston University*

Maribeth Carpenter, *SEI*

Clyde Chittister, *SEI*

Rick Cobello, *General Electric*

James Collofello, *Arizona State University*

Lionel Deimel, *SEI*

Charles Engle, *SEI*

Richard Fairley, *George Mason University*

Peter Feiler, *SEI*

Robert Firth, *SEI*

Gary Ford, *SEI*

Susan Gerhart, *MCC*

Norman Gibbs, *SEI*

Hassan Gomaa, *George Mason University*

John Goodenough, *SEI*

Harvey Hallman, *SEI*

David Lamb, *Queen's University*

John Maher, *SEI*

H. Dieter Rombach, *University of Maryland*

Rebecca Smith, *Hewlett-Packard*

Scott Stevens, *SEI*

James E. Tomayko, *The Wichita State University*

Nelson Weiderman, *SEI*

David Weiss, *SPC*

The *SEI Workshop on an Undergraduate Software Engineering Curriculum* was conducted to address a broad range of issues related to the establishment of undergraduate degree programs in software engineering. Participants were asked to submit position papers on relevant topics, such as the feasibility, desirability, or content of such programs. Twelve papers (not formally refereed) were selected for inclusion in these proceedings.

Norman E. Gibbs

Pittsburgh, Pennsylvania
April 1989

CONTENTS

SECTION I

Third SEI Conference

on

Software Engineering Education

Teaching Maintenance Using Large Software Artifacts

by

James E. Tomayko

The Wichita State University

Abstract

A method for teaching software maintenance at the graduate level using software artifacts is described. Objectives, the syllabus, and assignments are included in annotated form. A discussion of the actual events and lessons learned in a prototype course is presented.

Anyone who tries to teach the principles of software engineering without using realistic examples is doing students a disservice. The nature of large scale software development is such that merely talking about it does little good, even in graduate level courses. Software maintenance is a topic that suffers greatly if taught from a theoretical standpoint, both because there simply is no theory in the classic sense, and because the remainder of the typical curriculum in computer science or software engineering often gives the subject short shrift, despite its importance. Maintenance courses have to make up for the lack of specific background of the students, even those who have had actual experience. As systems become larger and more complex, their maintenance can not be left to ad hoc methods. Therefore, courses in software maintenance and evolution should have a significant laboratory component, both to introduce first principles and to cure bad habits.

Given the need for lab work, it is necessary to use large software artifacts in order to achieve the proper level of complexity. Two such artifacts are presently available from the Software Engineering Institute. One is documented in **Ford89**, the other is discussed below. Others were available to the author as products of project courses on software development. Two of these were used in a series of graduated exercises that were the core of a software maintenance graduate course taught in the spring of 1989 at The Wichita State University. This paper explains the objectives of the course, its structure, exercises, and the results of using the artifacts to teach the material desired.

Course Objectives

The course objectives are designed to prepare students to deal with the worst case: undocumented code inherited by them in an unprepared maintenance environment. For simplicity, the terminology presented in **Arthur88**, the textbook chosen for the course, is used both in the objectives and the syllabus. The meaning of this terminology is apparent in context.

<u>Behavioral Objectives:</u>

At the conclusion of the course, the student shall:

Be able to prepare undocumented code for maintenance activity by:

Establishing configuration control

Reverse engineering needed documentation

Gaining an understanding of the design of the software

Development of a foundation test suite

Be able to evaluate the impact of change in terms of:

Cost

Time required for implementation, and

Risk

Be able to perform corrective maintenance, including:

Development and testing of hypothetical solutions, and

Regression testing

Be able to perform adaptive maintenance, including:

Documentation changes

Implementation, and

Integration and regression testing

Be able to perform perfective maintenance, including:

Analysis of quality factors

Evaluation of improvements

Implementation and regression testing

It can be seen from the list of sub-objectives that the themes of configuration control and quality assurance are repeated as goals within each type of maintenance activity. One potential criticism of this list of objectives is that the topic of the proper design and production of code in order to enhance maintainability is not explicitly expressed. The reason for this is that the Wichita State undergraduate and graduate computer science and software engineering curriculum places significant emphasis on this point when design and implementation are taught. Within this course, the topic is reviewed when discussing perfective maintenance, as that is where enhancing the maintainability of existing code is presented.

Software Maintenance Project Activities:

The project activities used to achieve these objectives include the use of well-documented and poorly-documented artifacts. Well-documented artifacts in supposedly working condition are scheduled for early exercises in the course so that the principles of configuration management and the build process can be taught without undue distraction from non-functioning code. After these foundation activities, non-working code is used to teach reverse engineering of designs and to reinforce corrective maintenance procedures. The well-documented artifact is the AIM (APSE Interactive Monitor), a windowing system first developed by Texas Instruments and distributed by the SEI for university use. The non-working artifact is the Ares system, a simulation program that assists in activity planning for long-duration missions on the surface of Mars. It was developed as a project in an undergraduate software engineering course and described in **Tomayko87**. Even though at first glance it is a working program, it has several subtle bugs that have arisen in use. By withholding the existing documentation, save for the user manual, the internal structure of the system becomes much more difficult to understand.

The activities included:

I. With the AIM Installation and Maintenance Guide as the only hard
copy documentation, and the distribution tape, the students shall install
AIM, determine which items shall be under configuration control, place those
items under configuration control (including on-line documentation), and
establish a foundation test suite including some tests not on the
distribution tape.

II. If the installation of AIM results in errors, then they shall be
corrected to achieve these objectives, otherwise the instructor shall
introduce a series of bugs as exercises.

III. The students shall recommend enhancements to AIM, which shall be
evaluated and at least one implemented.

IV. The students shall recommend segments of AIM for quality
improvements, which shall be evaluated and at least one implemented.

V. The Ares system shall be installed and corrected, as in I. above.

Course Syllabus

The syllabus used to implement the specified activities and achieve the objectives is reproduced in annotated form here. The actual dates were left in to show the balance of time in a real instantiation of the course. Note that a key element of the time allocation is that significant periods are set aside for in-class meetings of the maintenance teams and project work. This reflects not only the emphasis in the course, but the fact that all the students are working full time as software engineers, and this is the only guaranteed meeting time available for the teams. The references are annotated in the bibliography. Following the syllabus is a description, due dates included, of the actual project assignments, which can then be mapped against the activities of the class meetings to give a two-dimensional perspective on the course.

Software Evolution Concepts

This segment of the course is used to establish the place of maintenance in the life cycle of software, review its importance to cost reduction and quality, and present some of the inherent difficulties in the field.

17 Jan.: Introduction to Software Evolution and the course

19 Jan.: Issues in Software Maintenance **[Lientz83]**

24 Jan.: Software Maintenance in the Life Cycle **[Arthur, Ch.1; Lehman80]**

Porting Well-Documented Software

This segment uses the AIM artifact to illustrate the use of configuration mangement and establishing a build process.

26 Jan.: Accepting a System Release **[Arthur, Ch. 10; AIM Installation Guide]**

31 Jan.: Discussion of Configuration Management for AIM

This class period is used to identify the configuration items of the AIM artifact, and to discuss the contents of the configuration management plan that the students will prepare.

2 Feb.: Metrics for Maintenance Management **[Schaefer85]**

Corrective Maintenance

First the principles of change management are presented, then the students create their own plan for change control and the principles are applied.

7 Feb.: Change Management **[Arthur, Ch. 2]**

9 Feb.: Impact Analysis **[Arthur, Ch. 3]**

14 Feb.: Corrective Maintenance **[Arthur, Ch. 5]**

16-21-23 Feb.: Conduct Corrective Maintenance of AIM

Adaptive Maintenance

Adaptive maintenance is the implementation of enhancements to software when it is ported to different environments or to different user communities. Suggestions for enhancements are solicited from the students and instructor, and at least one promising suggestion is implemented.

28 Feb.: Adaptive Maintenance **[Arthur, Ch. 6]**

2 Mar.: AIM Enhancement Meeting

This class period is used to discuss the various proposals for enhancements, conduct an impact analysis, and decide which to do. The students will have prepared proposals in advance.

7 Mar.: AIM Enhancement Lab

9 Mar.: Exam One.

14-16 Mar.: Spring Break

Perfective Maintenance

Often even working software has need for improvement, plus software that has been patched numerous times may have lost its structure and comprehensibility. Perfective maintenance tries to accomplish these goals. Note that it is not aimed at adding features.

21 Mar.: Perfective Maintenance **[Arthur, Ch. 7]**

23 Mar.: Reengineering Code **[Arthur, Ch. 8]**

28 Mar.: Perfective Maintenance Meeting

This class period is used to identify candidates for perfective maintenance, conduct an impact analysis, and decide which to do.

Porting Poorly Documented Code

By this time in the course, the students know how to establish change control, have a build process in place, and know how to do the three principal types of maintenance. At this point the poorly-documented and probably failing code is introduced to enable them to practice reverse engineering of documentation, and to learn how to devise and use tests to localize problems.

30 Mar.: Software Testing in Maintenance [Arthur, Ch. 9]

4 Apr.: Design Recovery [Arango85]

6-11-13 Apr.: Design Recovery of Ares

During this period the students install, configure and test Ares. They also prepare a design document similar to one prepared as a product of the high-level design stage of original software development.

18 Apr.: Ares Design Review

20 Apr.: Ares Corrective Maintenance Meeting

25-27 Apr.: Ares Corrective Maintenance Lab

Maintenance Management Issues

The final segment addresses issues that will be important when the students take over as managers of maintainers.

2 May: Management Issues I: [Arthur, Ch. 11, 12]

4 May: Management Issues II: [Bendifallah87]

Final Exam during the exam period.

Project Assignments

The following are the project activities in this course. The first date is the date that the activity begins, the last date is the date at which it should end.

26 Jan.: Install AIM on the WSUIAR VAX, complete by 31 January.

31 Jan.: Place AIM under configuration control, prepare change control procedure and build plan, complete by 23 February.

16 Feb.: Corrective Maintenance Assignment for AIM, complete by 28 February.

28 Feb.: Write a proposal for an enhancement of AIM, due 2 March.

2 Mar.: Choose AIM enhancement and implement, complete by 21 March.

21 Mar.: Write a proposal for an improvement to AIM, due 28 March.

28 Mar.: Choose improvement to AIM, complete by 4 April.

4 Apr.: Install Ares on the USIAR VAX, complete by 11 April.

11 Apr.: Design Recovery of Ares, complete by 18 April.

18 Apr.: Diagnose Ares faults, determine corrective action, due 20 April.

20 Apr.: Decide which Ares faults will be corrected, complete by 4 May.

Reports of the work done during corrective, adaptive, and perfective maintenance contained the following information:

1. Description of the original problem, including how it was discovered, side effects, and why it was determined to change it.

2. Impact analysis: how many and which modules affected, estimated code changes, time estimates, etc.

3. Design of the change: interface changes, PDL of code to be added/deleted, imports and exports, etc.

4. Copy of code changes, showing 'before and after' versions of the changed units.

5. Copy of tests devised to specifically verify the change in question.

6. Results of regression testing.

7. Brief review of the efficacy of the change, including an analysis of how accurate the impact analysis was.

Lessons Learned Teaching the Course

As noted, the course as it is structured here was taught in the spring of 1989. Six students enrolled, all full time software engineers working at companies doing large scale data processing, embedded systems in weapons, software research, operations analysis, and special purpose software. Since their formal software engineering backgrounds were relatively even, they were divided by random lot into two groups, each of three persons. The artifacts were dumped from tape in raw form into a common directory on a VAX8650 with the VAXSet tools available for configuration management, make files, and debugging. The groups could not access each other's directories.

Both groups had to exert more effort into putting AIM under configuration control and in acceptance testing than expected. They discovered that the CMS files containing the documentation were inaccessible since they had been built using a CMS release much older than the one on their machine. This was solved by locating a 'CMS convert' utility that convinced the new CMS that the old files were readable. The teams also found sections of dead code and missing sub-documents that became candidates for perfective maintenance. The major bug in the initial installation process was that the functions assigned to special keys did not match up to the special keys on the local keyboards. Keys that might actually be needed for routine work, such as the up arrow, had bizarre AIM commands associated with them. This delayed the completion of the acceptance tests, as several could not be run unless some of the keys could be identified.

Most of the corrective maintenance on AIM was in the form of documentation fixes where the actual performance of the product did not match the user manual. The manual was changed in lieu of the more expensive code changes in cases where is was obvious that it did not really matter which way it worked. Several 'bug' reports actually turned out to be 'features,' not an unusual experience. For instance, the 20 character limit for names, number of lines in a window, and number of windows, all immediately reported, were actually part of the product, though the students did not find those requirements documented anywhere. As an example of one problem actually tackled, the TERMINATE command did not work. One team repaired this, but not without considerable code-searching in an attempt to base the design of the fix on existing related commands such as suspending a process.

Enhancements to AIM included changing the functions assigned to the arrow keys to other keys and the addition of a prompt line in the windows displaying the function keys. The former enabled the use of the keys for line editing and was accomplished with minimal effort. The latter turned out to be much more expensive due to the considerable 'hard coding' of parameters relating to the size of windows and others affecting the display of the function keys.

AIM perfective maintenance was centered on reengineering code. **Arthur88** has a good chapter on this subject and the instructor decided to pursue it in the project because Ada code lent itself to reengineering concepts not presented by Arthur, such as the proper construction of package bodies and the use of packages in general. The emphasis then was on taking Ada written by relatively beginning Ada programmers, and making it into something more advanced Ada programmers could use effectively.

At this point in the course, the 'well-documented' artifact was abandoned in favor of working on a 'poorly documented' one. This gave the students a chance to see how techniques of configuration management, change control, and impact analysis are effective when working with such code. Since they already had the 'good' experience with AIM, the Ares experience was less frustrating. Due to time limitations, the work on Ares was limited to design recovery and preparing the software for use by eliminating obvious bugs. During the AIM section of the course, test cases were developed to supplement the existing tests in the case of enhancements, with the existing tests used for regression testing. The Ares portion of the course required the generation of a new test suite based on the user manual, the only document available to the students.

In summary, the students were in a constant state of excitement and challenge from the beginning of the course to the end. This situation made it one of the easiest courses to teach of any in the software engineering curriculum. It certainly dispelled the notion (at least for these students) that maintenance is not a creative activity, or that it is less creative than the production of original software. As the students struggled with introducing changes to the fragile scaffolding that the artifacts turned out to be, they gained increased respect for the task of maintenance. They also clearly saw the effects of poor design on later enhancements and adaptations of the software. This is one positive result of the use of the artifacts, as these results would not have been so impressive if software developed by other persons (and unavailable persons at that) had not been used.

Acknowledgement

I would like to acknowledge the 'guinea pigs' who survived the first offering of this course: Ida Evans, Eric Herrmann, Tom Kelley, Dave Remmel, Keith Rhodes, and Richard Strunk.

Bibliography

Arango85 Guillermo Arango, Ira Baxter, Peter Freeman, and Christopher Pidgeon, "Maintenance and Porting of Software by Design Recovery," in the *Proceedings of the 1985 Software Maintenance Conference*, pp. 42-49.

This work is from the Reusable Software Engineering Project at the University of California, Irvine, and is a valuable framework for developing the support material needed when placing undocumented code under maintenance.

Arthur88 Lowell Jay Arthur, *Software Evolution*. New York: John Wiley, 1988.

This particular textbook on maintenance does a good job of placing the activity in the context of the total life cycle of software, plus it has a number of examples and a useful language for describing maintenance activity.

Bendifallah87 Salah Bendifallah and Walt Scacchi, "Understanding Software Maintenance Work," in *IEEE Transactions on Software Engineering,* Vol. SE-13, No. 3, Mar. 1987, pp. 311-323.

This paper expands on Scacchi's previous work on the social aspects of software development organizations. It makes a comparison between two different software evolution organizations that illuminates many of the principles presented in the technical part of the course.

Ford89 Gary Ford, Charles B. Engle, and Tim Korson, "Software Maintenance Excercises for a Software Engineering Project Course," SEI-89-EM-1.

This outstanding piece of educational material is a guide to the use of maintenance excercises, and contains actual problems usable in software engineering project courses. It comes with a fairly substantial piece of 'broken' software.

Lehman80 Meir M. Lehman, "Programs, Life Cycles, and Laws of Software Evolution," in *Proceedings of the IEEE*, Vol. 86, No. 9, September 1980, pp. 1060-1076.

In this classic paper, Lehman first separates programs into types, then derives laws of software evolution that are illustrated in an example. Very useful for sparking discussion.

Lientz83 Bennet P. Lientz, "Issues in Software Maintenance," in *Computing Surveys*, Vol. 15, No. 3, September 1983, pp. 271-278.

This is a useful survey of the main problems confronting maintainers. It makes a good jump-off reading for the course.

Schaefer85 Hans Schaefer, "Metrics for Optimal Maintenance Management," in the *Proceedings of the 1985 Software Maintenance Conference,* pp. 114-119.

The author suggests that certain data be kept by maintainers to help identify modules that would be candidates for perfective maintenance, and also to facilitate estimation of time and costs of future maintenance work. Even though this is a 'management' article, it is useful to discuss it just prior to starting serious project work to give the students some idea of the reasons for collecting such data.

Tomayko87 James E. Tomayko, "Teaching a Project-Intensive Introduction to Software Engineering," Software Engineering Institute, SEI-87-SP-1.

This contains the documents about Ares. The user manual was the only item given to the students.

Project Work in Software Maintenance Education

B.J. Cornelius, M. Munro and D.J. Robson
Centre for Software Maintenance
University of Durham
Durham DH1 3LE
UK

Abstract. *Software engineering education has traditionally focussed on the development phase of the software life cycle. It is recognised that maintenance is the most expensive phase of the life cycle, yet it receives very little direct attention in the software engineering curriculum. This paper contrasts a development based approach with a maintenance based approach to project work in software engineering education.*

1. Introduction

In this paper software maintenance is defined to be any work that is undertaken after delivery of a software system. It is often split into four categories, namely perfective, adaptive, corrective and preventive maintenance [1; 2]. Perfective maintenance is the enhancement of the system to incorporate new tasks which were not previously part of the requirements. Adaptive maintenance tasks are the amendments required when the system is moved to a new machine or when changes are made to the external environment in which the system operates. Corrective maintenance is defined as that part of the maintenance effort which is devoted to the correction of errors. Finally, preventive maintenance is the modification of parts of the system to ease the problems of future maintenance activity.

It has been recognised that software maintenance consumes approximately 70% of the costs during the life cycle of a software system[3]. Thus the maintenance phase is a vast consumer of resources, both financial and human. The education of software engineers, however, has largely concentrated on techniques applicable to the development phase[4], ignoring much of the work which will be undertaken in the future by a large number of the course graduates. There is a correlation with the research activity in software engineering where there is a similar emphasis on development as opposed to maintenance[5]. Lientz and Swanson's survey[3] also showed that 60% of the maintenance phase is taken up with perfective maintenance, whereas only 20% is corrective maintenance. Thus even if new development techniques reduce corrective maintenance, they will have little effect on the most expensive component, perfective maintenance.

Although modern techniques can be used to develop new software, there is still considerable investment in existing software. It is often not cost effective to throw away existing systems and rewrite them with the latest development technique. Thus software will be subject to continual modification and correction [6]. In practice, the accompanying system documentation, if any, and requirements may or may not be updated as the program is modified and this can make future maintenance more difficult. Thus future maintenance activity often utilises the code as the only authoritative source of information as to the exact function and construction of the system.

The main emphasis in many software engineering courses is the development phase. Such courses often involve practical work, but this is usually based on the development of new software rather than the modification of existing software. In an industrial environment perfective maintenance is a common activity and it was felt desirable that students should be exposed to such activity.

In section 2 of this paper we briefly describe our original approach to practical work in software engineering and the problems that we encountered. We describe an alternative to this approach which involves practical work in software maintenance. In the following section we describe the current implementation of the course at the University of Durham. The final section discusses some conclusions of this work.

2. Practical Work in Software Development

The University of Durham started teaching courses in software engineering in 1984 and the courses have since developed and expanded so that they now form a substantial part of the curriculum and are taught in all three years of the degree courses. Accompanying the second year course there has been practical work similar to that used at the University of Southampton[7] which was originally based on the software hut principle[8] [9].

In this practical work the students are divided into small teams within which they have to develop a software system. The project is divided into a number of phases each of which has a document as an end product. The phases are based on a simple waterfall model of the development life cycle. Each phase has a strict deadline and the documents which are the end products of each phase are:

requirements documents
requirements appraisal document
design document
implementation document
acceptance testing document

The requirements appraisal and the testing documents are reports on work completed by other teams.

The objectives for the introduction of this practical work were

(1) to give the students experience of the concepts and techniques discussed in the formal lectures.
(2) to introduce the students to the experience of working in a team. Prior to this course the students had only written relatively small programs and were positively discouraged from working in a team.
(3) to attempt to illustrate the need for the requirements and design phases. Students who have no experience of working on large pieces of software often fail to appreciate the need for such documents until they have had actual experience in a practical project.

Our experience of this practical work over the last five years has been that the students gain a great deal from the project and we have found that in general, the students spend more than the allocated time on the project. The practical work serves as a reinforcement of the concepts presented in the lecture course. We feel that we have satisfied the first two of the original objectives. The third objective has not been so easy to fulfill. At the beginning of the project, some students see little need for requirements documents as they only have experience of the construction of small programs. However, by the end of the project they need a requirements document to carry out the acceptance testing phase. They also usually realise that the requirements document is an essential statement on the functionality of the product. In contrast, the other documents which are produced at the end of each phase are rarely referenced once they have been submitted for assessment and it is not always easy to convince students of their worth.

To overcome this difficulty, it was decided to motivate the need for design documents by using a different approach. The basis of this approach would be to let the students maintain an unfamiliar piece of software which was supported by information on its design. We would expect this to reinforce the need for design documentation.

A second objective of this work was to introduce the students to the management of the maintenance process by involving them in such tasks as handling change requests and assigning priorities to the requests.

The practical work in software maintenance would be divided into the following phases:

familiarisation
receipt of change requests
allocation of priorities to change requests
design of change
review of proposed changes
implementation of change
validation

The change requests would involve all four categories of software maintenance. Thus, the change requests would include bug reports to simulate corrective maintenance, suggested enhancements to simulate perfective maintenance and requests to implement the system in a new environment to simulate adaptive maintenance. There would also be an internal request from management to allocate some time to upgrading certain parts of the system to ease future maintenance activity, i.e. preventive maintenance.

It was decided to split the students into teams and each team would have to allocate priorities to these activities, but they would also have to undertake a minimum amount of work in each category, so that they gained experience in all areas. Some of the change requests would be too large and complex to complete within the allocated timescales and this would force the teams into estimating the difficulty and selecting the most appropriate change requests.

3. Current Implementation of the Course

The practical work was accomplished in a workshop lasting six weeks. During this period the students were undertaking three other workshops of similar length. The time schedule for the maintenance workshop was divided into two periods with deliverables at the end of each period. The first deliverable would be the rationale and design of the changes. The second deliverable would be a single copy of the enhanced system from each team and a report of the testing.

One of the problems that had been encountered in previous practical work is the desire of students to start programming at the earliest opportunity. In order to get the students to think about the design of their changes rather than develop them by trial and error, it was decided to only give them a printed version of the source code during the familiarisation phase. They would also have access to a binary version so that test programs could be executed. A machine readable version of the source code would only be released at the implementation stage.

The students would only have a limited amount of time for this workshop and they would have to decide which of the change requests was the most important and whether they could be implemented within the limited timescales. The first deliverable document would contain a rationale for the choice of change requests. The team would then allocate the work between individuals and design the changes to the code to satisfy the selected change requests. After the group allocation of work between individuals, students would work on their own changes. Each student would produce a change design document (CDD) which would give details of how the changes could be accomplished.

In the week before the first deadline, students would undertake reviews of the CDDs with each member of the team taking turns at the roles of chair, reviewer and reviewee. The workshop instructors would be present, but would not allocate any marks for the review. The reviews would follow the normal pattern of software reviews[10], but adopt some of the techniques of the active design review technique[11]. In particular, the student whose work was being reviewed would supply the reviewers with a questionnaire which forced the reviewers to study the sections of the code which were being modified. The questions would not be passive such as 'Will the required modification work ?', but active such as 'What are the postconditions of the modified procedure ?'. The chair of each review committee would produce a report on the problems discovered in the review and the reviewee would produce an updated design document that would be reviewed again before commencing implementation.

During the remaining three weeks the students would implement the selected changes and amalgamate their individual versions into a single version of the system, with the modified parts clearly commented with the initials of the person responsible for the modification. They would work as individuals during the implementation phase, except when they needed to produce the final system or when some of their changes conflicted.

The program chosen as the object to be maintained was a compiler and interpreter for the language Pascal-S[12], which is a subset of Pascal. This system was supported by a book[13] which fully described the system and avoided the problem of the students spending too long on the familiarisation phase or on mastering the compilation techniques employed (the students had not yet taken a course in compiler construction). The system contained a tracing mode and a debugging mode which enabled the students to follow the internal procedure calling within the system and to obtain dumps of the symbol table and the generated code. The supporting book contained a source listing of the system. It could be argued that providing the students with a fully documented and well structured system was not exposing them to the realities of the outside world,

---

Summary of Change Requests

The students were given the following change requests. Each change request could not be undertaken by more than one person:

- Implement checks on for loop control variables. Check for threats, non-local and non-structured variables.
- Implement the loop and exit construct of Modula-2.
- Implement an otherwise arm in a case statement, ranges for case labels and improve the efficiency of the code generation for a case statement.
- Improve the symbol table routines by implementing the symbol table as a binary tree or hash table.
- Implement string operations and a string data type as in Turbo Pascal or UCSD Pascal.
- Implement conformant array parameters as in Pascal.
- Implement pointers as in Pascal.
- Implement the goto statement as in Pascal.
- Improve the error message handling by having a file of compile-time and run-time error messages, by suppression undeclared identifier messages and by improving error diagnostics.

Figure 1

---

but this compromise was necessary because of the time constraints and it was felt that this reinforced the usefulness of design documentation in the maintenance phase.

The students were given a number of change requests (see figure 1) some of which were infeasible within the time constraints. The time constraints also led to a decision by the instructors to limit the change request to those involving perfective maintenance. Perfective maintenance forms the largest part of maintenance work and so this was not expected to compromise the original aims of the workshop.

The reviews took place at the end of the third week, but again because of time constraints, it was decided not to have a second round of reviews, but only require that students submit a revised design document. To illustrate the benefits of good design documents, the students implemented a design other than their own, the allocation being random.

4. Evaluation of the Implementation

The workshop took place in the spring of 1988 with a group of five students. Due to the small numbers, they were formed into a single team. The familiarisation stage went smoothly, but the students did not explore the binary version very thoroughly. In order to evaluate the thoroughness of their exploration, three errors were deliberately seeded in the binary version to see how well the students exercised the system, but none of them was detected. The machine readable copy of the source code which was supplied did not contain these errors, but the binary version that was generated from this source was not compared with the original binary version, so the errors remained undetected. This was probably a reflection of the student's lack of experience in maintenance work.

There was some uncertainty by the students about which of the modifications to undertake as there were some conflicting constraints, such as the amount of time available, the perceived difficulty of the enhancements and the possible amount of marks available for different enhancements. With hindsight, the instructors did not give this problem enough thought and a clearer strategy will have to be applied in future versions of the course.

The reviews were particularly successful, revealing a number of errors in the proposed changes of all the students. All the final versions of the design documents were significantly different from those presented at the reviews. The reviews also revealed that the full impact of one of the changes had not been understood and that the suggested changes were insufficient. In the second phase of the workshop, this particular modification, the implementation of the symbol table as a binary tree, was redesigned rather than implemented.

Examples of the questions asked of reviewers are illustrated (see figure 2). There were fears that some of the reviewees might interpret criticisms of their design as personal criticism, but this did not occur. This particular problem may arise when the workshop is undertaken by a larger group of students in future years.

The majority of the modifications were successful, but there were errors which were largely due to some of the subtle semantics of the programming

---

Examples of Questions given to Reviewers

1. Exactly how is the Jump instruction at the end of the case table used ?

2. What information is logged about each compilation error and how is the information stored ?

3. In what order are the symbol table entries displayed ?

4. How do the proposed changes detect attempted exits within procedures and functions, and what error message is produced ?

5. In what other ways could a variable's usage as a control variable be indicated ?

Figure 2

---

language constructs. For instance, the precise circumstances under which a control variable in Pascal can said to be threatened were not fully understood.

The students were supplied with the machine readable copy of the source code contained within a revision control system. To the disappointment of the instructors, the revision control system was not utilised, and greater emphasis will be given to the benefits of such a system in future courses.

5. Conclusions

The study of software maintenance is usually neglected in software engineering education. Too often students only get exposure to development techniques with maintenance largely ignored. The aim of this project was to attempt to balance the students education in software engineering and give them experience of the type of activities usually undertaken during maintenance.

The workshop also introduced the students to a disciplined approach to software maintenance, where all changes are fully documented and subject to review. The reviews were particularly successful in highlighting errors in the proposed changes. The project supported the instructors view that group based project work in software engineering is extremely valuable. The course was popular with the students and will be repeated with a much larger group.

6. Acknowledgements

The authors would like to acknowledge the assistance of Andrew Brabban, Russell Collingham, Yuet Ip, Nick Saville and Mike Smith who acted as guinea pigs for this project.

7. References

[1]   SWANSON, E.F. : 'The Dimensions of Maintenance', Proceedings of the 2nd Int. Conf. on Software Engineering, IEEE, 492-497, 1976.

[2]   PRESSMAN, R.S.: 'Software Engineering - A Practitioner's Approach' (McGraw-Hill, 2nd Ed., 1987).

[3]   LIENTZ, B.P. and SWANSON, E.F.: 'Software Maintenance Management' (Addison-Wesley, 1980).

[4]   GIBBS, N.E. and FAIRLEY, R.E.: 'Software Engineering Education: The Educational Needs of the Software Community' (Springer Verlag, 1987).

[5]   BENNETT, K.H., CORNELIUS, B.J., MUNRO, M. and ROBSON, D.J.: 'Software Maintenance: A Key Field for Research', *University Computing*, **10**(4), 184-188, 1988.

[6]   LEHMAN, M.M. and BELADY, L.A.: 'A Model of Large Program Development', *IBM Systems J.*, **15**(3), 225-252, 1976.

[7]   GARRATT, P.W. and EDMUNDS, G.: 'Teaching Software Engineering at University', *Information and Software Technology*, **30**(1), 5-11, 1988.

[8]   HORNING, J.J. and WORTMAN, D.B.: 'Software hut: A computer program engineering project in the form of a game', *IEEE Trans. on Software Engineering*, **SE-3**, 325-330, 1977.

[9]   WORTMAN, D.B.: 'Software projects in an academic environment', *IEEE Trans. on Software Engineering*, **SE-13**(11), 1176-1181, 1987.

[10]   FAIRLEY, R.E.: 'Software Engineering Concepts' (McGraw-Hill, 1985).

[11]   PARNAS, D.L. and WEISS, D. : 'Active Design Reviews', Proc. 8th Int. Conf. on Software Engineering, IEEE, 132-136, 1986.

[12]   WIRTH, N: 'Pascal-S: a subset and its implementation', in BARRON, D.W. (Ed), 'Pascal - The Language and its Implementation', Wiley, 199-260, 1981.

[13]   REES, M.J. and ROBSON, D.J.: 'Practical Compiling with Pascal-S' (Addison Wesley, 1988).

Improving Software Maintenance Skills in an Industrial Environment

Dr. James S. Collofello
Computer Science Department
Arizona State University
Tempe, Arizona 85287

Mikael Orn
AG Communication Systems
P.O. Box 52179
Phoenix, Arizona 85027–2179

Abstract

Software maintenance activities consume the majority of software life cycle costs in organizations which support a software product over an extended interval of time. These maintenance activities include error corrections as well as enhancements to the software. In addition to being extremely costly, software maintenance activities are very error prone. As a result, if an organization is to improve its productivity and quality, improvements in software maintenance skills would provide an effective return on investment. This paper describes a two–fold approach to improving software maintenance skills which entails a practical "hands–on" training course coupled with performance management focusing on positive reinforcement for new skills.

Background

Although software maintenance is widely regarded as being the dominant activity performed in most software development organizations, very little attention has been paid to software maintenance in either university or industrial training courses. Even in software engineering programs, most of the emphasis is on developing new software as opposed to maintenance approaches. Therefore, most software professionals performing software maintenance tasks have rarely had university–level education or formal industry training in software maintenance activities. This is, of course, an undesirable situation, especially in light of the large and complex systems with high reliability requirements which must be maintained in today's marketplace.

Software Maintenance Skills

AG Communication Systems Corporation (AGCS), similar to many companies, has significant portions of the R&D staff perform software maintenance activities. Software maintenance activities include both adding new functions/features to an existing system and corrections of deficiencies. Few employees have had formal education in software maintenance. A decision was, therefore, made to enhance R&D's software maintenance skills. The approach taken consists of an AGCS developed software training course coupled with the application of Performance Management* principles. The software training course was developed to reflect both a state–of–the–art and a realistic view of software maintenance. The software maintenance literature and experienced software maintenance practitioners were consulted to identify effective industry practices.

Hands–on Practice

Feedback from an earlier in–house software maintenance course had indicated that "yes, software engineering ideas are great for development, but how do you apply them in our maintenance environment." This criticism was directed at the fact that exercises were "academic" in nature (not real AGCS problems) and did not demonstrate a realistic application of new techniques. Therefore, many employees were not convinced of the practical use of many of the ideas in the course. Their argument was that in their software (a few million lines of source code) those "fancy software maintenance ideas won't work."

To overcome this problem, exercise material from the actual AGCS environment was developed. We wanted exercises that were real, but still brief enough to be useful in a training setting. Course evaluations confirmed that the "real life" exercises were effective in demonstrating that the software engineering principles for software maintenance can be applied at AGCS.

Ensure Management Support

The next problem was the application of skills back on the job. Most students leave a course more knowledgeable and trained, but will they start applying the newly learned skills? This issue can be explained from a behavioral perspective [1]. Training is merely an antecedent or cue for a set of new behaviors (e.g., a new skill or activity, such as a more systematic approach to code reading). To maintain the new behavior, positive consequences must be applied. Management must encourage and reinforce the use of the new skill learned in the course. Our approach at AGCS is to solicit management support through an abbreviated course. Management

---

* Performance Management (PM) is a systematic, data–oriented approach to managing people at work that relies on positive reinforcement as the major way to maximize performance [1].

attends a short overview of the key material in the course so that they become familiar with the new concepts. We follow this with a work session to identify specific ways management can support and reinforce their staff in utilizing the new skills. See Figure 1.

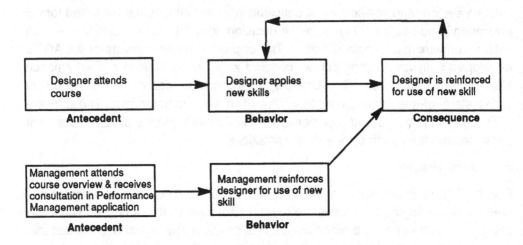

Figure 1. Management reinforces the use of new skills.

Reinforce the Skills

As a follow–up to the course overview, Performance Management plans are developed by management as a strategy to implement the new skills. Each plan consists of five critical ingredients:

1. Pinpoints   Specific desired results and the desired methods for achieving those results (behaviors) are identified. These pinpoints are the foundations for the plan.

2. Measurement   A tracking system for measuring the progress on the pinpointed results is developed. The measurement system is necessary for determining if improvements have occurred.

3. Feedback   Collecting metrics and measuring performance and results requires providing feedback to the engineers for the measurement system to be effective. Learning is not possible without feedback. Therefore, a feedback system (preferably via a graph) is developed.

4. Goals   Goals and subgoals are set and communicated on the graph. Subgoals should be as frequent as practical (typically weekly). All goals should be realistic; "stretch

goals" should be avoided. Research has shown that high achievers tend to set frequent and realistic (but challenging) subgoals. This allows them to establish a history of success and build their confidence.

5. R+   A positive reinforcement (R+) plan is developed, listing specific reinforcement for each subgoal. Social reinforcement associated with meeting a goal is crucial. "A word of well–deserved praise can go a long way . . . . praise generates energy, but only if it is justified. Receiving unmerited accolades can be an insult." [2]. Well–defined pinpoints and an accurate measurement system ensure that the right people get acknowledged for the right results and methods.

One such Performance Management plan currently being piloted tracks the quality of solutions released to our customers. Examples of pinpoints in the plan are "Improve review package completeness and timeliness" and "Improve test plan quality." Each solution (and corresponding test plan and documentation) is evaluated according to eight criteria, each on a scale one through five. Thus, each solution can receive a maximum score of 40 points. The data is collected through checklists. A solution quality index is averaged once a week and is plotted weekly on a graph (see Figure 2). Once a baseline has been established, goals will be set; and each time a goal is reached; the participants will be reinforced.

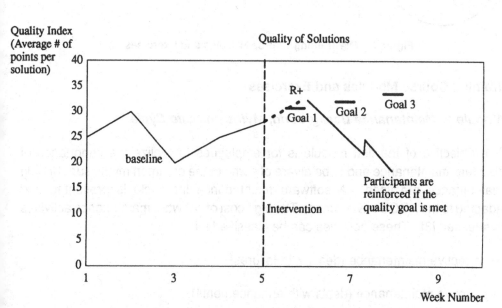

Figure 2. Example of a Performance Management graph.

The remainder of this paper describes the focus and intent of each of the training course modules and exercises (see Figure 3).

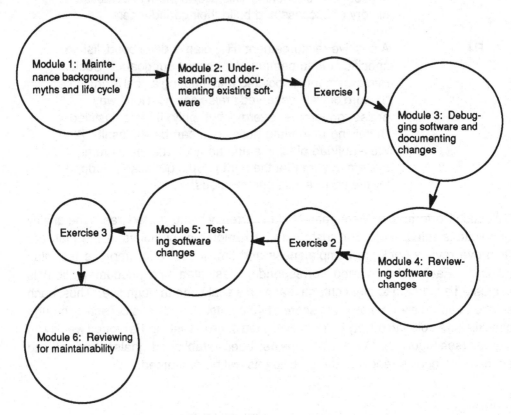

Figure 3. The Training Course Modules and Exercises

Training Course Modules and Exercises

Module 1: Maintenance Background, Myths and Life Cycle

The objective of the first module is for employees to realize the importance of software maintenance and to be aware of some of the common myths surrounding maintenance practices. A software maintenance life cycle is presented and adapted to the AGCS environment. The high cost of software maintenance activities is stressed [3]. These activities can be classified into:

– corrective maintenance (deals with failures)

– adaptive maintenance (deals with enhancements)

– perfective maintenance (deals with optimization) [4].

The typical phases of a software maintenance activity are also described. These consist of:

– understanding the software

– generating maintenance proposals

– accounting for ripple effect

– retesting the modified code [5].

Common problems in performing these tasks as well as their causes are also described [6]. Finally a set of maintenance myths are presented such as those discussed in [7] and summarized below:

1. "A special department for maintenance? Ridiculous. Our development programmers can maintain a system or two each in their spare time."

2. "We can't really control maintenance or how well the crew is working. After all, every fix or change is different."

3. "You don't get anywhere doing maintenance."

4. "Any of my programmers can maintain any program."

5. "Maintenance is all 3 a.m. fixes and frantic hysterics. It's nothing we can anticipate and it doesn't take up that much time anyway."

6. "You just can't find anyone who wants to do software maintenance."

7. "Maintenance is the place to dump your trainees, your burnouts and Joe, the boss' nephew, who thinks that hexadecimal is a trendy new disco. How can they hurt anything there?"

8. "Why bother to provide maintenance programmers with new software tools? After all, they're just patching up."

Module 2: Understanding and Documenting Existing Software

Module 2 offers some practical approaches to understanding existing software and documenting this understanding. The two basic approaches to understanding existing software are presented, top down and bottom up. Top down understanding assumes a well–documented program in which it is possible to proceed from an overall specification and design of the program through levels of documentation until the actual code is reached. This requires clear traceability of functionality throughout the software documentation. An important message is that software should be developed in a manner such that top down understanding can be later utilized by those who will perform maintenance on their product. Bottom up understanding is necessary for poorly documented software. It is also sometimes referred to as "stepwise abstraction" since the goal is to proceed from the code and try to discover intermediate abstractions which facilitate program understanding.

Regardless of the approach followed, there are several basic questions which must be answered in order to comprehend what a program is doing. The employees are made aware of these questions as well as approaches to answering them. Six questions are summarized below and explained in more detail in [8].

1. What actions are performed by the program?

2. What data is utilized?

3. Where does information come from?

4. Where does information go?

5. How are actions performed?

6. Why are actions performed?

Some additional questions are listed below.

7. What data is used elsewhere?

8. What data is modified elsewhere?

9. Are there any external dependencies?

Once understanding is acquired, it is essential that it be documented to facilitate future maintenance activities. This documentation normally takes the form of in–line comments and data dictionaries. Employees are made aware of the types of comments which aid software maintenance and those which do not. An important practical approach is defining the role and goal of variables where the role is a description of the variable and the goal is the reason why the variable exists [9].

Exercise 1

The objective of the first exercise is to practice top down and bottom up techniques for understanding software and then to effectively document their new knowledge. Actual code segments, excerpts from the User's Guide and Data Dictionary entries are provided. Groups are asked to add in–line comments and role/goal information for four variables. Each group presents their documentation to the other groups. Finally, as a test of the effectiveness of the documentation, other groups (than the authoring group) attempt to answer previously written questions concerning the software segment. If the code was adequately documented, those people seeing the program for the first time should have little problem addressing the questions.

Module 3: Debugging Software and Documenting Changes

The objective of Module 3 is to sensitize employees to the extremely error prone nature of changing software, and the importance of carefully and thoroughly documenting all software changes. Published statistics are presented, which demonstrate that every three fixes introduce a new error and that there is a very high probability that adding a new feature to a program will break an existing one [10]. Internal statistics are also presented to show the current trends within the company.

Employees are also made aware of the information necessary to effectively diagnose an error and the basic approach to follow in defect removal. Some typical information usually found on those forms includes:

– a description of the problem

– a description of the scenario in which the problem occurred

– an identification of when the problem occurred

– location of where the problem occurred

– technical contact if more information is needed

The "Scientific Method for Debugging" is also reviewed and includes the steps in Figure 4.

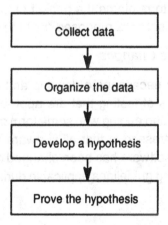

Figure 4. The "Scientific Method for Debugging"

The last important topic in this module is documenting the changed software. This step requires documenting what was changed, why it was changed and ensuring that all documentation has been updated to reflect the changes. (Some examples and further guidelines are presented in [11].)

A good exercise to support this module involves providing a program and a documented error in the program. The task is to diagnose the problem, fix the error and document the changes which were made.

Module 4: Reviewing Software Changes

Module 4 attempts to provide practical checklists for reviewing software changes. Software reviews must be performed for each change to ensure that:

- the change is correct

- the change does not introduce side effects

- the change does not degrade the quality of the software

- all documentation is updated

Some practical review checklists and guidelines are contained in [12]. A strong message conveyed is that all software changes be reviewed. This review must ensure that the software has been changed correctly without adverse side effects.

Exercise 2

The objective of the second exercise is to ensure adequate practice reviewing a software fix. Groups are given a package containing a change request (and printouts from the lab confirming the malfunction), the failed code (the error was seeded and is quite obvious), and a proposed fix to the problem. The proposed fix also has a seeded error in it to reinforce the benefit of the review. Each group is asked to present their checklist and a proposed "fix to the fix."

Module 5: Testing Software Changes

Module five focuses on skills necessary to develop and document a change test plan. There are several levels of testing that are appropriate, beginning with the developer testing the change and ending with some form of system level regression testing. An important point stressed is that all software changes be tested. This testing must ensure that the software has been changed correctly without adverse side effects. Some basic testing guidelines applicable during software maintenance are included in [13, 14].

Exercise 3

The objective of the final exercise is to practice writing test procedures for a software fix. The same fix as in Exercise 2 (but now corrected) is used. Groups attempt to develop a test plan for the proposed change to ensure that the change is correct and does not have any side effects.

Module 6: Reviewing for Maintainability

The last module in the workshop attempts to provide the students with skills for assessing the maintainability of a software product. This maintainability assessment is often performed prior to the transfer of a software product from a development organization to a separate maintenance group. The basic ideas of maintainability assessment, however, should be followed by maintenance programmers to assess the quality of the changes which they introduce into the product.

There are several approaches to maintainability assessment. One controversial approach consists of "bebugging." In this approach errors are seeded into a product and trained maintenance programmers are monitored in terms of their ability to debug and fix the errors. Their experiences serve as an indicator of the future maintainability of the product.

Another, more practical, approach to maintainability assessment is the utilization of checklists. These checklists address quality characteristics such as understandability, modifiability and testability. The software engineering literature contains an abundance of checklists, particularly at the design and code levels.

Conclusion

This paper has described an approach for improving software maintenance skills. One immediate and widespread benefit of this approach has been an appreciation on the part of participating employees of the importance of effective software maintenance and an appreciation of the skills required to perform maintenance activities effectively. In addition, by utilizing effective training in combination with Performance Management, customer satisfaction of design maintenance releases has increased.

References

[1]   Daniels, A. C. and Rosen, T. A., *Performance Management: Improving Quality and Productivity through Positive Reinforcement,* Tucker, GA: Performance Management Publications, 1984.

[2]   Carlzon, J., *Moments of Truths,* Cambridge, MA: Ballinger Publishing Company, 1987.

[3]   Lehman, M.M., "Survey of Software Maintenance Issues", Proc. 1983 Software Maintenance Workshop, *IEEE Computer Society Press*, 1984, pp. 226–242.

[4]   Swanson, E.B., "The Dimensions of Maintenance", *Proc. 2nd International Conf. on Software Engineering,*1976, pp. 494–497.

[5]   Yau, S.S. and Collofello J.S., "Ripple Effect Analysis of Software Maintenance", Proc. *IEEE COMPSAC 78*, 1978, pp. 60–65.

[6]   Lientz, B.P. and Swanson, E.B., "Characteristics of Application Software Maintenance", *Communications of the ACM*, vol. 21, no. 6, June 1978, pp. 466–471.

[7]   Schwartz, B., "Eight Myths about Software Maintenance", *Datamation*, vol. 28, no. 9, Aug. 1982, pp. 125–128.

[8]   Zvegintzov, N., "The Eureka Countdown", *Datamation*, vol. 28, no. 4, April 1982, pp. 172–178.

[9]   Letovsky, S. and Soloway, E., "Delocalized Plans and Program Comprehension", *IEEE Software*, May 1986, pp. 41–49.

[10] Collofello, J.S. and Buck, J.J.,   "Software Quality Assurance for Maintenance", *IEEE Software*, Sept. 1987, pp. 46–53.

[11] Fay, S.D. and D.G. Holmes, "Help! I have to Update an Undocumented Program", *Proc. 1985 Software Maintenance Workshop*, IEEE Computer Society Press, 1986, pp. 194–202.

[12] Freedman, D.P. and G.M. Weinberg, *Handbook of Walkthroughs, Inspections and Technical Reviews*, Little Brown and Company, 1982.

[13] Wallace, D.R., "The Validation, Verification and Testing of Software: An Enhancement to Software Maintainability", *Proc. 1985 Software Maintenance Workshop*, IEEE Computer Society Press, 1986, pp. 69–77.

[14] Fischer, K.F., "A Test Case Selection Method for the Validation of Software Maintenance Modifications", *Proc. IEEE COMPSAC 1977*, pp. 421– 426.

An Onsite Education Program for Software Quality

Abbas Birjandi and Cynthia A. Brown
College of Computer Science, Northeastern University
360 Huntington Ave., Boston, MA 02115

Abstract. *A software engineering education program consisting of three intensive courses was developed by Northeastern University in cooperation with a local company, and taught at the company's facility. The courses cover advanced C programming, software engineering, and peer code reviews. We describe the contents of the courses, the process of developing them, and our experiences in presenting them.*

Introduction

Early in 1988, Northeastern University was approached by a mid-size company located in the Boston area's Route 128 technology belt for help in designing and implementing an in-house education program. The company, which produces mostly business systems (e.g., operating systems, file systems, transaction processing subsystems, compilers, and network software, as well as office applications software, departmental office products, and data base applications) was interested in improving the quality and maintainability of their code, and in making software development more efficient. They had already decided to move away from assembly language and into C as one part of this effort; they had also decided to seek outside help in developing new software engineering methods and in implementing an education program to train their personnel in the new methods.

The first stage of our interaction with the company involved setting specific goals for the education program. The most straightforward aspect of this was in the area of developing C expertise. The choice of C as the standard language for software production was natural. Projects in the company were being done in a suprising variety of high-level procedural languages as well as in assembler. By converting most of the new software development activity to C, the company expected to produce more maintainable code faster on the projects that would otherwise use assembler, and to facilitate communication of ideas, sharing of software, and movement of personnel among projects that would otherwise be written in high-level languages other than C. Given the desire to standardize on a single high-level language to replace most of the assembler coding and most of the other languages, the additional constraint that a compiler for the chosen language would be produced in-house, and the intention to explore the use of commerically available CASE tools, C was the only reasonable choice. About 25% of the software developers in the company already knew C, and some were using it for their current projects; still, there remained a large body of people who would need to be trained in the language.

The management was aware that simply switching to C would not be a panacea for their problems. In order to address the larger software development issues, it was decided to offer a course in software engineering in addition to the course on C. The software engineering course would be a survey of the material usually covered in a graduate course, but would concentrate on topics of particular relevance to software developers: specification, design, modularity, testing, and maintenance.

Just introducing software engineering principles to the programmers would probably have some beneficial effect, but management was also interested in instituting a systematic check that good principles were being applied. As with many companies, the people (and even departments) that maintain code are usually not the same as the developers; yet the principal benefits and economies of well-engineered code appear in the maintenance phase. Developers are often under time pressure to produce a working product; under such pressure, programming style, careful documentation, and thorough testing may be neglected, unless there is some intervention by a higher level of management. It was decided that code reviews would provide an effective mechanism for ensuring that these aspects of program development were properly addressed.

Our initial program thus consisted of a series of three courses: C programming, software engineering, and peer code review. Pulling engineers off their projects to attend classes is expensive for the company and disruptive to schedules; we therefore decided to limit each class to two working days. This tight schedule meant that the three courses had to be carefully designed to meet their objectives. In the next three sections we describe the contents of each of the courses in more detail; this is followed by a discussion of the process of designing the courses, and an evaluation of the effectiveness of the program.

The C Course

The company had purchased a videotaped introductory C course, which was used to begin the process of retraining programmers to use C. The tapes were perceived by the programmers as too elementary and as rather boring. They were perceived by the management as extremely cost-effective. Both groups saw the need for additional training beyond the elementary level. As a result, we decided that the C course taught by Northeastern would assume that the participants already had a basic working knowledge of C. The focus of the course would be on programming style, pitfalls, and subtleties: the aspects of programming which are not usually covered in elementary books, which are typically learned through long and painful experience, and which are particularly critical for users of C.

The format for the first day of the course centers around a review of C syntax. As each construct is covered, issues relating to it are raised and discussed. Such issues include, for example, precedence of operators, the = versus == pitfall, and the problems that result from not parenthesising parameters in macro definitions. The company has a C style manual which prescribes standards for indenting and layout of each construct; these are reviewed also. (A source code formatter is under development but has not yet appeared.)

The remainder of the course is devoted to various deeper issues that tend to cause problems for beginning C programmers. Some of the topics are: organization of include files, semantics of pointers, C idioms, the preprocessor, casting of pointers, pointer arithmetic, and portability issues. An effort is made to promote good idiomatic C style through the use of examples; each student is given a copy of the course notes containing all the examples. Andrew Koenig's recent book [4] makes an excellent supplementary text for this course. Given the short time-frame of the course, there is no opportunity for lab work; the assumption is that the people in the class are using C in their daily work and will get plenty of practice with it in the work situation.

The Software Engineering Course

This is probably the most conventional of the three courses. The chief reference around which the course is structured is Fairley's book on software engineering [3], which is the main text for our regular graduate software engineering course. We also drew heavily on the SEI curriculm modules [for example, 5], which contain more up-to-date and thorough discussions of many topics. We are continuing to revise and enrich the course as new modules [such as 1, 6] appear.

The course begins with an overview of the field of software engineering and a section motivating the need for such a discipline. This is important since the company has many long-time programmers who did not have the benefit of a formal computer science education and who have to be persuaded to consider changing the way they do things. (Informal polls taken in the classes suggest that few of the software developers belong to either ACM or IEEE, and the ones who do tend to be more recent graduates, so the long-time programmers are not exposed to new ideas through the technical societies either.)

The next phase of the course is a discussion of the software life-cycle. This provides a framework for the remaining topics. Along with the waterfall model, we present prototyping and incremental construction of software as alternatives. We then go into requirements analysis and specification, and software design. We find that [1] gives an excellent overview of the requirements and specification phase, and we are adopting its terminology for our course. We introduce a number of specification and design methods using brief examples. Naturally there is not enough time to train the students in the use of any method; instead, we try to give them a feeling for what each method is like, the kinds of problems it applies best to, and sources to consult for further information. A part of this section is devoted to a discussion of modularity, including the standard parameters of cohesion and coupling and a discussion of object-oriented design versus top-down functional decomposition. Many of the students told us they felt this was the most helpful part of the course.

At this point we are about half-way through the second morning of our two-day course. We continue with a discussion of software complexity measures, data flow analysis, and testing. We also include a section on estimating the cost of software projects. We finish up with configuration management and maintenance.

After the formal presentations are over, we walk the students through a short annotated reading list and encourage them to follow up on the class by reading some of the materials and applying the ideas they have learned in their work. We also encourage them to join a professional society. In addition to the course notes, we hand out copies of several interesting papers from recent issues of the CACM which relate to topics we have covered; we hope that reading these articles will lead people to explore the literature further on their own. We also try to stimulate discussions in class (as time permits) about methods the students are currently using and how the ideas we are presenting relate to them.

Our goal in this course is to persuade the students that (1) there are ideas and methods in the computing literature which can help them become better at their jobs, (2) that these methods are accessible to them through classes, study, and discussion with their co-workers, and (3) it is worth the effort to learn about and implement such methods. If we are successful then the workers may begin to implement changes in their procedures on their own; they will also be more receptive when management introduces software engineering methods or CASE tools into the company.

The Code Review Course

This is the most innovative course of the three. As a starting point, we used Collofello's module on the technical review process [2]. While the C course and the Software Engineering course are done in a lecture format, this course is part lecture and part workshop. The goal of the course is to train the students to do peer code reviews of the type in which one or two people who are at the same professional level as the author of the code review it for style and correctness. There are two important aspects to doing a good job on such a review: a technical one, relating to what to look for, and an interpersonal one, relating to how to communicate what is found.

We begin the class with a one-morning lecture session; the first topic we address is the stressful nature of a review for both the reviewer and the reviewee, and methods for making the experience a positive one for both parties. Our viewpoint is that the review should be seen as an educational experience for both people, rather than as a confrontation or a test. A skillful reviewer should attempt to improve both the program being reviewed and the coding skills of the reviewee; the reviewer may also pick up good points of style or technique by reading other people's code. We model good and bad ways of communicating information in a review, and encourage positive as well as negative feedback.

The second part of the lecture material is concerned with the technical aspects of the review. To facilitate the work of the reviewer, we distribute a checklist for use in the reviews. The checklist is divided into four sections. The first is concerned with easily-checked and syntactic considerations: for example, good layout of the program (this will no longer need to be checked once the formatter is available), adequate use of parentheses, proper declarations and types, reasonable variable names, and the presence of certain required comments. The requirements of this section are mostly adapted from a C style manual the company produced. The second section is concerned with somewhat deeper or more subjective issues: such things as use of defined constants, avoidance of unnecessary global variables, use of switch statements in preference to complex nested ifs, adequacy of comments, meaningfulness of variable names, and avoidance of overly complex or obscure C code. The third section is concerned with global issues of program structure, such as length of functions, choice of algorithms, modularity, exception-handling, and efficiency of the code. The fourth section addresses the special concerns of maintained code: that changes are clearly indicated and adequately documented, that the style of new code is reasonably consistent with the old, that parameters passed to procedures are in the correct order, and so on.

We next discuss the code review procedure in detail. We encourage the students to make several passes over the code, one for each of the first three categories in the checklist. We present small examples of sub-optimal code and suggest appropriate responses for the reviewer. This completes the first morning's session.

The second session is devoted to reviewing some code provided by us. The code consists of two different solutions to a programming problem given in the systems programming course at Northeastern: one quite well written and one rather ordinary. We distribute a modified version of the assignment, which gives a careful functional specification, and the code, which has been modified to conform to the company's formatting standards. Each program is about 5 pages of C code. The students are given a chance to read and review the code of the well-written program (this typically takes about 45 minutes), and we then go around the room and let each person review the code to the group at large. Each reviewer is given feedback about his or her style of presentation. We then break into teams of two people. Each person reads the second piece of code, and then each reviews it as if it had been written by his or her partner. The reviewers are given feedback on their performance by their partners.

Our original plan was to spend the second day reviewing code written by the students on their projects at work. This has proved to be impractical, because the projects are usually very large and it is impossible for someone who is completely unfamiliar with a project to learn enough to review a component of it in a single morning. In addition, the programmers typically do not write small self-contained pieces of code. On the other hand, we feel it is important for the students to have a piece of their own code reviewed. We therefore hand out a small programming assignment to be written on the second morning. The program takes as input a month and a year, and produces a simple calendar. This assignment is about the right level of difficulty for reasonably experienced C programmers who are using C in their daily work. It is a bit too hard for novices. To help minimize feelings of self-consciousness, we tell the participants not to make their code perfect; we want code that has mistakes for the reviewer to comment on. This code is used as the basis for the third code review exercise, which takes place the second afternoon.

We finish the course with a group discussion. By this point most of the students are enthusiastic about doing code reviews. We talk about the projects their groups are doing and how code reviews can best be worked in. One result of the classes is an appreciation of the difficulty of doing a good review, so we also discuss the need to schedule time for this activity, and to reward the efforts of the person who does the review. (This addresses a concern of the students, namely that they will be asked to do reviews in addition to the work they are already doing, without any extra time being added to the schedule.) We also discuss who is an appropriate reviewer; our experience in the class suggests that the best reviewer is a person from the same project, since that person will already understand the context in which the reviewed code is written. Finally, students who have completed all three courses are given a certificate of achievement by a manager.

The Course Preparation Process

The process of designing the three courses had its own dynamics. The company wanted the courses to reflect their software development culture and methods; they did not want the curriculum to suggest radical changes to what they considered good practice. On the other hand, we at Northeastern did not want to create a series of courses to basically preach what they were (supposed to be) practicing. The company has a strong committment to education, and some of the employees had developed internal mini-courses; these people saw us as a threat to their domain.

To resolve any differences, it was decided to establish a committee which would oversee course content. The committee contained three people from the company and two from Northeastern. The committee would first review the internally-created education program, and then decide whether to incorporate their efforts into the final product or start from scratch.

The most complex issue, surprisingly, involved the C course. One of the people in charge of creating internal courses had developed a "higher-level" notation for programming in C. This notation was implemented as a set of macros, known collectively as "Nouveau C". Nouveau C had been adopted by some of the programmers and a major project was done using it. The language was strongly recommended by two of the company's members of the committee as the language to be taught in the C course.

After a careful review of the package and after looking into some examples done using it, we at Northeastern decided that the package did not offer any help in protecting programmers from the subtleties of the C language, and that using it would make programs far more difficult to debug than straight C programs. It would also eliminate the possibility of using commercially available CASE tools designed for C programs. Our next task was to convince the committee of the disadvantages of this approach and the benefits of focussing on C itself.

The third member of the committee from the company side was the manager of the section in which a major communications package had been developed using Nouveau C. Fortunately, this person was very open-minded and also up to date on recent developments of productivity tools such as interactive debuggers for C. He had also had some exposure to C++. In our informal chats with him we discovered that he was very knowledgeable in the area of object-oriented programming. We decided to base our case on two issues: the existence of software tools for original C, and the prospect of building on C with an eventual transition to C++ as a successor which provides higher-level constructs to support object-oriented programming. Using these arguments we were able to persuade him to drop the idea of Nouveau C, without having to attack its weaknesses directly. The net result was positive and we succeeded in our effort, by far the most tricky task of this project.

The process of suggesting and creating course materials was as follows. First we came up with a syllabus showing the course contents, and explained the motivation behind proposing them. After discussions with the committee we created a draft of the course materials and had them reviewed to cross check notations and style standards. Because of the close cooperation of the committee members, we rarely had to make changes in the course materials. For the later courses, as the company members of the committee gained confidence in us, the process became much less formal and they became increasingly willing to let us establish the course contents and format with only minor checking and corrections from them.

Evaluation and Future Directions

The education program we described has been in place since the summer of 1988. We began with the C course, which was introduced in July; the first software engineering course was given in September and the first code review course in November. A full schedule of all the courses is planned for 1989, with eight sections of each course spread throughout the year. Overall, our experience with these courses has been very positive. The students enjoy them and find them useful. In order for the program to have its maximum impact on the company's productivity, however, certain concerns remain to be addressed.

The software developers in the company fall into roughly two categories. One group, which tends to be younger, consists of people who have formal academic training in computer science, some from leading institutions, and who are actively interested in improving their skills and staying current with the field. The second group tends to be older, to have less formal training, and to feel satisfied with their present skills. Students are chosen for the courses by their managers, but in practice most students come to the courses at their own request, rather than on the manager's initiative. Thus, the courses do not always reach the audience that might benefit from them the most. We expect this situation to change as the number of people who have had the courses increases: it will become more the norm to have taken the courses, and the managers are expected to begin taking more initiative in sending people to the courses.

With only two days for classes, some might wonder why homework was not assigned, perhaps in advance or as a follow-up. For example, the exercise for the code review course could be handed out in advance. We have found that many workers are reluctant to do assignments outside of regular hours, and that managers find it difficult to allocate more than the two days of their work time already required. With the code review course, another factor is the reluctance of the students to expose their work to others for criticism. After the experience of the first day of the course, students are much more willing to produce a piece of their own code for review.

Projects in the company are done by people working in relatively stable groups. We have found it most beneficial to have several people from a group go through the courses together. This provides a "critical mass" of advocates for new methods within the environment, and makes it much more likely that procedures will actually change. Such changes also require the enthusiastic cooperation of first-level managers. The courses as currently taught are not really appropriate for managers, but it is essential to educate them in new methods and convince them of their benefits. We are therefore designing a one-day overview of software engineering for managers, and a half-day session on the code review process. Our plan is to eventually put the majority of software developers and low to middle level managers through the program. The company is also working to identify CASE tools to aid in the software development process. Once these tools are selected, we will work with them to develop a training program in the use of the tools. The process of technology transfer is notoriously difficult, but we expect that this program will result in significant improvements in the software development process within the company and in its products.

References

1. John W. Brackett, *Software Requirements*, SEI Curriculum Module SEI-CM-19-1.0, Carnegie-Mellon University Software Engineering Institute, 1988.

2. James S. Collofello, *The Software Technical Review Process*, SEI Curriculum Module SEI-CM-3-1.4, Carnegie-Mellon University Software Engineering Institute, 1988.

3. Richard E. Fairley, *Software Engineering Concepts*, McGraw-Hill, New York, 1985.

4. Andrew Koenig, *C Traps and Pitfalls*, Addison-Wesley, Reading, MA, 1989.

5. Everald Mills, *Software Metrics*, SEI Curriculum Module SEI-CM-12-1.1, Carnegie-Mellon University Software Engineering Institute, 1988.

6. Larry J. Morell, *Unit Testing and Analysis*, SEI Curriculum Module SEI-CM-9-1.1, Carnegie-Mellon University Software Engineering Institute, 1988.

The Rockwell Software Process Training Program

Part I

Herbert L. Reed
Manager, Professional Development
Rockwell International
Space Transportation System Division
Downey, California

Part II

Sam Harbaugh, PhD
President
Integrated Software, Inc.
Palm Bay, Florida

Part I - The Pre-development Phase

Abstract

Part I describes the pre-development phase of "The Rockwell Software Process Training Program" (SPTP) currently under development at Rockwell International Space Transportation Systems Division (STSD), Downey, California. Part II describes the development phase. Part I describes the sequence of events leading to the award of a contract to develop the Rockwell SPTP and gives STSD's perspective of this effort to date. Included in Part I is a discussion of the following:

- A short description of STSD's needs for a Software Process Training Program
- STSD's program objectives and project plan
- SEI support of curriculum development at Rockwell
- The invitation and response to quote
- Evaluation and selection of a training vendor
- Transition to the M.S. Degree in Software Engineering at a local University
- Planned Funding through the State of California Employment Training Panel
- Lessons learned

Background

In 1985, Rockwell divisions in Southern California initiated a major training effort to train its employees in the Ada language. Through this training program, with STSD acting as the lead division, a total of 475 Rockwell members of the technical staff including 175 from STSD have completed Ada language training. The success enjoyed through Ada training and continued pursuit of enhancements in the software development process has encouraged STSD to pursue total software process training.

In April 1987, the Space Transportation Systems Division's Human Resources Professional Development Group initiated a software engineering training needs assessment among Rockwell International Southern California Divisions. Software engineering department heads were asked to determine the extent of their requirements for software engineering training. Feedback from this inquiry indicated there were over 400 current or future employees who would need software engineering training or retraining for current or planned projects. It was generally agreed upon by management that the right source for software engineering training was not immediately available, and that required training in software engineering would be expensive.

Software engineering is concerned with the orderly, methodical development of reliable, usable software, and since the software process is labor intensive where adequate attention must be paid to establishing a consistent process, the training of people in understanding that process becomes an important strategy for continued productivity. STSD Human Resources professional development unit in conjunction with experts from the software engineering unit were tasked with a goal of developing a software process training program that would develop key competencies (knowledge, skills, and attitudes) by providing learning experiences which enable individuals to perform current or future jobs in the software process environment.

An overview of the Software Process Training Program, which resulted from this development is shown in Part II, Figure 4. It consists of 21 topics organized into 7 courses with a total of 408 video taped lecture-hours. In addition there is an integrating laboratory problem scheduled to be completed in 164 lab-hours plus 28 hours of comprehensive tests.

Introduction

Rockwell International Space Transportation Systems Division (STSD), Downey, California, provides systems, services, and technologies for access to and use of space, both manned and unmanned. STSD markets are national and international, involving both government and private customers. STSD provides systems and software engineering, integration, production, operations, and leadership capabilities to meet customer needs from concept formulation through full program life.

STSD's software development mission is to produce reliable high-quality systems and software products for commercial, military, and NASA programs. The software for systems required by these customers is steadily becoming more complex and the size of programs is increasing. Many of these systems have to be modified extensively during their life cycle due to changes in the operational environment and customer demands. Such complex and dynamic programs have to be properly engineered and their development must be well managed. This requires increasing numbers of people trained in the use of modern software development techniques.

This notion of a need for training was also echoed in a September 1988 article titled, "Can the US win the other space race? Space Science Education", by Senator Dan Quayle, now Vice President of the United States. In the article, Mr. Quayle indicated that trained scientists and engineers are critical to maintaining the US international competitiveness in such key areas as computer technology, robotics and advanced electronics. Mr. Quayle went on to say, "the problem is real".

The National Academy of Science forecasts a 40 percent decline in the number of aerospace engineering graduates in the US between now and 1990 even though the demand for such graduates will increase by 70 percent. There will be a shortfall of 140,000 computer scientists and 30,000 electrical engineers in the US by 1990, according to the Academy. [1]

Compounding this situation on training in software engineering even further, it appears that the number of computer science graduates is very limited, and most of the ones graduating today lack the engineering background needed in the development of embedded computer systems software. Furthermore, currently employed programmers and systems analysts lack a thorough education in modern systems and software engineering technologies for the development of complex software systems. [2]

At STSD, software products are produced through an integrated software process environment that assures adequate and cost effective use of software tools, people and methodologies (process). According to Bill Selfridge, a Rockwell project manager and software engineering expert, the software development process is labor intensive and adequate attention must be paid to establishing a consistent process and training people in understanding that process. [3] Facing these challenges, STSD decided to develop its own internal Software Process Training Program (SPTP).

STSD systems and software engineering personnel development programs are planned through the Systems Engineering Technical Advancement Committee (SETAC). SETAC is a formal work committee that meets bi-monthly to explore ways of improving employee performance through in-house training and educational programs. SETAC members represent a cross section of systems and software engineering managerial units.

SETAC provides a focal point for formulating domain specific training requirements, serves as a course content specialist body, recommends resources and development methods, identifies trainers and trainees, communicates course availability, and resolves training issues resulting from performance measurement and feedback during training program implementation.

Technology transfer training and development programs are focused on maintaining STSD's competitive edge through prevention of obsolescence in systems/techniques, methods, and technical staff. At STSD the in-house sources of education and training for members of the technical staff are obtained through a two pronged approach. The first approach involves cooperative ventures with local high-tech universities to provide after working hours training programs targeted for domain specific high technology skills development needs. The second approach is through tapping the scientific and engineering capabilities of nationally known experts from academia and private institutions, and large and small businesses to ensure delivery of state-of-the-art products. The latter approach is being used for the SPTP.

Software Process Training Development Model

The training development model used for the SPTP has six major steps, or phases, as described in Figure 1. This training development process embodies the principles of both the linear approach and the geodesic approach. [4] (Figure 2) Through the linear approach the first five steps are performed in sequential order, with the sixth "step" being performed simultaneously with the other five. The geodesic approach is employed in the development process through activities and tasks being performed simultaneously for all steps in the process. In addition, there was often more than one way to complete a given step.

PHASE (Step)	DESCRIPTION
1. Analysis	Is training needed? If so, what skills and knowledge must be addressed? Can the development of the program be justified in terms of costs?
2. Objectives and tests	What must the learner be able to do upon completion of the course? How will completion be measured?
3. Instructional design	What is the best way to present the course information to make learning effective?
4. Materials	How should the course materials development (texts, media, and lectures) be produced and then tested to ensure validity and effectiveness?
5. Implementation	How should actual delivery of training to the target audience be handled? There must be periodic maintenance to ensure course integrity.
6. Evaluation	How will the effort be evaluated? There must be ongoing assessment of the effectiveness, validity, and need for course material through phase 4. In phase 5, an assessment of the effectiveness and impact of the entire course in must be made.

Figure 1. Six phases of training development

The training development model shown in Figure 1 best describes the framework from which development of the Rockwell SPTP follows throughout the life cycle of this project. Even though implementation of the program is incomplete, the model is shown in this paper to provide the reader with a sense of direction for this effort.

Linear Approach

Linear thinking is a process of organizing knowledge by explaining objects and events in terms of their component parts and the sequence or priority of those parts in relation to each other. The linear approach brings the following advantages to the training process:

- Order and logic are imposed on a complex set of interrelated tasks.
- Accurate and measurable goals are created through attention to detail, and these goals can be used as evaluation tools.

Geodesic Approach

Geodesic Thinking is the process of organizing knowledge by explaining objects and events in terms of their wholeness, their impact on the environment, and the interrelationships and interdependencies of their component parts. Some of the advantages of using the geodesic approach include:

- Viewing the course development effort as having one major goal, to create a program that will positively impact human behaviors.
- Perceiving the whole as well as the parts, thus ensuring a consistent and thorough approach. Treating each task and activity in the process of course development as an interrelated and interdependent element.
- Recognizing and managing the environmental factors that would impact the course development effort.
- Making the project management aspects of course development more effective by allowing for flexible decision making, providing many alternative ways to complete a given phase or task, providing a conceptual frame upon which a course can be created, establishing an environment that encourages creative, innovative thinking and problem solving.

Figure 2. Linear and Geodesic Approach [4]

Needs Analysis and Training Requirements Analysis for SPTP

Lessons learned from presenting Ada language training to over 18 classes have been valuable in providing a sound foundation for embedded systems development. In addition to training experience, STSD is successfully involved in several Ada work projects including the displays and controls software development and testing of Ada for the Boeing 747-400 program. The impact of Ada has provided STSD with a practical understanding of software engineering.

In addition, in 1987, a needs analysis was performed by Software Engineering Department heads as described previously in the Background section of this paper.

SPTP Terminal Objectives

The terminal objectives of the Software Process Training Program are to:

1.   Maintain/increase the base of trained Rockwell software process personnel (e.g. test and design engineers) for existing and new contracts.

2.   Maintain/increase efficiency and productivity by providing Rockwell divisions with competent system and software requirement analysis, design, test and programmer specialists, project managers, and other supporting personnel.

3.   Produce software process personnel who can assume positions of increased responsibility within the software organizations.

SPTP Enabling Objectives

Extensive research of the software engineering literature and known sources for software engineering training were undertaken in order to develop the enabling objectives for the SPTP. These are objectives that support related terminal objectives and cover a large portion of the course, topic, and subtopic units. Establishment of enabling objectives have been perhaps one of the most critical and difficult phases to accomplish in the SPTP development process. During this phase one must answer the question, what content is required in a program for developing the desired terminal objectives established for the program? This phase took more than 10 months to complete. It involved the manager of professional development in a role as an instructional technologist, and experts from the software engineering department in their roles as technical subject matter experts and course designers. All concerned parties spent many hours of discussion and debate before an agreement was reached about what constituted a software engineering curriculum that mapped well with Rockwell software process environment. This was a complex and difficult subject upon which to reach a consensus. It required geodesic thinking, in that the group started with the whole and built out to the parts, thus requiring an understanding of how the parts interact and depend upon one another.

SEI's Draft Software Engineering Curriculum as ITQ Specification

The breakthrough for establishing the enabling objectives for the SPTP came when the Software Engineering Institute (SEI), a federally funded research and development center operated by Carnegie Mellon University, published a work draft software engineering curriculum. [5] This draft was rewritten by Rockwell into a Statement of Work (SOW) for development of a software engineering training program as a part of an Invitation to Quote (ITQ). This document presented an organizational structure for software engineering curriculum content, and served as an excellent vehicle for communicating software engineering curriculum/course content requirements among Rockwell software process experts. All five Rockwell Southern California division's software engineering departments reviewed the specification for completeness when mapped across their individual software engineering environments. Each division provided a few minor modifications, which were integrated into a final SOW.

Invitation To Quote

In August 1987, Rockwell mailed an Invitation to Quote (ITQ) to eleven training vendors and two universities, with an expected response date three weeks after receipt of the ITQ. This ITQ indicated that Rockwell International would accept proposals from the training vendors and Universities for a Software Engineering Training Program, in accordance with the specifications contained in the SOW. The ITQ instructed respondents to adhere to the following format in submitting their response: Volume I - Technical Proposal, Volume II - Cost Proposal, Volume III - Management, and Volume IV - Proposal Documentation.

Excerpts from the Rockwell ITQ are shown in Figure 3. The intent of these excerpts is to give the reader an idea of the extent to which the SEI's working draft software engineering curriculum was used by Rockwell as the basis for solicitation for the development of a Software Engineering Training Program (SETP). The name for the program was changed from SETP to SPTP shortly after contract award.

Response to ITQ and Evaluation

Seven training vendors and the two universities responded to the ITQ by submitting full or partial proposals. Evaluation committees were established composed of software engineering department personnel representing the five Rockwell divisions. These committees were given one and a half months from the date that bids were received to

What is being proposed through this solicitation is the development of a Software Engineering Training Program (SETP). The Rockwell SETP must be designed to create and present a program of training for the professional enhancement of its system and software requirements analysts, design, test and programmer specialists, project managers, and other supporting software development personnel.

The program should consist of the following six major categories of software engineering activity:

1. General   4. Design
2. Planning   5. Testing
3. Analysis   6. Maintenance

The Scope of the Procurement includes:

The development of individual course content materials, overhead projector viewgraphs, instructors notes, trainee materials, and tests, all of which meet the course requirements set forth.

The development of appropriate tests to be given to trainees at the completion of a course to determine the effectiveness of the courses, its presentation, and the knowledge acquired by the trainee during the course.

Presentation of individual courses by qualified instructors is to be video taped by Rockwell, at Rockwell's facility.

Figure 3. Excerpts from Rockwell ITQ

review and recommend the source for this effort. The committees were given all volumes submitted by the respondents except for Volume II, the Cost Proposals. The evaluations were based on the following criteria:

1. Responsiveness to the SOW
2. Judgment of the credentials of proposed personnel who would prepare and present course material, based on resumes in the proposal
3. Judgment of the perceived ability of vendor(s) to achieve schedule commitment

The organization of the written evaluation was in three parts. Part I of the evaluation rated the vendors from one to ten on each component of the criteria. When computing the score, a weighting factor was applied where criteria 1 and 2 had a weighting factor of one (1.0), and criteria 3 had a weighting factor of one-half (.5). Criteria 3 was rated lower because the schedule, although important, did not seem as important as the quality of the vendor's personnel who would prepare and present the material and their technical response to the ITQ SOW. Part II of the evaluation provided rationale for the score given to each vendor. Finally, Part III of the evaluation provided a summary of some observations and recommendations. The summary and recommendation from Part III follows. The respondents' names are intentionally omitted, except for the vendor chosen through this process.

It was expected that the recommendation contained in the technical evaluation would form just a part of the total evaluation. The cost submitted by the vendor played an important part in the final selection.

Summary and Recommendation for Developer Selection (Part III of the evaluation report)

The vendors fell into three categories: 1) those that declined to bid, 2) those that were partially responsive or offered an alternative to the SETP SOW, and 3) those that were responsive to ITQ SETP SOW.

Based on the response given by one vendor, Rockwell concluded that the terms and conditions of the ITQ SOW might have been a contributing factor in "no bid" decision returned by qualified vendors.

The vendors in category 2 (partially responsive or offered alternative) were ranked in the following order:

1.	University A	3.	Vendor C
2.	Vendor B	4.	University D

In category 2, the first choice was University A. It proposed its software engineering curriculum as an alternative to the Rockwell SETP and provided the added advantage of University credits. However, the objectives of SETP are to meet Rockwell's training needs. These objectives are: to be adaptable and incorporate evolving Rockwell standards, methods, and tools; to be flexible and to provide training when the need arises to meet project schedules, and to have in-house trainers who can bring recent project experience to the courses being taught.

Only two vendors fell into Category 3 (responsive to the SETP SOW), Vendor E and Vendor F. The evaluation scores of the two vendors did not indicate a clear winner and the evaluation team's recommendation of Vendor F was more intuitive than empirical. Some considerations that led the team to their recommendation of Vendor F were:

1. Attention to detail in the ITQ SETP response.

   Vendor F clearly identified its proposed approach, and the personnel to be involved in the development and presentation of each course.

   Thought was already given to the topics to be used throughout the SETP.

   A judgment that Vendor F would assume responsibility for course planning and development without an undue burden on the buyer's staff.

2. Vendor's Commitment to Rockwell's goals

   Identification of the specific SETP trainer personnel (and their qualifications).

   A judgment that individuals identified to fulfill the contract requirements would be available after contract award.

   A judgment that this development would be taken seriously. Upon completion, the product would be Rockwell's property, and would not be sold to others.

3. A top-down approach versus a bottom-up approach

   To define and plan the top level objectives of the SETP courses and prepare an overview of the content of those courses instead of building each course and then, lastly make an overview.

4. Cost

   A judgment that the recommended vendor's product would have less initial cost, and that future changes to the SETP could be made by Rockwell without further help from the vendor.

In summary, the SETP evaluation committee recommended the proposal from Vendor F, Integrated Software, Inc., ands its teammates BTG, Inc. and Software Productivity Solutions, Inc., and believes that the vendor will provide a high quality training program.

SPTP Developers

The Integrated Software, Inc. team, composed of nationally known experts in various software engineering areas, was awarded the contract as developers for the SPTP in March 1988. The development team member's names are shown in Figure 4 of Part II of this paper. Phase 3, Instructional Design, is also covered in Part II of this paper.

Excerpts from the Rockwell ITQ

Excerpts from the ITQ are shown here so that the reader may better understand the Rockwell requirements for the instructional design phase.

The Development Phase consists of the preparation of: Course Contents, Overhead Projector Viewgraphs, Trainee Materials, Instructor Notes, and Tests by the Seller for each of the courses identified .

Course Contents — Because of the body of knowledge known as Software Engineering is sufficiently large, the Rockwell SETP will concentrate on twenty-one topic areas that can be redistributed into three training tracks with varying level of proficiency in the subject matter in each track.

There is a strong relationship among topics and sub-topics. A top-down approach is required to focus on the software engineering process first because the overall view is needed to put the individual activities in context. Software management and control activities are presented next, followed by the development activities and product view topics. Viewed in this manner, there are three distinct levels in the Program.

LEVEL 1   The Software Engineering Process Software Evolution
          Software Generation
          Software Maintenance
          Technical Communication

LEVEL 2   Software Configuration Management
          Software Quality Issues
          Software Quality Assurance
          Software Project Organizational and Management Issues
          Software Project Economics
          Software Operational Issues

LEVEL 3   Requirement Analysis
          Specification
          System Design
          Software Design
          Software Implementation
          Software Testing
          System Integration
          Embedded Real-Time Systems
          Human Interfaces

The first level is an overview of the software engineering process, including how software evolves, how it is generated, and how it is maintained. The educational objective is to give the trainees a minimal degree of knowledge and comprehension.

The second level stresses the control and management activities of software engineering. These are the activities that most clearly distinguish software engineering from programming; they also complement the trainee's knowledge of programming to provide the total conceptual framework for more detailed study.

The third level presents in-depth coverage of development activities in the context of programming-in-the-large. The trainee should achieve a level of skill in using tools, applying methods, and synthesizing software work products.

Overhead Projector Viewgraphs — The Course Contents developed by the Seller shall be used by the Seller as the basis for the development of Overhead Projector Viewgraphs summarizing and highlighting the main points to be presented during the course. One viewgraph, at a minimum, shall be prepared for each major-point and sub-point set forth.

Trainee Materials — The Course Contents developed by the Seller shall be used by the Seller as the basis for the development of Student Materials to be provided to each trainee attending the course. Trainee Materials shall include copies of all Overhead Projector Viewgraphs developed, as well as any other materials used by the instructor during the video taping of the course, for subsequent reference use by the Trainee.

Tests — The information to be presented by Seller's instructor during video-taping and the information contained in the Overhead Projector Viewgraphs and Trainee Materials shall be used by the Seller as the basis for the development of Tests to be given to Trainees by Rockwell upon completion of the course, to measure knowledge gained from the course.

Reviews — During the Development Phase, the Seller shall participate in Preliminary Course Content reviews, Final Course Contents reviews, Monthly Program reviews, and other reviews as required with Rockwell to provide complete visibility over the progress of the Seller. The Course Content, Overhead Projector Viewgraphs and Trainee Materials and tests developed by the Seller for each course shall be reviewed by Rockwell during a Preliminary Content Review to be held within the period specified. During this review the Seller shall present the form, format and draft contents of all such items being developed, for Rockwell's approval.

Similarly, all such items shall also be reviewed by Rockwell during a Final Content Review to be held within the period specified. During this review the Seller shall present for Rockwell's approval the final contents of the Course Content, Overhead Projector Viewgraphs, Trainee Materials , Instructor Notes, and Tests for each course.

Monthly Program Status Reviews will be held in accordance with the Delivery and Completion Requirements set forth. During these meetings the Seller shall present schedule status reports and other information, as required, to keep Rockwell fully informed as to the Seller's progress.

Monthly Reports — The information presented in the Monthly Program Status Review shall be summarized and submitted by the Seller in a written Monthly Report, in Seller's format, due in accordance with the Delivery and Completion Requirements.

Items to be Delivered — The Seller shall provide to Rockwell a reproducible master, 8 1/2 inches by 11 inches, for each page of each Course Content, Trainee Materials, Instructor Notes, and Tests, which have received Final Approval under the Development Phase, to be delivered in accordance with the Delivery and Completion Requirements.

Seller shall provide instructor(s), to present each of the courses as set forth in the approved Course Content, Viewgraphs, Instructor Notes, and Trainee Materials developed by Seller, to be Video-taped by Rockwell personnel and equipment at Rockwell's Downey, California facility.

Instructor Qualifications — Each instructor provided by the Seller shall be experienced in the subject of the specific course to be presented and shall also be proficient in the art of transference of knowledge to be imparted during such course.

Instructor Responsibilities — Instructors shall be well-groomed and properly attired for a business instruction environment; clothing colors shall be compatible with video-taping requirements.

Instructors shall promptly arrive and initiate presentation of course materials to be video-taped in accordance with the specific times mutually established between Rockwell and Seller under the requirements.

Acceptance or Rejection of Instructor Personnel — Before being assigned to perform Instruction, Seller shall submit the names and qualifications of all Seller-proposed personnel so that Rockwell may review such qualifications and conduct personal interviews, if desired. Rockwell shall accept or reject personnel as the result of such reviews and interviews.

Rockwell may request the replacement of any Seller's Instructor whom it considers to be unsuitable for instruction to be performed. Seller's instructors so removed shall be replaced within 48 hours of such removal by Seller unless otherwise directed by Rockwell.

Multiple Course Instruction — When selecting instructors, the Seller shall consider grouping courses to be instructed by one particular instructor, so that video-taping can be completed at consecutive taping sessions.

Instructor Travel Arrangements — Seller shall be responsible for making all travel arrangements and paying all approved expenses of its instructors.

Program Implementation

This program is scheduled for implementation involving the personnel from the software engineering department. Career tracks based on personnel job assignments have been developed for participation.

The scheduled implementation date is October 1989 for the target audience as identified by the terminal objectives. The first implementation is being presented concurrently with the video tape production activities. The course(s) are being presented to a select audience for the purposes of facilitator training and review.

Formative evaluations have taken place throughout the course(s) development process. These evaluations assess the potential effectiveness of courses through analysis and testing of component parts prior to actual course delivery.

A summary evaluation procedure is currently in the planning stage. This will be the process of assessing the actual effectiveness of the SPTP via testing, observations, surveys, and other means.

Plans for State of California Funding Support

The State of California established an Employment Training Panel (ETP) with the enactment of AB346, Johnston, September 14, 1982. It is the policy of the ETP:

1. To help people retrain to get a good job and keep it;

2. To promote the economic vitality of California by providing employers the skilled workers they need to successfully compete around the world;

3. To train skilled workers to help bring new business to California;

4. To operate a training program, not a social work or welfare program;

5. To train only when there are jobs for those who successfully complete training;

6. To eliminate bureaucratic interference and keep paperwork to a minimum;

STSD, as lead division, initiated Rockwell's Southern California organizations involvement with the State of California Employment Training Panel (ETP) through a subsidized Ada training program for members of the technical staff, August 1985. Subsequent to "Ada", other training programs have commenced including Artificial Intelligence/Expert Systems (AI/ES), and Computer Aided Design and Manufacturing (CAD/CAM). To date, reimbursement from the State to Rockwell for the retraining programs "Ada", "AI/ES", and "CAD/CAM" totals approximately $2 million dollars.

Rockwell involvement with the State of California ETP has provided a cost effective approach to personnel retraining in critical skill areas needed to build a technology base for current and future advanced aerospace transportation vehicles and components, at a time when the demand for trained personnel significantly exceeds the supply. This retraining focus has assisted in the enhancement of technical resources for high quality, high tech deliverable products and systems, and better response to new business demands.

Rockwell is in the planning stage for State of California ETP involvement with the SPTP. Rockwell anticipates an ETP agreement by October 1989.

Plans for MS Degree for SPTP

In addition to seeking state subsidy for the SPTP, Rockwell is seeking academic accreditation for SPTP. California Polytechnic University, Pomona, California, has been employed to review SPTP course materials to ensure that the pedagogical approach is consistent with requirements for graduate level academic credit. Cal Poly participates in review meetings and makes recommendations concerning inclusion/exclusion and/or modification of course content for each course.

Upon completion of each final course review meeting between Rockwell and Integrated Software, Inc., representatives of Cal Poly meets with Rockwell and Integrated Software representatives. The purpose of these meetings, which total approximately 178 hours, is to determine the additional student work requirements, such as research papers, in each of seven courses in order to be granted university credit. The meetings set the basis for the award of academic credit for completion of the course(s) in accordance with standards set by the University.

Lessons learned and experience gained

The effort involved in the preparation of the SPTP has been extensive. Many lessons have been learned and many more lessons will be learned before this development process is completed. Lessons learned thus far during the development phase of the program are:

- Developers are not too willing to develop courses at buyer's expense without the right to sell the finished product on the open market.

- During the early stage of needs and requirements analysis, it became apparent that decisions concerning program or course content could not be made by the user or developer until certain terms were mutually defined. An agreement of terms was needed to allow the user to describe the subject in terms of tasks and activities, skills and knowledge, and attitudes required to perform the job.

- Prior to the start of this type of project, management must have a clear vision of the total program in terms of benefits to be gained, such as increases in software development productivity. Management must commit the necessary resources for long term gains to be realized.

- Good results can not be expected without a well defined project plan.

- The success of program development depends heavily on the selection of well qualified and committed developers with sufficient industrial experience and theoretical knowledge.

- In a program development effort of this size, conduct as many reviews as resources will allow. This helps to ensure the inclusion of software engineering technology changes over the life of the development cycle.

Part II - The Development Phase

Abstract

Part II presents the development phase of the "Rockwell Software Process Training Program" described in Part I. It describes the program content, the tests and laboratory problem. It also presents the laboratory environment and the way in which the student can obtain partial college credit. The video taping studio and equipment is described. Lessons learned and future directions for the program are presented.

Background

The Rockwell Corporation, in 1984, began an extensive Ada language Train-the-Trainers educational effort in Southern California. Integrated Software, Inc. was contracted to develop the 80 hours of course material and delivered the lecture material in a classroom setting to the first team of 20 Rockwell trainers. This program was very successful and continues to function today. The State of California has reimbursed Rockwell for each of the approximately 475 students who have successfully completed the course.

Over the next 3 years it was recognized by Rockwell that a comprehensive Software Engineering Training Program was needed to educate and train all of their people involved in the software life cycle. During that time The Software Engineering Institute was formed and produced a "Draft Software Engineering Curriculum" [5]. Rockwell used this draft curriculum as the basis for a Solicitation for a Train-the-Trainers program. This is not to imply that the SPTP is an implementation of the current SEI curriculum recommendation for a MSE program.

Integrated Software, Inc. with its teammates BTG, Inc. and Software Productivity Solutions, Inc. responded to the Solicitation with a proposal to design, develop and deliver a program exactly as requested, with reuse of their existing teaching materials at the viewgraph level only. At this time 288 of the 408 lecture hours have been video taped.

Please refer to Part I of this paper for further background.

Introduction to the Rockwell SPTP

The Rockwell Software Process Training Program (SPTP) is a *large* industrial training effort by any measure. It consists of 21 topics organized into 7 courses with a total of 408 video taped lecture-hours. In addition there is an integrating laboratory problem scheduled to be completed in 164 lab-hours plus 28 hours of comprehensive tests. The development effort by the ISI, BTG, SPS team is 7862 labor hours (4.2 labor years).

An overview of the SPTP structure is shown in Figure 4. The reader will note the 7 courses consisting of 21 topics. The first topic of each course starts with a course overview but otherwise each topic is a separate physical entity so that topics may be rearranged into new courses if desired. The video time is expressed in hours where each hour is between 45 and 55 minutes of video taping. There are approximately 6000 transparencies plus 6000 associated instructor notes for the entire program.

The video tapes are used by the Rockwell instructors, who are called Facilitators, in a classroom scenario. The video tapes are played and the Facilitator answers questions and then leads a class discussion on related topics. Each student is given a workbook which

Integrated Software, Inc.
(407) 984-1986
BTG   SPS

Rockwell International

COURSE NAME & NUMBER	TOPIC NAME & NUMBER	VIDEO TIME Hours/Topic	LAB TIME Hours/Topic	TEST TIME Hours/Topic	INSTRUCTOR
1 Introduction to the Software Process	Software Process	16	:00	1:00	
	Software Evolution	8	:00	1:00	
	Software Generation	16	:00	1:00	Mark Lantzy
	Software Maintenance	4	:00	:30	
	Technical Communication	4	4:00	:30	
2 Software Quality	Software Quality Issues	16	1:00	2:00	Mark Lantzy
	Software Quality Program	24	3:00	2:00	
3 Software Project Management	S/W Project Issues	24	3:00	1:30	Doug Ingram, PhD
	S/W Project Economics	16	2:00	1:00	
	S/W Configuration Management	20	2:30	1:15	
	S/W Operational Issues	4	:30	:15	
4 System Design	System Design Process	24	16:00	2:00	Ed Comer
	Embedded Real-Time Systems	16	:00	1:15	Steve Von Edwins
	Human Interfaces	8	:00	:45	Cammie Donaldson
5 Software Requirements & Specification	Requirements Analysis	24	6:00	2:00	Al Davis, PhD
	Requirements Specification	24	6:00	2:00	
6 Software Design & Implementation	Software Design	40	16:00	1:00	Kaye Grau, PhD
	Software Implementation	40	32:00	1:30	Sam Harbaugh, PhD
	Advanced Ada Topics	40	32:00	1:30	Sam Harbaugh, PhD
7 Software Testing & Integration	Software Testing	32	32:00	3:00	Mark Lantzy
	System Integration	8	8:00	1:00	
TOTALS		408 Video Taped Lecture Hours	164 Lab Hours	28 Test Hours	

Software Process Training Program
FOUNDATION FOR EXCELLENCE

Figure 4. Integrated Software, Inc. Development Team

consists of each transparency and associated instructor note plus a list of reference material. The reference material itself is available to the student in a training reference library. The test time of 28 hours is allocated to all topics so that tests can be conducted progressively throughout the program. Attendance is recorded and tests are graded.

The laboratory time of 164 hours is allocated to 15 topics. A unifying laboratory problem is used such that the students gain practice with all aspects of the software development life cycle. The students perform the laboratory exercises in teams of 4-5 people. The first laboratory assignment is a flight simulator to execute on an IBM PC/AT. The students are given a Operational Concept Document, a skeleton Software Requirements Specification and device drivers and then they produce a DOD-STD-2167A documentation set and working model. Students on a career track which skips some laboratory assignments are given prerequisite laboratory solutions as input for their laboratory assignment.

The course instructors listed in Figure 4 are the ones who prepared the course material and delivered the videotaped lectures.

The SPTP Development Life Cycle

The SPTP development life cycle is shown in Figure 2 and consists of 5 temporal phases, Program Design, Preliminary Design, Detailed Design, Finalize and Video Taping.

Program Design was accomplished mostly during proposal preparation when the team members, as a group, determined how much time to allocate to each topic, laboratory and test and which instructor was responsible each topic and course. Each instructor then designed their topic to the level of sub-subtopics based on the educational objectives stated in Rockwell's requirements and their personal teaching experience. After contract award a 3 day group meeting was held to review and refine the program design, define standards for presentation format and production tools and formulate a detailed development schedule. The program design phase culminated with a one day Kickoff Meeting at Rockwell for their approval of the design, standards and schedule.

During Preliminary Design each instructor designed their topics to the slide title level including slide number, objectives to the subtopic level and 1 hour tape boundaries. Slide content hierarchy was shown by relative indentation level of the slide title. The preliminary design of course 1, "Introduction to the Software Process" was the subject of the first preliminary course review (PCR) at Rockwell which lasted one day. This review gave a good forum for discussing the extent and depth of material to be covered in the entire program. The remaining 6 courses were then reviewed by team members and then PCRs were subsequently conducted at Rockwell in 4 consecutive days to maintain continuity of material and, if necessary, move material among topics and courses.

The detailed design phase produced the individual transparency masters and corresponding instructor notes (6000 of each), lab assignments, reference list and tests. Each team member reviewed the output of the other 2 team members and then a one day Final Course Review (FCR) was held at Rockwell for each course. The FCRs were spread out over the 12 month development schedule. The finalization phase resulted in final edits and reproducible masters. The video taping phase was conducted in Rockwell's studio which is described in the following section.

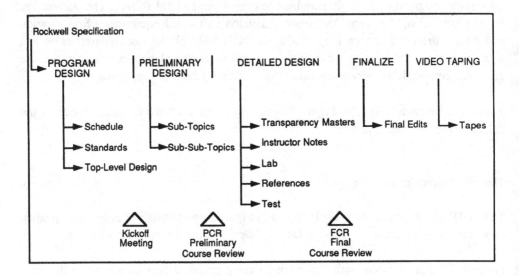

Figure 5. SPTP Development Life Cycle

The Rockwell Video Taping Studio

Between the time of the 1984 Ada Train-the-Trainers effort and the current SPTP effort, Rockwell designed, built and staffed a video taping studio at their Space Transportation System Division in Downey, California. The 900 square foot (100 square meters) studio is designed to produce instructional video tapes of lectures given by one lecturer to an audience of up to 15 people seated at tables. The lectures are viewed by 3 cameras on mobile floor pedestals, each with a cameraman, under the control of a director in an adjoining control room. The instructor wears a wireless microphone while an array of ceiling mounted microphones pick up any audience participation.

The lecturer utilizes 2 overhead transparency projectors while the cameras are viewing the projector screens, the instructor and audience. Four video tape recorders simultaneously record each camera's output and the line output from a mixer panel. A character generator for titles and other documentation is also input to the mixer panel. Future mixer input from a Macintosh computer is planned. An audience member is assigned to change transparencies for the instructor in order to save time and to avoid unflattering views of the instructor. The audience members each have a copy of the transparencies for reference and note taking. Recording 6 tapes per day stressed the durability of the instructor and audience. Four tapes per day would be a better plan.

The Laboratory

The software process training laboratory at Rockwell, Downey, California consists of 20 networked IBM PCs with Ada compilers and CASE tools. In addition the students will utilize VAX-based CASE tools for portions of the laboratory problem. Other Rockwell divisions will have their own laboratory facilities.

Career Tracks and College Credit

There are four career tracks through the SPTP course material as shown in Figure 6; Software Project Management, System Design, Software Design and Software Evaluation. Each track can carry with it a certain amount of college credit toward a degree at California State Polytechnic University, Pomona, California. The course design and content has been reviewed by Cal Poly faculty to determine the amount of credit that will be awarded on a Cal Poly transcript to students who successfully complete the SPTP and an additional amount of related library research work. The credit will be awarded toward a Masters Degree in Computer Science, Bachelor's Degree in Computer Information Systems or Master's of Business Administration Degree.

Lessons Learned

Communications are vital:

The geographical distribution of the development team and customer has stressed the interpersonal communications. The development team had two "all-hands" meetings, one for overall program design and a second for individual course and topic design. These were invaluable; however, electronic interchange of slide material via electronic mail and/or facsimile machines would have lowered costs and increased quality. Describing slide changes by telephone is a costly, trying experience.

Tool capabilities and flaws limit creativity:

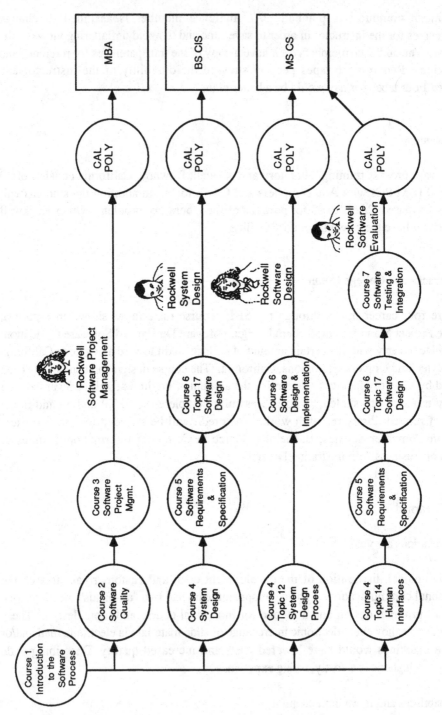

Figure 6. SPTP Career Tracks

The Microsoft Powerpoint slide production software, for the Macintosh, was chosen for production of hard copy slides and instructor notes. The most notable Powerpoint limitations and flaws are:

1) Lack of management features - Powerpoint is fine for presentations of about 25 or so slides but there are no functions to aid management of 6000 slide presentations. A configuration management system and the ability to write a slide title list to a file would be a great help.

2) Problems importing MacDraw files - MacDraw slides imported into Powerpoint exhibit strange anomalies when printed, such as gaps in the printing and unexpected new-lines.

3) Lack of programmatic interface - Powerpoint is basically a paper-maker. The ability to write machine processable output files is not in its architecture. Therefore the ability to perform global edits to slide material is frustrated. No material regarding internal file formats could be found.

4) Personality traits - Sometimes What You See Ain't What You Get (WYSAWYG). For instance, a white oval on the screen may be printed in solid black. In a number of cases the reduced slide on the instructor notes gets noticeably distorted from the full sized slide.

Course material is never "finished":

Creative people never stop creating. That is a desirable trait and certain mechanisms were provided to accommodate this. The instructors carried updated pages to the taping to replace pages in the presentation. During the taping Rockwell Facilitators were able to call for discussion and clarification or inject a point themselves. After taping the director edits out "flubs", "bad shots", etc. using the tapes from each camera as raw material. During use of the tapes the Facilitator can enhance taped material by lecture and discussion. Each course's Instructor's Manual contains a section for discussion topics.

Need to Consciously Adjust to Train-the-Trainers Scenario

The course developers are in every case experienced teachers who are accustomed to preparing and delivering viewgraph material. It has required conscious effort for them to adjust to preparing material for other teachers. They have had to direct their instructor notes to the next instructor rather than to themselves. Usually this means adding much more material. For instance, an instructor note which read "tell the Emu story" had to be replaced by the actual Emu story.

The course material quality had to be much better for Train-the-Trainers than for a seminar. A seminar instructor can effectively use some last minute viewgraphs, perhaps hand-drawn enroute to the seminar. With the extensive review cycle of TTT the viewgraph quality must be uniformly high at all times. Laser printers and MacIntosh software made this economically feasible.

A seminar instructor can often get by with using slang, acronyms, in-jokes etc. by reading the audience's reaction and adjusting accordingly. These same expressions fall flat when stated in "cold-print" on instructor notes. They had to be systematically removed from the TTT material along with any expressions which could possibly be offensive to any potential audience.

(Re)Scheduling is a Complicated Activity:

Scheduling of the reviews and video taping among the subcontractors, Rockwell's engineers and video studio was a very complicated activity. It was accomplished only by the fortitude and cooperation of everyone concerned and the luxury of being able to slip the schedule when conflicts could not be avoided.

Reuse of existing course material is not as high as desired:

Technology is rapidly evolving and existing material must be updated. For instance, the change from DOD-STD 2167 to DOD-STD-2167A required much more rework than adding the "A" suffix.

The instructor improves the presentation technique. For instance, the way that Ada can be presented has evolved over the past years from a language orientation to a software engineering orientation.

The course material is intended for a specific, rather than general, audience. For instance, terms which can be used loosely for general audiences, may have a precise historically established meaning at Rockwell and must be used only in that precise way in their SPTP.

Future Directions

The SPTP must evolve along two directions; intellectual content and presentation technology.

The "half-life" of software process technology may be about 5 years, that is, in 5 years 50% of the course material will be obsolete and it will be desired to replace it with newer technology. The SPTP has been constructed modularly so that, in time, certain material can be skipped and new material inserted to replace it.

Presentation technology is evolving at a rapid rate as new, low-cost devices and authoring software become available for interactive, PC based teaching machines. Once again we will be looking toward the SEI for guidance through such avenues as the workshop on Intelligent Tutoring. The challenge will be to reuse the intellectual matter contained in the slides, instructor notes and video tapes with a minimum of rework but gain the advantages of self-paced, individualized training offered by intelligent tutoring machines.

Acknowledgements

Acknowledgement is due to Herb Reed, Bill Selfridge, William Wimberly and many others at Rockwell who are tirelessly dedicated to the success of the program.

A special thanks is due to Mary Smith of Integrated Software, Inc. for editing and production of this paper.

References for Part I

[1]   Senator Dan Quayle, "Can the US win the other space race? Space Science Education", Defense Science, September 1988

[2]   Winder, R et al., "Software Engineering in A First degree", Software Engineering Journal, July 1987

[3]   W.P.Selfridge. "SA and OOD Methodology Study", (October 29, 1985), Rockwell Internal Publication

[4]   Meier, David, "New Age Learning: From Linear to Geodesic", Training and Development Journal (May 1985): 40-43

[5]   Ford, Gary, Gibbs, Norman, and Tomayko, James, "Software Engineering Education", An Interim Report from the Software Engineering Institute, Working Draft for 1987 SEI Conference on Software Engineering Education. This work was sponsored by the U.S. Department of Defense

References not cited

Preparing Instructional Objectives, revised 2nd edition, Robert F. Mager, David S. Lake Publishers, Belmont, CA ISBN -0-8224-4341-4

Taxonomy of Educational Objectives, Book 1 Cognitive Domain, Benjamin S. Bloom editor, Longman Inc., New York ISBN 0-582-28010-9

Data Structures, Algorithms, and Software Engineering

*Christian S. Collberg**
Lund University, Sweden

Abstract. *Traditionally, students in undergraduate computer science curricula have to wait until their third or fourth year until they are confronted with the problems which arise in the design of large programs. The rationale behind this is that programming-in-the-small has to be mastered before programming-in-the-large. In this paper we will argue that the elements of software engineering must be present at all levels and in all computer science courses and that it is feasible, with the proper tools and precautions, to assign large and complex programming assignments even at the introductory level. An experiment to this effect has been carried out in a data structures and algorithms course given at the University of Lund. A non-trivial program (a make-utility for Modula-2) was specified and partially modularized by the instructor and assigned piecewise to the students. The assignments trained the students in the implementation of data structures and algorithms as well as software tool design, modularization, information hiding, reuse, and large system design.*

1 Introduction

We believe that the principles of software design must permeate every part of a computer science program, and should not be confined to one upper-level course in software engineering. Every course, even ones at the introductory level, can contribute to the students' understanding of large systems - how they are designed, implemented and tested, and how they evolve with changing needs. In this sense our views coincide with the ones expressed in the ACM recommended curriculum for CS2 [5]. This paper describes how a traditional undergraduate data structures and algorithms course was given a software engineering flavor by careful choice of programming language and assignments.

2 The course

The Lund University computer science program, like most other computer science curricula, offers a course in the fundamentals of data structures and algorithms. The course contains, among other things, sections on lists, trees, and graphs, algorithms

---

*Author's present address: Department of Computer Sciences, Lund University, S-221 00 Lund, Sweden. email: collberg@dna.lth.se

for searching and sorting, and elements of the design and analysis of algorithms. The students come from a variety of backgrounds; some have almost two years of mathematics training as well as an introductory course in Pascal programming, others are starting their third year in a business computing program, and others are still freshmen with an introductory Pascal course as their only computing experience.

The students are supposed to spend an equivalent of ten weeks of full time work on the course. This includes twenty-four ninety-minute lectures and twelve ninety-minute labs, six to eight programming assignments, and a final.

For many years the assignments were written in Pascal, each assignment being a self-contained (small) program. A typical set of assignments might have included the following:

- An arithmetic RPN calculator using a stack.

- A polynomial calculator using linked lists to represent polynomials.

- A telephone directory using binary search trees or hash tables.

- An index generating program using an $O(n \log n)$ sorting method.

- An implementation of Dijkstra's algorithm for the Single Source Shortest Path Problem.

2.1 Objectives

The emphasis of the course is on data structures and algorithms and their implementation. Certain topics have to be included in the course material and this limits the amount of extraneous material, such as software engineering, which can be covered. The mandatory sections are:

abstract data types their definition and use.

data structures dynamic and static implementations of lists (one-way, two-way), stacks, queues, trees (k-ary, general), and graphs.

recursion implementation and elimination.

sets bit string, sorted array (binary and interpolation search), binary trees, hash tables (with chaining, and with linear, quadratic, double, and double ordered collision resolution), AVL-trees, 2-3-trees and B-trees on external memory.

sorting $O(n^2)$ algorithms, quicksort, heapsort and mergesort on external memory.

priority queues heaps.

analysis of algorithms Asymptotic complexity, analysis of iterative and recursive algorithms, solution of recurrence relations.

3 The language

Choosing a suitable implementation language for novice computer science students is not an easy task. Apart from obvious factors such as simplicity, expressiveness and suitability for the assignments at hand, the availability of affordable and reliable compilers also play an important role. For the present course the choice was further complicated by the fact that the only prerequisite was a rudimentary knowledge of Pascal. Deciding on a language radically different from Pascal, perhaps in a different paradigm such as functional (ML) or object oriented (Eiffel), might force the students to spend more time getting acquainted with the new language than with the programming problems. An imperative language in the Pascal tradition was therefore deemed the most suitable choice.

Furthermore, it was felt that in order to teach the basic concepts of abstraction and software design the language ought to support modularization, information hiding, generics and generalized iteration. We concluded that Modula-2 would be the best, although far from optimal, choice:

- Modula-2 is in many ways similar to Pascal and should be easy for the students to learn.
- An acceptable compiler was already available.
- In Modula-2 information hiding is achieved through so called *opaque types*. This is a restricted form of information hiding since opaque types are essentially limited to pointers. Also, constants may not be hidden.
- There is no support per se in Modula-2 for generics. Generic ADTs can, however, be implemented using techniques discussed in [1, 9].
- Generators/iterators (in the style of CLU) are not available. They can, however, be simulated using Modula-2's procedure types.

Koffman [4] favors Modula-2 over Ada, PL/1, and Pascal for CS1 and CS2. Ada and PL/1 are rejected on the grounds that they are too large and complex and that compilers are not readily available for small computers. Pascal is rejected because of its lack of important software engineering features and because of its syntax, which is more complicated than that of Modula-2.

4 The project

The objective of the course was to give the students an idea of what they might encounter when they enter their career as computer professionals. Therefore, the programming project was given as a set of small, self-contained projects assigned at different times during the semester. The students were unaware of the ultimate goal of the project until presented with the last assignment. Thus, they may be thought of as having played the roles of *starting programmers*: largely ignorant of the overall structure and goal of a project, repeatedly given small, informally specified assignments, and unaware of how their contributions would eventually fit into the complete picture. But as the students reached the last assignment, they switched roles to become, in a sense, *project managers*. They were given a vaguely formulated description of a project which they should be able to design and implement with the aid of the tools they had constructed in previous assignments.

One of the major obstacles in the design of the course was to find a suitable, non-trivial assignment. It was felt that the following keywords described the criteria which had to be met:

usefulness To simulate the real world as closely as possible, the project should result in a useful product, not a toy.

tool-building It would be beneficial to the students' long-term understanding of software engineering if the product was a software tool which they could use in future class projects.

reuse To show the students the benefits of *reuse*, some general software component should be used more than once in the project.

relevance The course is *primarily* a course in data structures and algorithms. Hence, the individual assignments should be relevant to the material presented during class. Specifically, students should be trained in the areas of lists, trees, graphs, searching, and sorting.

non-irrelevance The students should, as little as possible, be required to implement functions unrelated to the course material. In other words, the assignments should not force the students to spend an inappropriate amount of time producing code which would not aid in their understanding of the problem area.

A *make*-utility [2] for Modula-2-programs was deemed a suitable project. Such a program was not available (this would take care of the *real world*-requirements), and it would require most of the data structures and algorithms on which the students needed training. Also, those parts which would require knowledge not obtained in the course, primarily a Modula-2 parser and certain system-dependent facilities, could easily be provided by the instructor.

The *make*-utility was envisioned as two separate programs, *dgen* (for *dependency generator*) and *m2make*. Basically, *dgen* would, by examining the source code of the modules making up a given program, build a directed acyclic graph on the import-export relationships between the modules and write this graph to a binary file. *m2make* would, when invoked, read this dependency graph and initiate the compilations necessary to bring the program up to date.

The input to the dependency generator is a text file, the *program description*, which contains a list of the modules used in the program. Two source files and two compiler-generated files are associated with each Modula-2 module: definition- and implementation files which are compiled into symbol- and object files, respectively. The *program description* must therefore contain references to the directories where these files reside. *program descriptions* may also define *aliases*, short forms of frequently used strings. The format of the *program description* is shown in figure 1.

It is important to remember that students in a second computer science course are novice programmers who have not yet reached the level of sophistication where they can take informal specifications of complex problems through the normal stages of design, formal specification, implementation, and testing. Careful wording of the assignments is therefore essential: the students must be guided over the worst pitfalls while, at the same time, be given enough latitude to explore different design strategies.

```
ALIAS      home        /usr/chris
ALIAS      m2          $home$/m2
ALIAS      bin         $m2$/bin

MODULE     AliasSet
DEF        $m2$/alias
IMP        $m2$/alias
SYM        $bin$
OBJ        $bin$

MODULE     GenericBST
DEF        $m2$/bst
...        ...         ...
```

Figure 1: The layout of the *program description*. X should everywhere be replaced by the value of the alias X.

Hence, the early assignments were specified in detail, giving only minor room for student design errors, whereas the later ones were more vaguely formulated.

In each of the first five (out of six) assignments the students were asked to perform three tasks: to implement a generic package for a certain data structure or algorithm, to create an instantiation of the generic package, and, lastly to extend the dependency generator in some way using the newly designed packages. Students were expected to turn in each assignment complete with user-, system-, and program documentation, as well as with a simple interactive main program that would enable easy testing of the functions implemented thus far. The program and its documentation was, in other words, developed in parallel and in an incremental fashion.

The sixth assignment was an exercise in design and reuse. The students were given a brief sketch of a Modula-2 make-utility and were asked to design one using previously constructed tools.

Assignment # 1: Lists.

1. Implement a generic two-way linked list package, *GenericLists*.

2. Use *GenericLists* to implement a package *ModuleList* which stores names of modules and for each module the names of the directories in which its corresponding files reside.

3. Implement a program *dgen* which loads the contents of a *program description* text file into the *ModuleList*.

Assignment # 2: Binary Search Trees.

1. Implement a generic binary search tree package, *GenericBST*.

2. Use *GenericBST* to implement a package *AliasSet* which stores variable-value pairs. Both variables and their values are character strings.

3. Extend *dgen* to handle the definition and use of aliases in the *program description*.

Assignment # 3: Hash Tables.

1. Implement a generic hash table package, *GenericHashTables*.

2. Use *GenericHashTables* to implement a package *ModuleSet* which stores a set of module names and data about each module. This data will include the complete names of the files which belong to the module.

3. Extend *dgen* to load data into *ModuleSet* from *ModuleList*.

Assignment # 4: Graphs.

1. Implement a generic directed graph package, *GenericGraphs*, using the adjacency-list technique. Use *GenericLists* to implement the adjacency-lists.

2. Use *GenericGraphs* to implement a package *ImportGraph* where each vertex represents a file and each edge a dependency between two files.

3. Extend *dgen* in the following way:

   - Create a graph node for each file in *ModuleSet*.
   - Store references to the nodes created in the *ModuleSet* entries for the corresponding modules.
   - Build an import dependency graph for the modules in *ModuleSet*. Use *M2Parser*, a parser for Modula-2 provided by the instructor.
   - Test the graph for circularity. A circular graph represents a non-compilable Modula-2 program.

Assignment # 5: Sorting.

1. Implement a generic sorting package, *GenericSort*, using an $O(n \log n)$ algorithm.

2. Use *GenericSort* to extend *GenericHashTables* with a function to iterate over the elements in the table in sorted order.

3. Extend *dgen* to create a listing file containing:

   - A list of the modules and their corresponding files, sorted on the module names.
   - The dependency graph.
   - A list of the aliases and their values, sorted on the variable names.

Assignment # 6: A Make-utility.

1. Implement a dependency generator *dgen* for Modula-2. *dgen* should as input take a text file, the *program description*, containing a list of the modules used in a program. It should generate two files, a listing file and a binary file containing a dependency graph.

2. Implement a *make*-utility, *m2make*, for Modula-2. *m2make* should as input take a dependency graph-file for a program, traverse the graph in reverse topological order, and update the program by initializing the compilation of the modules which are out of date.

5 Software engineering issues

Although primarily an exercise in the implementation of data structures and algorithms, the *make*-project covered many, albeit not all, pertinent software engineering issues. The choice of Modula-2 as the implementation language provided a natural stepping stone for training the students in the design of low-level specifications and in the hiding of representational details of modules. The concept of *reuse* was introduced in two ways: by making all low-level abstract data types general and generic and by forcing the students to structure their programs in such a way that major parts could be used more than once. *Maintenance* is, by nature, always difficult to teach within the constraints of an educational setting. Here the students were introduced to some of the issues involved when the incorporation of new code into their program required changes to old code. In order to promote a sound attitude towards *testing* and *documentation* each assignment was regarded as a program in its own right, complete with documentation and routines for testing.

6 Student reactions and results

A survey administered to the students at the end of the course revealed some expected but also some surprising results. A majority of the students were enthusiastic about the project as such, but, as might be expected, thought the workload was too heavy. A typical project contained approximately 2300 lines of code in implementation modules and another 300 lines of code in definition modules (see table 1). One of the primary reasons for the present project design was to minimize the amount of extraneous code, i.e. code unrelated to the subject matter. According to the students this goal failed. Some claimed that as little as 10% of their total programming time was spent implementing important data structures and algorithms, and as much as 50% was spent on "mindless hacking". We feel that these figures should be taken with a grain of salt. They are most likely a reflection of the frustrations programmers often experience: more time is spent structuring and restructuring one's program into appropriate units and subunits than on code which "gets the job done".

Many students had problems with string manipulation which is virtually nonexistent in Modula-2. Only a few had caught the hints from the instructor that designing

	DEFINITION	IMPLEMENTATION
Source code lines	633	3085
Source code lines (stripped)	298	2335
Number of modules	13	15
Number of procedures	138	168

Table 1: Project statistics. Numbers are per project averages. Blank lines and comments have been removed from stripped source code.

ones own string manipulation package might be a good idea. Those who did turned in cleaner and simpler solutions.

The relationship between generic modules and their instantiations also puzzled many students. Perhaps this problem can be attributed to Modula-2's limited support of generic modules and could have been alleviated if another language, such as Ada, had been used.

Abstractions were, as always, a great mystery to the students. Typically they had problems distinguishing between a *Mapping-ADT*, such as the module *AliasSet*, and its implementation, in their case a binary search tree. Complaints about the fact that "everything has to be hidden" were frequent at the beginning of the course but thinned out as the students' programs grew in size and complexity.

Students often complained that the assignments were too informal and unprecise. When the instructor pointed out that a student's program did not catch a certain error condition, the student invariably replied that that particular error was not defined in the assignment. Many students failed to see that the lack of details in the specifications of the assignments was not an oversight on the part of the instructor, but an indication that they should think for themselves and, if that was not enough to resolve some ambiguity, ask the instructor. When queried about some fairly obvious design flaw in their program, many responded that they had wanted to do a different design but did not know whether *they were allowed to*. These and other problems can in part be attributed to the students' lack of maturity and in part to the instructor's inability to explain to the students the primary objectives of the course.

All in all, students reacted very favorably to the project and preferred it to the set of many small assignments they had had in earlier courses.

7   Relation to previous work

Courses with similar objectives have been described before [3, 6, 8]. None of these courses, however, have the strong emphasis on incrementality of implementation and documentation, tool design, real world applicability, and reuse as the one described in this paper. Also, the programming languages used (Pascal, PL/I, and FORTRAN, respectively) are unsuitable for teaching large system issues.

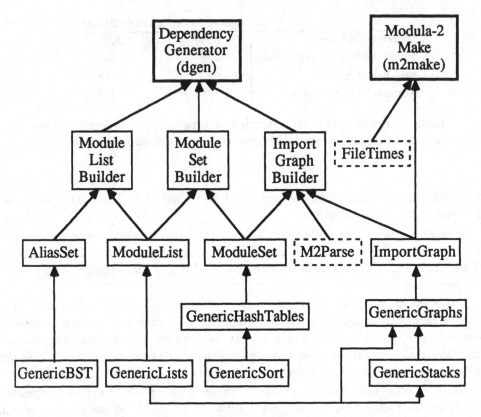

Figure 2: The module structure of the complete project, as envisioned by the instructor. Dashed boxes indicate modules made available to the students. *FileTimes* contains routines operating on file modification times. The stack handler is used in graph traversals.

8 Conclusions

In introductory computer science courses students are usually assigned programming projects that amount to little more than toy programs. The reason is the students' lack of programming maturity which makes it impossible for them to successfully manage a complex project from beginning to end. The consequence is that the students will not be confronted with the inherent complexities of large programs until they are approaching the end of their undergraduate computer science program. Even worse, if a programming project course is not required students may not even see, let alone design, a large program until well after graduation. The present course tries to alleviate this problem.

Essential parts of large system design, namely team effort and management, were not a part of the present course. There were three primary reasons for this: Firstly, it was considered important that each student would implement all major data structures and algorithms. Secondly, team coordination takes time and effort which, in this case, could be better spent learning the subject matter. Thirdly, students who drop the class will make problems for the remaining team members. We are not entirely happy with the lack of training in management skills and in future courses this may change.

Modula-2 was chosen both as the implementation- and target language. Modula-2 has many advantages over other languages frequently used in teaching. Other languages, such as Ada or Mesa, which support software engineering principles would have worked equally well. One important point to consider, however, is that in order to automatically generate dependency graphs, the target language should make module dependencies explicit in the source code. Automatic extraction of dependencies in languages such as C which rely on *include*-files for modularization is difficult and error prone [7]. Such languages should therefore be avoided.

Acknowledgements

We would like to thank Anders Edenbrandt and Sheila Dooley Collberg for their careful reading of this paper. Special thanks, as always, to D. Ed. Nils G. Hult.

References

[1] CZYZOWICZ, J., AND IGLEWSKI, M. Implementing Generic Types In Modula-2. *SIGPLAN Notices, Vol. 20*, No. 12, June 1985, pp. 26–32.

[2] FELDMAN, S. I. Make - A Program for Maintaining Computer Programs. *Software-Practice and Experience, Vol. 9*, No. 4, Apr. 1979, pp. 255–265.

[3] GILLETT, W. The Anatomy of a Project Oriented Second Course for Computer Science Majors. In *11th SIGCSE Technical Symposium on Computer Science Education*, Feb. 1980, ACM, pp. 25–31.

[4] KOFFMAN, E. B. The Case for Modula-2 in CS1 and CS2. In *19th SIGCSE Technical Symposium on Computer Science Education*, Feb. 1988, ACM, pp. 49–53.

[5] KOFFMAN, E. B., STEMPLE, D., AND WARDLE, C. E. Recommended Curriculum for CS2, 1984. *CACM, Vol. 28*, No. 8, Aug. 1985, pp. 815–818.

[6] TEAGUE, D. B. Computer Programming II: A Project-Oriented Course. In *12th SIGCSE Technical Symposium on Computer Science Education*, Feb. 1981, ACM, pp. 41–45.

[7] WALDEN, K. Automatic Generation of Make Dependencies. *Software-Practice and Experience, Vol. 14*, No. 6, June 1984, pp. 575–585.

[8] WERTH, L. H. Integrating Software Engineering into an Intermediate Programming Class. In *19th SIGCSE Technical Symposium on Computer Science Education*, Feb. 1988, ACM, pp. 54–58.

[9] WIENER, R. S., AND SINOVEC, R. F. Two Approaches to Implementing Generic Data Structures In Modula-2. *SIGPLAN Notices, Vol. 20*, No. 6, June 1985, pp. 56–64.

Teaching Software Maintenance

J.C. van Vliet

Department of Mathematics and Computer Science
Vrije Universiteit
De Boelelaan 1081
1081 HV Amsterdam
The Netherlands

Abstract. *An often-cited problem in software engineering education is that many of the relevant topics are difficult to address in a university setting. Though project work is a useful supplement to the lectures, it is very difficult to make the project truly realistic. In our environment therefore, we decided not to try to mimic all aspects of reality. Rather, we try to concentrate on a few aspects which can be realistically dealt with in a university environment. In this paper we describe a project which concentrates on maintenance activities. Independent evaluations by both students and project instructors reveal that these maintenance activities were most seriously hampered by inappropriate documentation at the component level.*

1. Introduction

The Vrije Universiteit in Amsterdam is a medium-sized university. The Department of Mathematics and Computer Science has about 500 undergraduate students, 350 of which take a major in Computer Science. The yearly intake for Computer Science is about 100 students. The undergraduate program lasts 4 years, though most students need 5. Students may specialize in Software Engineering, Information Systems, Computer Systems, Artificial Intelligence and Theoretical Computer Science. There is quite a large core program that is mandatory for all students. The specialization shows itself in a few advanced CS courses, a project to be done near the end of the program, and in a minor, such as Economy for Software Engineering students, or Cognitive Psychology for Artificial Intelligence students.

The software engineering course that is being dealt with in this paper, is given in the first half of the second year. Before attending this course, students have followed an introductory computer science course, a programming course (using Modula-2), a course on data structures (using [Stubbs87]), and a course on computer organization (using [Tanenbaum84]).

In the fall of 1988, some 140 students took the software engineering course. (Due to a change in the curriculum, a number of students in their third or fourth year took the course as well. Moreover, students majoring in physics, biology, economy, mathematics, and the like, may also take a minor in computer science, including the software engineering course.) All in all, it is fair to say that most students taking the software engineering course have not been exposed yet to very advanced topics in CS.

The text book used is [Van Vliet88]. The topics covered in this book do not drastically differ from those in other books, like [Fairley85] or [Pressman87]. The book does include chapters on (algebraic) specifications and reusability, topics that are generally not widely covered in other text books.

A recurring problem in software engineering education is phrased by Brooks: "you cannot teach it, you can only preach it" [Brooks87]. Lacking a solid theory, the instructor is left with good advice. It is easy to say that discipline is important, or that proper documentation is a critical success factor. Students will readily believe so. They will even think they practice those principles. Practicing good discipline or making proper documentation is hard to realize, though.

Courses in software engineering are therefore usually supplemented by some sort of project work. These projects are intended to give students a feeling of how software is really being developed. Several authors have stressed the importance of this project work, and advocate to bring in projects from outside the university itself [Gibbs87].

Such is not feasible with the number of students we have. Nor is the level of expertise of students in their second year such that realistic problems can be tackled successfully. We therefore took another approach, one which does not try to mimic all aspects of reality. Rather, we try to expose students sufficiently to some of the important aspects of real software development projects. The central objectives of the project were to expose students to:

- problems incurred by working in a team;
- problems incurred by imposing strict deadlines for various milestones;
- maintenance problems.

The degree in which the first two types of problems can be addressed realistically is seriously hampered by our environment. The project can only give students a feeling of the importance of these aspects.

We expected to be able to realistically address maintenance problems, though. In one of the first lectures, we stressed the importance of having a clear and precise requirements specification. Through a careful analysis, one may hope to build a sound perspective of user requirements and anticipate future changes. It was also noted that, no matter how much effort is spent in a dialogue with the prospective users, future changes remain hard to foresee. In this respect, specifying requirements has much in common with weather-forecasting: there is a limit as to how far the future can be predicted.

Problem description 1

You are to develop an interactive program which allows the user to move a cursor around in a maze. The maze to be used is specified on a file. {Follows a description of the input format.} When the program is started, part of the maze is shown on the screen. The part initially shown contains the entrance. The maze only contains horizontal and vertical corridors. Note that the maze need not entirely fit on the screen.

When the program is started, the cursor is positioned at the entrance. The cursor can be moved in four directions (left, right, up, down). The program stops if an exit is reached.

In the project discussed here, students were first asked to develop a certain application. Next, they had to maintain a version of that same application, developed by another group of students. Section 2 gives a short description of this project.

Both project instructors and students gave an evaluation of the software that had to be maintained in the course of this project. Section 3 discusses these evaluations. The difference in rankings given by project instructors and students yields valuable insight into some of the major causes of maintenance problems. It turned out that the quality of the documentation at the component level was particularly troublesome, much more so than the (technical) quality of the design and code.

2. The project

The course consisted of 12 weekly lectures, of 1.5 hours each. The project started in week 1 and ended by the end of week 12. Students were grouped into teams of 4 during week 1. Students were allowed to choose their own partners. Assistance with respect to this team organization was only given on request. During week 1 too, a one-page problem description was handed out. A summary of this problem description is given in Problem description 1. Each team was supposed to finish this project within 6 weeks. The following milestones were identified:

1. At the end of week 2, the requirements specification had to be completed and agreed upon by the project instructor;

2. At the end of week 4, the design had to be completed and agreed upon;

3. At the end of week 6, the program and documentation had to be completed. (A number of test files was provided by the instructor.)

For both the requirements specification and the design documentation, students had to adhere to a strict scheme. We decided to follow IEEE Standards 830 and 1016, respectively [IEEE84, 87]. Students were supposed to write their documentation in SGML-style. SGML is an ISO-standard for marking up structured documents [ISO86]. In SGML, one writes a context-free grammar for some specific document type.

Problem description 2

You are to maintain the maze program handed out to your group. You have to incorporate at least three changes, one out of each of the categories given below.

Category 1:

- Commands to move the cursor should be extended such that one may move 'nr' positions in any direction. It should also be possible to indicate that a corridor should be traversed up to its end.

Category 2:

- The maze should be allowed to contain corridors with an angle of 45 degrees to the horizontal axis.

- The screen should only show the part of the maze that has already been traversed.

- Each corridor has a certain width. The cursor has a certain width too. Thus, it may not be possible to enter some corridor.

- One may allocate penalties with certain locations within the maze. Each play starts with the player having a predefined number of points. Each time a location with a non-zero penalty is visited, that penalty is subtracted from the running number of points. If the number of points reaches zero, the play ends and the player has lost.

Category 3:

- The screen shows two windows, each with its own cursor. Both windows show a, possibly different, part of the same maze. Thus, two persons may play in one and the same maze via their own window.

- One or more mazes are placed above each other. The mazes are connected by one or more stairs.

Subsequently, documents of that type are marked up according to that grammar, and a parser may then check these documents for consistency with the corresponding grammar. We provided the students with templates for both the requirements specification and design documentation, and parsers for those document types. These parsers were generated, using an SGML parser-generator [Van Egmond87], from simple grammars derived from the IEEE-standards. Moreover, simple backends to generate nroff-code were supplied.

In this way, students were forced to pay attention to a number of aspects in the documentation. They had no need to bother about layout problems; every aspect hereof was taken care of by the tools provided. To the project instructors, this way of doing had the added advantage that all documents had the same appearance and the same order of treating things.

Students were allowed (and even urged) to have weekly meetings with their project instructor. They could reserve a slot in the instructor's agenda to discuss problems or the documentation delivered. For each milestone, the corresponding documentation had to be approved of by the instructor before the next phase could start. (We could not really enforce those rules. For instance, we have the suspicion that some teams wrote the program first, and made the design afterwards.)

During the second half of the project, each team had to maintain a program written by some other group. To this end, the results of the first stage were, largely at random, divided amongst the groups again. The teams were given some freedom with respect to the exact maintenance activities to be performed. For the types of maintenance activities allowed, see Problem description 2. The schedule for week 7-12 was the same as that for week 1-6.

3. Evaluation

At the beginning of week 7, each group was given both the source files and all documentation of the program they had to maintain. In week 11, they were given an evaluation sheet that contained a number of questions addressing various quality aspects of the documentation and program received. These evaluation sheets were, independently, also filled in by the instructors that assisted during the first six-week period. The rankings of both the instructors and students are summarized in Tables 1 and 2. The figures in the average-column are computed by counting the hopeless, bad, reasonable, good and excellent markings as -2, -1, 0, $+1$, $+2$, respectively.

The discussion in this section will concentrate on the difference in rankings between instructors and students, and possible explanations therefore. These differences give us some valuable clues.

A first observation seems to reveal that, on the average, project instructors gave higher rankings than students. To see whether this pattern is consistent, we have to take a closer look at the individual rankings. We therefore counted, for each question, the number of times the instructors gave higher rankings than the students for the same program and documentation, and vice versa. These figures are given in Table 3.

The figures in Table 3 show that the trend is not all that consistent. For some questions, notably 2a, 3a, 3b, 3c, 4a, 5a, 7, the pattern is rather chaotic. For others, it is much more consistent. The results of applying the two-sided sign test with null hypothesis (H_0) that instructors and students give equal rankings, is given in the last column of Table 3.

Questions 3a–c asked for an assessment of the maintainability of the program received. These questions address the changes mentioned in Category 3 of Problem description 2 (these changes were considered to be more difficult to realize than those in Categories 1 and 2). Both instructors and students have similar opinions about the effort needed to accommodate these changes. Somewhat to our surprise, the actual changes decided upon by the students do not agree with their assessment. A large majority (24)

question	answer					average
	hopeless	bad	reason-able	good	excellent	
Requirements specification						
1. Completeness reqs spec		3	12	17	1	.48
Design						
2. Modularization:						
a. Cohesion of components		3	17	11	3	.41
b. Coupling between components		5	17	9	3	.29
c. Information hiding		2	11	18	3	.65
3. Generality/adaptability of modules						
a. More than 1 maze possible		9	3	20	2	.44
b. More than 1 window possible		14	8	11	1	−.03
c. More than 1 cursor possible	1	13	11	8	1	−.15
4. Design documentation:						
a. Global structure	1	2	14	13	3	.45
b. Individual components			12	17	4	.76
Program						
5. Modularization:						
a. Cohesion of components		4	17	10	3	.35
b. Coupling between components		6	19	8	1	.12
c. Information hiding	1	2	17	11	3	.38
6. Individual components:						
a. Neat, understandable code	1	1	12	17	2	.55
b. Documentation/comment	1	5	10	12	6	.50
7. Result of testing		7	12	14	1	.26

Table 1: Assessment by project instructors (a few answers are missing,
so not all rows add up to the same number)

decided to implement multiple windows, though they generally thought this change more difficult to realize.

A possible explanation is that they very well knew the difficulties incurred by the change actually realized, while they only had a global opinion about the change not realized. Thus, they may have overseen intricacies that would have cropped up had they decided to actually incorporate that change. Though this is in line with some other observations discussed below, it is somewhat unsatisfactory, since the project instructors gave a similar assessment of the difficulties involved in these changes.

A further analysis of free-form evaluations written by the students reveals that the actual effort required to augment the program differs widely. For some groups, the changes were easy to accomplish, for others it turned out to be a major undertaking. Fairly often also, some of the changes were easy, while others required a substantial re-design and/or re-implementation of part of the program.

question	answer					average
	hopeless	bad	reason-able	good	excellent	
Requirements specification						
1. Completeness reqs spec	1	8	16	9		−.03
Design						
2. Modularization:						
a. Cohesion of components		1	15	18		.50
b. Coupling between components		12	17	5		−.21
c. Information hiding	1	8	15	10		.0
3. Generality/adaptability of modules						
a. More than 1 maze possible	1	7	6	17	3	.41
b. More than 1 window possible	2	12	9	11		−.15
c. More than 1 cursor possible	4	7	7	15	1	.06
4. Design documentation:						
a. Global structure	4	5	9	15	1	.12
b. Individual components	1	8	18	7		−.08
Program						
5. Modularization:						
a. Cohesion of components		4	17	13		.26
b. Coupling between components		14	16	4		−.29
c. Information hiding	3	8	11	12		−.06
6. Individual components:						
a. Neat, understandable code	1	10	13	9	1	−.03
b. Documentation/comment	6	14	6	6	2	−.47
7. Result of testing		9	11	14		.15

Table 2: Assessment by students

Before the course started, a pilot implementation of the maze program was written by one of the instructors. This person was not involved in the planning of the changes contained in Problem description 2. It turned out that some changes were easy to realize in this pilot implementation, while others were very hard to realize.

These observations confirm our earlier statements about the unpredictability of change requests. The project carried out was a success in this respect.

Project instructors could only assess project results fairly globally. Each instructor had to supervise 8 to 9 teams. Since the schedule was fairly tight, they often had less than one day to evaluate the next set of milestone reports. Conversely, the students had to really work with the end product of some other group. They got hit by all the details that were missing, simply wrong, or ill-documented.

Such is reflected in the difference in rankings. A further analysis of free-form evaluations written by students confirms this opinion. Quite a few of them contain

question	instructor>students	instructor<students	H_0
1	18	4	.004
2a	9	13	.52
2b	17	6	.035
2c	17	3	.003
3a	8	8	1.0
3b	8	9	1.0
3c	10	13	.68
4a	12	8	.50
4b	21	2	.0000
5a	13	11	.84
5b	14	4	.031
5c	16	7	.093
6a	19	6	.015
6b	23	4	.0004
7	14	8	.29

Table 3: Difference in rankings between instructors and students

phrases of the form "at first sight, the requirements specification/design/program looked OK, but on closer inspection we encountered the following problems: ...".

The most prominent difference in assessment concerns questions 4b and 6b. Students have a rather more negative opinion about the quality of the documentation at the component level. (Note that the global structure of the design documentation was fixed in advance, and adherence to it was taken care of by the tools provided.) Analysis of the free-form evaluations gives us some insights into possible reasons for this negative assessment. The comments given can be roughly categorized into two classes:

1. Documentation is wrong or inconsistent;

2. Documentation is incomplete, or not clear.

Documentation is wrong or inconsistent if a description at one level does not agree with the corresponding description at another level. Most often, the requirements specification or design documentation tells one story, while the program tells another. Examples vary from different names for one and the same variable (like InputMaze versus ReadMaze) to cases where the program has been changed and the corresponding documentation has not been updated.

It is difficult to separate this type of problem from the one where documentation is incomplete or not clear. In most cases, people seem to have really done their best to provide clear documentation, but it just does not seem to be adequate. Some programs, for instance, contain abundant documentation where it is not needed, while important facts remain hidden in the code. A particular class of such problems is exemplified by the following reactions:

- "Quite unexpected to us, the Main module checks for Signals"

- "It is strange that this module updates Position, rather than TerminalCursor"

- "The key-function NewScreen was not documented, while it turned out to be very important to know that it calls ChangeMaze"

- "The close cooperation between NewScreen and Maze was not documented"

- "The postcondition of routine X does not specify that the routine checks for negative values. This is important to know, since it is explicitly used by some other routine"

- "In other parts of the program too, the fact that connections have length 1, was used"

From these comments, we conjecture that the negative opinion of students is partly caused by the occurrence of 'delocalized plans' [Soloway88]. According to Soloway, "Basically, the idea is that experts have and use knowledge structures that are a schematic representation for stereotypic behavior patterns [...] Correspondingly, plans in programming are stereotypic action structures [...] In a delocalized plan, pieces of code that are conceptually related are physically located in non-contiguous parts of a program." The study by Soloway et al. indicates that the occurrence of delocalized plans is one particular source of maintenance problems.

Our students are no experts. They do not have a vast body of stereotypic program plans. Their conception of what the various components do is largely inferred from the documentation they get. One could argue that their ideas are based on them having implemented the same problem before. Their evaluations, however, do not indicate serious problems in mismatch between those preconceived ideas and the solution they had to work on.

Thus, the comments given by our students reveal that hidden, i.e., undocumented, relations between non-contiguous parts of a program are insidious. Questions which indirectly relate to the same phenomenon, such as those concerning the coupling between components (2b, 5b) and information hiding (2c, 5c) have relatively low scores as well, certainly when compared with those given by the project instructors.

In setting up this project, we anticipated problems with the documentation. The results show that the maintenance activities asked for were indeed seriously hampered by the inadequacy of the documentation. The analysis further revealed some particularly insidious problem areas.

4. Conclusion

The project described in this paper aimed at exposing students to some important aspects of real-life software development projects, and software maintenance in particular. The project showed students that even a careful requirements analysis and design phase is no guarantee that maintenance will be easy.

An analysis of evaluations by both project instructors and students shows that, in particular, the importance of documentation presented itself in this project. When the students were asked to maintain a program written by others, they almost invariably found problems with the documentation at the component level. In particular, inconsistencies in the documentation at different levels (requirements specification, design, program) and improperly documented relations between components, showed itself as major causes of trouble.

By presenting the above analysis to the students at the end of the project, they were made aware of the significance of proper documentation for maintenance activities. They could similarly reflect on their own performance in this respect during the first phase of the project. To us, the exercise was helpful in that it gave further insight into problem areas that can be realistically tackled in our environment.

5. Acknowledgements

This project could not have been carried out without the help and interest of the project instructors: Sylvia van Egmond, Frans Heeman, Klaas Sikkel and Jos Warmer. My special thanks go to Sylvia, who devised the problem and took care of the day-to-day management of the project.

6. References

[Brooks87] F.P. Brooks, *People are our most important product*, in N.E. Gibbs & R.E. Fairley (Eds.), Software Engineering Education, Springer Verlag (1987) pp 1-15.

[Van Egmond87] S. van Egmond & J. Warmer, *The Implementation of the Amsterdam SGML Parser*, Report IR-159, Department of Mathematics and Computer Science, Vrije Universiteit, 1988.

[Fairley85] R. Fairley, *Software Engineering Concepts*, McGraw-Hill, 1985.

[Gibbs87] N.E. Gibbs & R.E. Fairley (Eds), *Software Engineering Education*, Springer-Verlag, 1987.

[IEEE84] *IEEE Guide to Software Requirements Specifications*, IEEE Std 830, 1984.

[IEEE87] *IEEE Recommended practice for Software Design Descriptions*, IEEE Std 1016, 1987.

[ISO86] *Information Processing – Text and Office Systems – Standard Generalized Markup Language (SGML)*, first edition, 1986-10-15, Ref no ISO8879-1986 (E).

[Pressman87] R.S. Pressman, *Software Engineering*, McGraw-Hill, 1987.

[Soloway88] E. Soloway et al, *Designing software documentation to compensate for delocalized plans*, Comm. of the ACM **31**, 11 (1988) pp 1259-1267.

[Stubbs87] D.F. Stubbs & N.W. Webre, *Data Structures with Abstract Data Types and Modula-2*, Brooks/Cole, 1987.

[Tanenbaum84] A.S. Tanenbaum, *Computer Organization*, second edition, Prentice-Hall, 1984.

[Van Vliet88] J.C. van Vliet, *Software Engineering*, Stenfert Kroese, 1988.

A Proposal for a Bachelor's Degree Program
in Software Engineering

Paul A. Bailes
Eric J. Salzman
Key Centre for Software Technology
Department of Computer Science
University of Queensland
St. Lucia QLD 4067 AUSTRALIA

Andreas Rosel
School of Computing Science
Queensland University of Technology
GPO Box 2434
Brisbane QLD 4001 AUSTRALIA

Abstract. *Perception of Software Engineering as a multi-disciplinary profession like established branches of engineering justifies its treatment in a specialised bachelor's degree. Identification of the essence of professional engineering education in general, and the instantiation of this essence with the particular content requirements of SE, provide precise SEE design criteria. The critical role of the introductory Programming course in establishing the importance of correct SE methods dictates the adoption of functional programming for its purposes. Necessary resources for teaching functional programming to introductory classes are either available or easily accessible. The curriculum overall builds upon this foundation, avoiding mistakes in existing CS curricula, providing quality academic education with the extensive practical and integrative work required for professional preparation.*

INTRODUCTION

To date, existing and proposed initiatives (Ford, 1988) in Software Engineering (SE) Education (SEE) seem condemned to be of limited influence. As postgraduate programs they are by their nature practicably available to only a small proportion of practising programmers. An additional, pedagogical doubtfulness of the postgraduate approach is the difficulty likely to be experienced by students with prior Computer Science (CS) exposure in integrating the "correct" SE approach to software development, with bad habits otherwise acquired through experience or even education! The alternative, of teaching SE as single courses, or streams thereof as mere components in undergraduate (bachelor-level) CS programs while increasing accessibility, still stimulates the above pedagogical reservation.

We submit that such limitations are due to flaws in the underlying perceptions of the relationships between CS, SE and Programming. Typical flawed comments are those to the effect that there is more to CS than Programming. Typical flawed questions are those which ask how best can CS curricula accommodate teaching SE. In refutation of the first (the comments), the very distinctive nature of computers is that they are programmable devices, implying that any distinctive study of computers and their uses (i.e., CS) must be Programming-focussed. For example, theoretical studies in Complexity Theory and Formal Semantics have as Programming-focussed ends the development of more efficient and correct programs. Likewise, the end of Artificial Intelligence (from a CS as opposed to, say, a Sociological point of view), is the development of ambitious applications through the discovery of Programming-related models of human intelligence. And so on.

In refutation of attitudes which give rise to the second (the question), we observe that it is most atypical to view a profession (such as SE) as a contributor to a single academic discipline (CS). Rather, we see professional education as a multi-disciplinary exercise, to which recognised academic disciplines make contributions of appropriate elements as needed. Consider, for example, how professional education in Electrical Engineering draws upon scientific knowledge in Mathematics and Physics, and even elements of Economics and Psychology.

Thus, SEE is an activity to which CS is but one contributor (albeit a major, but not an exclusive or exhaustive one). Just what others are important will emerge below. The challenge is to achieve an integrated presentation of the various disciplines, primarily so that learning by students of the basic knowledge and equi-importantly the methods of the SE profession will be facilitated.

CRITERIA FOR SOFTWARE ENGINEERING EDUCATION

Software Engineering is Engineering

Engineering works are usually thought of as involving the manipulation or taming of *physical* phenomena, often with extreme physical manifestations (e.g. sturdy dams, mighty turbines, miniature circuits). However, this view is open to challenge when engineering is regarded as a *process*, and not in terms of merely apparent results. What distinguishes the engineering professional from the dangerous amateur is the former's conscious application of proven techniques in accord with an ethic of practice that takes account of wider social responsibilities. We therefore submit that *these* are the essential attributes of the engineering concept, and that the incidental technical context in which they are applied is relatively unimportant.

It follows that SE is truly "engineering" because of the correspondence between this abstract characterisation and more concrete characterisations of SE *per se* (Bentley, 1988; Hoare, 1983).

The Engineering Education Paradigm

Traditional branches of Engineering are well-established disciplines and the technical soundness and thoroughness of engineering education is relatively satisfactory. We therefore examine the major aspects of general engineering education in order subsequently to derive guidelines for the education of software development professionals.

First, the most obvious commonality between all traditional (i.e., Civil, Electrical, Mechanical, etc.) engineering curricula is the overwhelming amount of general foundation material in the early semesters. At Australian Universities, for example, more than 20% of the total degree content is comprised of basic science and engineering-related mathematics, most of which is taught in the first year (Lloyd, 1980). Second, the ethic of the engineering profession is its application for social benefit, leading to the inclusion of an increasing amount of material relating to professional responsibility and the social context of engineering decisions. Third, considerable amounts of project work and compulsory industrial practice are undertaken in the later years of the curriculum. Thus the traditional professional engineer is one whose education provides practical experience supported by a strong background in physical and mathematical science, and a lesser but still measurable background in social sciences (e.g. Economics). It is most important that the intellectual fundamentals of correct engineering practices are conveyed from the commencement of the program, so that correct methods of their employment can be practised throughout.

The Software Engineering Education Paradigm

In applying this paradigm to the education of software developers, we preserve the overall theme, but with appropriate content changes to account for the essential differences between "Engineering" and software development. In particular, physical science and continuous mathematics (e.g. calculus, applied maths.) will be supplanted by computer science (e.g. programming methods, languages and tools) and discrete mathematics (e.g. sets and logic). The precise criteria that we shall use to assess the adherence of software development curricula (including those currently available or previously proposed, as well as our own proposal) to the above paradigm, are as follows.

(1) By the extent to which fundamental principles and methods of software development are exposed early in the curriculum, and consciously applied in what follows, as opposed to their portrayal as optional alternatives to the use of "trade skills" for software development.

(2) By the thoroughness with which the pragmatic compromises with principles that are demanded in professional practice are eventually treated, as well as the fact that these compromises are explicitly represented as such.

(3) By the selection of appropriate mathematics (i.e., discrete rather than continuous).

(4) By the inclusion of an integrated package of social sciences elements, as opposed to the mere possibility of selecting options.

(5) By the extent to which application-specific skills can be dovetailed into a general curriculum.

(6) By the inclusion of large-scale software development projects, performed in a realistic setting, i.e., in teams as opposed to individually, and with respect to applications in addition to just systems programming.

(7) By the apparent relationship between these strands in both the structure and execution of the program.

We identify formal methods (Jones, 1980) as *the* correct approach to the production of quality software (1 above). It is therefore essential that they be practised throughout the curriculum.

Appropriateness of SE to Bachelor-level Study

As noted, most of the specific SEE activity is in the graduate (master's) field. Historical reasons provide one justification for this myopia (Sigiletto et al, op. cit.): many CS programs, which over the years gave birth or mutated into SE programs were established at graduate level to provide education in a discipline for which there were no existing bachelor's programs at the time their prospective students were undergraduates. Continuing advances in Programming technology beyond what has been taught in both undergraduate and graduate CS and SE programs continue to provide a niche for graduate SE programs, in the "in-service" or "professional development" role.

However, none of this excuses inertia in the bachelor-level field. It may be argued that the SE profession is too immature for its basic truths and methods of working to have been refined to a level appropriate for presentation to teenagers - if all we have to present is a chaotic message, let the students wait till they have grown up and can work things out for themselves (or attend graduate school)! In refutation, Richardson (op. cit.) testifies to the perils of such pedagogic anarchy, with the observation that if good professional habits are to be learned eventually, contrary prior experience is a severe handicap. Moreover, Hoare (op. cit.) and Mills (1988) suggest that SE *has* evolved to the stage at which it can be taught. The very specificity of the various graduate SE programs only serves to support the case that the material is appropriate for bachelor's students. Further, we exhibit below selected details of our proposed undergraduate SE curriculum, in which the technical material is patently digestible by such students.

It may be otherwise argued that SE is not sufficiently distinctive to warrant special programs of any sort, bachelor's, master's, etc. To re-iterate our introductory remarks, SE is a profession, not a branch of a discipline (CS). SEE involves a unique, multi-disciplinary combination which can only be achieved in the context of a dedicated curriculum.

THE DESIGN OF THE INTRODUCTORY PROGRAMMING COURSE

We pay special attention to introductory Programming: formally, the distinctive place of introductory technical material under the Engineering Education Paradigm, together with the fulfilment of that role in the particular case of SE by Programming, dictates such an approach; pragmatically, there is ample testimony (Dijkstra, 1972; Wexelblat, 1981) to the profound influence on the subsequent learning characteristics of students depending on different experiences of a first programming language. Granted, we would intend to operate at a level beyond mere linguistic idiosyncracies, but so also do the arguments advanced in these testimonies refer to the extent (or otherwise) to which desirable (abstract) principles can be expressed in (concrete) programming languages.

Criteria for Introductory Programming Teaching

For some two decades now, SEs have become ever more aware that *formal* (mathematical) *methods* of software development (Gries, 1978) are the only means by which adequate (i.e., both correct *as well as* efficient solutions can be crafted. How should the curriculum foster the adoption of such methods by its students, at least with respect to its introductory components?

The following pedagogical observations seem self-evident.

(1) If there is a "better" way to do something, then that way should be employed from the outset.

(2) While a professional, as opposed to a purely "academic" education must at some stage attend to contemporary norms, needs and even fads, this attention should be given towards the end rather than at the outset. Over a professional lifetime of around forty years, fads will come and go, but there will be a body of lasting truths, appreciation and understanding of which will be the most valuable acquisition gained by a student during his/her few years of formal education. The more the curriculum can be imbued with these truths, the better. Moreover, given that professional experience will involve repeated compromises with academically desirable methods (e.g. because of current or local technological limitations or fads), there is something to be said for the above-conceded teaching of such pragmatics to appear in terms of the compromises they entail. (For example, a civil engineer might learn to include various uneconomical safety factors in designs to cater for cases where the technology for precise strength calculations is unavailable). Thus, even a professional education should be founded both logically and temporally upon academic principles.

(3) Students' first experience of a new field is not one in which much in the way of concrete content will be assimilated. What will be picked up, however, is the often hidden agenda: methods of and attitudes to working. While the correctness of introductory content cannot be trifled with, it is most important to select such content on the basis of the attitudes it signifies.

Instantiating these points with the specifics of Programming, we carry on.

(1) The correct way of doing Programming is by the conscious application of formal methods. Formal methods are not easy (though they are the easiest way of achieving correct software), so need to be taught as long as possible, from the outset.

(2) While *complete* rigour in all examples may stretch current techniques beyond credibility, the more rigour that can be achieved the better. If there is one

lasting truth of SE that has been discovered in two decades of research, this surely is it.

(3) Ultimately, "process" skills such as required in Programming can only be learned via practice. The incidental factual knowledge required to apply and learn the correct SE approaches to Programming must be kept to a minimum (the germ of this idea can be seen in the oft-expressed desire "to teach Programming, not any particular programming language"). This is in order to avoid obscuring the essential message, and to redeploy instructor and student effort away from teaching and learning marginal facts.

At the same time, a legitimate function of the introductory Programming course is to introduce a generally-applicable and lasting vocabulary of linguistic concepts. It is important to avoid restricting the context (i.e., the chosen programming language) so severely that the omission of simple and general concepts from the initial treatment makes them appear exceptional and so complicated when they are eventually encountered.

A particular danger in the postponement of formal methods until large-scale programming exercises are attempted. This is because the successful (to all appearances) completion of smaller projects, without benefit of formal methods, will induce belief that formal methods can be ignored, until it is too late to remedy this situation (and, incidentally, until a stage in the *professional* curriculum is reached at which a free choice of programming notation to best expose formal methods is no longer possible). Therefore, nothing must be done that would undermine the credibility of formal methods as *the* means of creating quality software. To summarise, this credibility is *big lesson* that the introductory Programming course should be putting across.

Critique of Existing Introductions

The typical bachelor-level CS curriculum of today (ACM, 1978), founded on CS1 (ACM, 1984) and CS2 (ACM, 1985), in which most emergent SEs have been "educated", cannot satisfy these requirements. Rooted as they are in procedural languages (Pascal, Modula-2, Ada, etc.) and programming techniques, a credible treatment of formal methods is not possible. Either difficult constructs (with respect to formal treatments) will have to be omitted, or the application of formal methods across the languages constructs employed in teaching will have to be most selective. In the former case, the credibility of formal methods will be subverted by the restriction to artificial small examples forced by the complexities of the von Neumann model with respect to those methods. If handling the concept of state is hard enough, what about handling "standard" (in von Neumann terms) means of program composition: subprograms, with reference parameters, aliasing, etc.?

In the latter case, credibility is immediately forfeitted when students see "real" examples (requiring employment of hard concepts like reference parameters) performed without benefit of formal treatment: the big lesson learned by any half-perceptive mind would be that formal methods are just an academic game (as is currently too often the case).

It is worth noting that Pascal (and so its derivatives), despite claims to the contrary, are not pure pedagogical instruments. Pascal is a conscious compromise (Wirth, 1974) between design elegance (according to the programming methodology and language design norms of the late 'sixties) and prospective implementation efficiency (again according to 'sixties norms). As the balance moves from the latter to the former as better language implementation techniques emerge, so do the constraints under which language designers operate loosen (as if "efficiency" should be a concern for an introductory programming language, anyway). As well as punctuation irritations such as the placement of semicolons and periods etc., entire dimensions of experience in software construction (e.g. higher-order functions, polymorphism) are ruled out, leaving subsequent courses the task of correcting this narrow mind-set.

A New Introduction to Programming

The alternative is to adopt for introductory programming teaching a broad-spectrum software environment, in which the range of facilities offered by "real" languages is credibly mirrored, but which is controlled for the sake of credible applicability of formal methods. We immediately identify *functional languages* as providing just such an environment. They have simple mathematical structures (notably the maintenance of referential transparency) which make rigorous methods of derivation and proof relatively easy to employ. The better functional languages possess flexible program and data structuring mechanisms built-in, so that interesting motivating examples can be introduced at once. Of course, the concept of assignable store, undoubtedly one of utmost significant to SEs for the forseeable future, is not immediately presented. While this problem has a neat solution in terms of the overall curriculum that employs this functional introduction to Programming (see below), we note in passing that those who oppose the employment of alternatives to imperative programming for introductory teaching are in our experience those who would make loud claims as to the naturalness of the von Neumann model. We refer to the further discussion of this point below, but for the moment respond with the observation that if this claim were completely true, and that the state concept was quite without subleties and ramifications that complicated programs, then not much effort need be spent on teaching imperative concepts, and so it would be quite in order to do functional programming first!

Note that none of this denies the importance and usefulness of the concept of state for practical SE. Nor do we suggest that formal methods are incompatible with any other than the functional model. On the contrary, we profess the significance and sophistication of "state" and of other models (e.g. object-oriented), but with the reservation that a proper understanding of their employment in computation (a "mathematical" one rather than a "natural" one) should be postponed until students are sufficiently similarly sophisticated.

By way of concrete illustration of our proposal, we refer to Bird and Wadler's (1988) *Introduction to Functional Programming* which already serves as the introductory Programming text in a number of centres of learning, from Oxford to New South Wales, that share some of our ideas.

The book (and a course based on it) begins with the analogy between a desk calculator that the expression evaluation style of functional languages readily permits. The key difference between a mere calculator and a computer (here, the abstract machine presented by the functional language) is presented by extending the set of available facilities via function definitions, in the course the necessary vocabulary of types etc. is introduced. Some significant programming examples (at least, for beginners) are given in list processing. Basic algebraic concepts of program proof are presented as well. Only then is recursion met, the lateness of which is possible by the encoding of list processing paradigms as higher-order functions in which the "ultimate" recursions needed for list processing are hidden. The recursive programs are verified and sometimes derived using formal methods (inductive proof). Concepts of complexity and algorithm analysis, presented at a relatively higher-level than in von Neumann programming, are still detailed enough to allow different solutions to the one problem to be compared, mathematically. Final topics expose the special expressiveness of modern functional languages in the processing of infinite data structures and programmer-defined data types.

No Sustainable Objections

Some of the objections to the adoption of functional programming for introductory teaching, together with their refutations, are as follows.

"It's too hard!"

> Granted, Bird and Wadler are on an entirely different intellectual plane, compared to most (all?) other introductory texts (and their authors). However, this is not so much evidence of the stratospheric level of the former, rather of the subterranean "ambitions" of the latter. Indeed, the proposed introductory course offers little in the way of mathematical sophistication beyond proof by induction, as found in the introductory analysis courses often taken by students contemporaneously with their first programming course.

> If we further point to the successful experience of Oxford University, some may object on the grounds that its students represent the cream of British youth, and that they are clever enough to cope with such sophistication! Even for the sake of discussion conceding the alleged superiority of those students, our reply is of course that the overall aim is the education of SEs in the importance and techniques of use of formal methods, and that Bird and Wadler provides the easiest yet path thereto: as claimed above, a path originating with Pascal et al can only be harder. If the luminaries at Oxford need things made so easy, then surely do the rest!

> A related but more credible objection is that the supply of lecturers, instructors etc. capable (intellectually and attitudinally) of teaching functional programming is limited. If introductory functional programming is to be followed by mainstream programming courses (e.g. data structures) taught in the functional paradigm, many such personnel will be needed. Because functional programming is really very easy, intellectual difficulties can be overcome by mounting staff update programs, following e.g. the example of the MIT (Weiss, 1987) when the Scheme language was introduced at introductory level. Problems of attitude, with staff who refuse to accept the technology of functional programming or the pedagogy which mandates its employment, might somehow be overcome by judicious re-allocation of duties by those heads of department with sufficient management expertise and above all commitment to the interests of their students. The alternative is to hire persons with

a background in discrete mathematics (no CS necessary). That this practice has already proved successful in staffing other theory-based components of the CS curriculum only serves to demonstrate the intellectual bankruptcy of current training (a more honest description of the current state of affairs, than "education", we think) in CS, and hence the need for the changes we propose.

"It's un-natural!"

Some authors (e.g. Goldschlager and Lister, 1982) make much of the analogy between imperative programming constructs and the processes "naturally" executed by human beings in their daily lives. Thus, so the argument goes, because there are no such analogies between functional constructs (e.g. recursion) and "nature", functional programming is, notwithstanding the immediately preceding discussion, too shocking for introductory purposes. Our response is to point out the range of ideas, or approaches to understanding problems, that are in a sense quite un-natural, yet are easy to learn and which produce superior results in their contexts. For example, the earth looks flat, yet a spherical earth is a better approximation to reality. The sun appears to orbit the earth, but the heliocentric model better (i.e., more easily and so reliably) explains/predicts many interesting phenomena. Unary notation for numbers is indeed natural for infants, but any serious arithmetic requires higher bases and positional notation. Moreover, mastering such "un-natural" numeric representations is elementary (in every sense of the word).

Likewise, the "natural" state-oriented model of computation is, objectively, not a good basis for understanding computation (compare the elegance of a denotational, i.e. functional, description of an imperative language with the converse). The point is that "better" models do not come naturally to us, but have to be learned, by teaching the results and insights of our predecessors. In this way, one generation can learn from the experiences of the past. (The suggestion that individuals should not short-circuit the laborious processes of discovery executed by their ancestors is, in a word, anti-social.) Indeed, the development of mathematics may be seen as the development of better understandings of observed or perceived physical or logical phenomena than provided by intuition. Learning "un-natural" functional programming should be (and at some places, is) just as feasible as learning mathematics; moreover, the mathematics in functional programming is no harder than that found in other first-year university courses. If you can't cope with learning mathematics, you shouldn't be doing SE.

"It's too expensive!"

Yes, existing functional language implementations are greedy users of space and time. The advent of radically better implementations (Peyton Jones, 1987) could conceivably be awaited, so that re-equipping laboratories with e.g. more powerful workstations could be avoided, but that's just giving the game away to those who would keep CSE/SEE underfunded. A proposal to completely overhaul SEE, with a new curriculum based on new (i.e., functional programming and formal methods) technology, surely would have a reasonable chance of justifying a corresponding re-equipment bid. (The University of New South Wales, Australia when recently moving to adopt functional programming for introductory teaching was able to convince itself that its CS department had thereby provided adequate academic justification for a laboratory of some fifty Apollo 3000's, just for introductory teaching using the Miranda functional programming language.)

"It's not as exciting as Prolog!"

Our affection for functional programming in introductory teaching is not because of some faddish devotion to change, but as the result of calculating pedagogical needs. Prolog is a good idea for lots of things, some of them necessarily part of the SE curriculum (e.g. prototyping, AI), but by no means do they constitute a satisfactory *foundation* for the study of Programming. The cleverness of the examples facilitated by the logic programming paradigm are moreover heavily outweighed by the practical difficulties posed by the adoption of Prolog: lack of sophisticated data structuring; the need to employ non-declarative constructs in non-trivial programs; and the need to understand a complicated evaluation mechanism to explain the strange behaviour of some simple programs (e.g. why left-recursion is unreliable). Other difficulties with its use as a mainstream pedagogical vehicle for subsequent programming courses include:

(1) higher-order computations which manipulate relations as first-class objects are not uniformly feasible;

(2) a demonstration of logic programming as a useful basis for the rest of computation, corresponding to the role of functional style in denotational semantics, is yet to be achieved;

(3) Prolog is not a mature software engineering tool, lacking e.g. type structure and modularity, in sharp contrast to the maturity of functional languages as demonstrated above.

Finally, most recent developments in functional language design and implementation (Darlington, 1988) show that the most useful applications for logic programming can be programmed within an essentially functional model. The overall state of research into the integration of logic and functional programming (DeGroot and Lindstrom, 1986) suggests that the essence of functional style will persist, so that our above analyses will retain their validity.

Resources for Introductory Functional Programming

We have already referred to the immediate availability of a text for the ideal introduction. While there are a number of other books/texts of putative relevance, none in fact suit our purposes as well. For example, *Functional Programming* (Field and Harrison, 1988) covers rather less in the way of programming and more in the way of language implementation, as well as travelling at a pace suitable for more advanced students: we use it to teach a graduate-level course to students with a one-semester background in declarative (functional and logic) programming. Also, *Structure and Interpretation of Computer Programs* (Abelson and Sussman, 1985), as used for introductory teaching at MIT, does not measure up. Its emphasis on language technology makes it even less suitable than Field and Harrison, and its employment of Scheme (a LISP variant) is an irritating idiosyncracy.

In that light, a particular advantage accrues to Bird and Wadler through its employment of Miranda* (Turner, 1985) (actually a slight variant thereof) for purposes of concrete illustration. Just as Pascal represented the best of the language design exercises around the late 'sixties and early 'seventies, avoiding ill-starred speculations, so does Miranda represent both the best ideas of the recent upsurge in activity in functional language design as well as the virtues of being the product of the labours of a single gifted individual.

The practicality of this proposal is further enhanced by the availability of Miranda on many of the classes of machine that populate CS department teaching labs: DEC Vax, SUN and Apollo workstations (all UNIX† systems); maybe the Apple Macintosh before too long. Another language that *may* be used instead is Hope (Burstall et al, 1981), with implementations not just on UNIX machines (VAX and SUN), but on the IBM PC and Apple Macintosh. For those for whom Scheme poses no insuperable obstacle, it has availability at least that of Hope.

THE DESIGN OF THE SOFTWARE ENGINEERING CURRICULUM OVERALL

We first criticise the best existing approximation to undergraduate SEE - CS curricula as typified by Curriculum '78 and subsequent modifications and alternatives - then show how their faults are absent from a new proposal.

Critique of CSE

The abovementioned continued adherence in the foundations of existing CS curricula to conventional programming styles, and the consequent repudiation of formal software development methods, can only undermine the integrity of the whole from an SE point of view. For example, by the time students reach Curriculum '78's CS14 (Software Design and Development), they will have spent around four semesters is a mathematical void. The fact that CS14 has no mathematics pre- or co-requisites means that it can only prolong this void, together with the totally incorrect view of correct SE practice that conveys. Even were some implementation of CS14 to attempt to counter that impression, too much damage would already be done.

These primary consequences of the deficiencies of introductory programming teaching aside, the following overall criticisms apply.

(1) Absent from the core are treatments of topics such as concurrent programming, language processing and networking. While they are available (in varying degrees of thoroughness) outside the core, there is no guarantee that a graduate with the self-style of "software development professional" will have elected them. At most, knowledge gained from such electives will usually not be available nor applied while the single year-long project is undertaken.

---

* "Miranda" is a trademark of Research Software Ltd.

† UNIX is a trademark of Bell Laboratories.

(2) No non-technical material is included, except for some discussion of the social implications of information systems, and of group psychology as part of the project.

(3) The lack of a culmination point in the core gives the undesirable impression that certain topics cannot be related (e.g. information systems and theoretical computer science). Moreover, if the prerequisite relationships are taken seriously in the execution of the curriculum, they will never be linked. For example, it will not be possible to set projects that demand that students have integrated knowledge of e.g. information systems, language theory or functional programming.

Though implied by the above, it is worthwhile to repeat the sense of Berztiss' and Gibbs' (1983) criticism of Curriculum '78, regarding the mathematical illiteracy of the CS curriculum. Even without exploring the details of the mathematical knowledge required for developing effective and efficient software, it should be clear that the education of those who would create such complex logical (i.e. discrete mathematical) phenomena should necessarily depend heavily upon mathematical knowledge and processes.

Similar but less severe criticisms apply to other more recent CS curriculum proposals. For example, Shaw (1985) describes a proposed four-year computer science curriculum. However, it does not have an engineering orientation, nor does it accept software development as its focus. Large projects and integrated social sciences are lacking, information systems is neglected, for example. The presentation of programming and languages is basically pedestrian (i.e., Pascal-oriented). In summary, neither the content nor the processes necessary for good SE are adequately exposed.

A New Software Engineering Curriculum

We propose a specialised, eight(8)-semester program five core segments: *Foundations*; *Information Systems*; *Programming*; *Programming Languages*; and *Projects*. Figure 1 presents the timetabling of (by semester and year), relationships between the core subjects with respect to useful (but not necessarily prerequisite) prior knowledge, and indicates the division into segments.

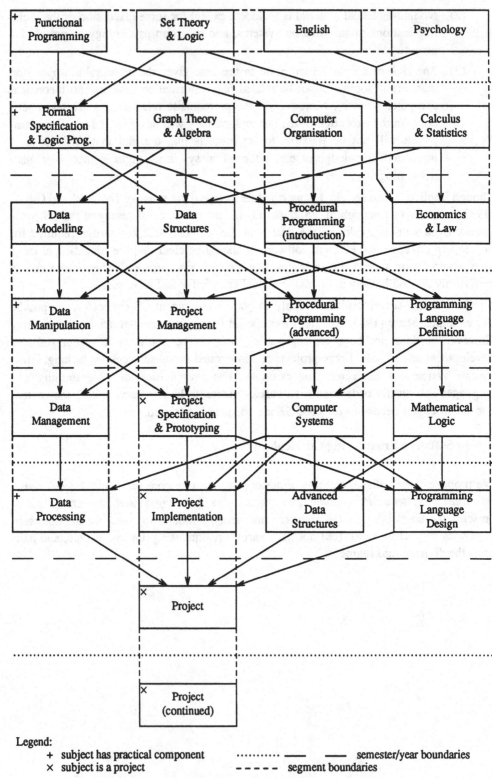

Legend:

    + subject has practical component   •••••••••• —— —— semester/year boundaries
    × subject is a project   - - - - - segment boundaries

Figure 1 - a new software engineering curriculum

Note that a group of six subjects in the fourth year remains unspecified, allowing for specialisations e.g. pairs of theory/prac. subjects in programming language implementation, operating systems, graphics, AI, computer hardware, information systems, etc.

Each subject is intended to represent approximately 20% of a student's full load, so allowing for further specialisations, additional prerequisites for specialisations in early years, or additional "liberal arts" studies. The coverage of content by specified subject and segment is as follows.

1. Foundations.

Functional Programming: essential programming concepts of information hiding, functional and data abstraction, recursion, dynamic data structures, data types.

Set Theory and Logic: set operations; propositional logic; predicate calculus; inductive definitions and proofs.

English: report writing; verbal communication and presentation.

Psychology: group dynamics; learning styles.

Formal Specification and Logic Programming: mathematical software specification; implementing specifications; specifications expressed as logic/Prolog programs.

Graph Theory and Algebra: boolean algebra; groups, rings, fields; graphs, lattices; models.

Calculus and Statistics: functions; sequences, limits, continuity; differentiation and integration; log. and exponential functions; elementary probability and basic distributions.

Data Structures: formal specification and implementation of data structures; practical application of techniques to selected examples.

Economics and Law: profitability; cost-effectiveness; copyright; contracts; computer mis-use; corporations.

2. Information systems

Data Modelling: conceptual schema; architecture and requirements analysis of information systems.

Data Manipulation: relational algebra, calculus; query languages; 4GLs; knowledge engineering.

Data Management: DBMS concepts.

Data Processing: file processing with COBOL; user interface design.

3. Programming

Computer Organisation: data flow, reduction and von Neumann machine organisations.

Procedural Programming (introduction): variables; sequencing; selection; iteration; arrays; pointers; files.

Procedural Programming (advanced): procedural language abstraction mechanisms (functional, data, concurrency).

Computer Systems: implementation models for languages; operating system concepts; data communications.

Advanced Data Structures: memory management; algorithm analysis; complexity theory.

4. Programming languages

Programming Language Definition: syntax, parsing; axiomatic and denotational semantics.

Mathematical Logic: incompleteness; computability; recursive functions.

Programming Language Design: evaluation of software development tools; effectiveness; efficiency; expressiveness.

5. Projects

Project Management: programming teams; cost estimation and scheduling; software life cycle.

Project Specification and Prototyping: development of a software system from analysis through formal specification and prototype implementation; CASE.

Project Implementation: revision of project specification and prototype; production of efficient implementation; maintenance.

Project: development of large software system from analysis through implementation to maintenance.

Discussion

With respect to our criteria, our proposal may be assessed thus by comparison with the criticisms aimed at existing curricula as typified by Curriculum '78.

- A highlight is the emphasis in the *Foundations* placed on discrete mathematics and on declarative (logic and functional) programming. The mathematics may be immediately justified as the straightforward adherence to the engineering paradigm, with particular content selected for "software" relevance. Sets and logic underlie formal program specification and verification. Graph theory and algebra are important for data structures, language semantics and advanced concepts in software specification.

  The introductory functional programming course leads naturally to formal specification, as the translation thereto from a mathematical description is relatively easy. It is also timely to simultaneously introduce programming in logic itself. We are incidentally open to the possibility that the developing maturity of logic languages and their integration with the functional style (de Groot and Lindstrom, op. cit.) will necessitate changes to the introductory subjects.

  Again, our policy is that if there exist correct ways to approach software design, then they should be exposed early and unequivocally. The correct process, via formal specifications, is encountered as soon as the basic notions of (functional) program and the necessary mathematical background are available.

- Because the functional introduction to programming is no more mathematically-demanding than an introductory analysis course, relatively no extra prerequisite mathematical knowledge is required. On the other hand, steps may have to be taken to persuade high school hackers that functional programming has something to offer them: there are now numerous examples in circulation of cute functional programs, each a fraction of the size of their imperative counterparts; perhaps that is the sort of thing that may appeal to such individuals.

- Pragmatics involving the employment of procedural languages in the efficient manipulation of von Neumann machines are treated at length and in comparably greater depth, especially in the segments *Programming* and *Projects*. Furthermore, the linguistic complexities of these languages can now be presented in the light of knowledge of the computer organisation that makes them so. Finally, all core subjects are completed before the final project, the value of which is additionally enhanced by prior completion of a trial (third) year of specification, prototyping and implementation.

- The four mathematics subjects (*Set Theory and Logic, Graph Theory and Algebra, Calculus and Statistics* and Mathematical Logic) included allow for ample mathematical core content and for ample time for its presentation. The amount of continuous mathematics relative to discrete mathematics reflects its importance to the *core* of SE: there is every reason to provide electives to strengthen this offering for students wishing to specialise in SE in an appropriate way.

- Issues of formal verification and validation are intended to suffuse the curriculum. The extent to which this would be achieved in practice quite depends upon the personnel involved, but it remains that our framework, in which the necessary mathematical and psychological preparation for such an approach is performed in first year, at least makes this at all possible.

- The (compulsory) humanities subjects in the *Foundations* give an integrated grounding in human interaction: written; verbal; non-verbal; legal; and financial. We submit that in implementing this proposal they be not just selected from established subjects but be designed to complement this curriculum, even to the extent of incorporating high levels of information technology in their presentation.

- All segments are closely inter-related. In designing an academic curriculum, the principle of loose coupling must be violated because the value of an education lies in the consequent ability to synthesise solutions to problems with multiple facets. Consequently, the curriculum must make inter-(sub-)disciplinary links obvious.

  The *Project* is the culmination of the curriculum. Students will be able (and expected) to draw on skills in e.g. database, management, programming and language design to analyse a problem, specify, implement and maintain a solution. Another example of integration is how students of the subject *Programming Language Design* can (indirectly) draw upon knowledge of all classes of language: data manipulation; procedural; logic; and functional.

The project occupies one-fifth of a student's full time in the final year: supervision will of course be a non-trivial duty for teaching staff. Experience with such projects suggests that while administrative and pedagogical needs may be better served by undertaking such projects in conjunction with industrial organisations, mounting in-house projects is within the bounds of feasibility.

The seven criteria of the *Software Engineering Education Paradigm* are satisfied as follows.

(1) Basing introductory programming on the functional model allows a clear exposition of powerful programming methodologies from the outset.

(2) The *Programming* and *Projects* segments incorporate large amounts of SE pragmatics.

(3) A complete coverage of relevant mathematics content is provided.

(4) Humanities subjects form 1/3 of the *Foundations* segment.

(5) Electives in years 1 - 3 and most of the fourth year provide ample opportunity for specialised subjects in the application of SE to any number of fields, including commerce.

(6) The final *Project* is attempted only after a trial in year 3, after all essential technical expertise has been presented, and in conjunction with application-specific electives.

(7) Unification of various content strands is brought about by the culminating project and by the explicit links between segments throughout the curriculum.

One potential criticism is that our adoption of the engineering paradigm violates the sound pedagogy of moving from the specific to the general. Our response is to suggest that this principle is one of tactics, of how a single subject should be taught, and not one of strategy, of how the subjects should be arranged in a curriculum. We do not accept that material with a general significance cannot be taught without appropriate motivating examples. A related criticism would be that our high proportion of pure maths. and theoretical computer science could appear far-removed from the exciting reality of "computing" and so lead to student boredom and impaired performance. Our response is again that it is a matter of how individual subjects are taught. Moreover, the significant practical components of our curriculum suggest that "hands-on" experience will be much more than adequate.

More positively, our curriculum emphasises intellectual rigour and stimulation, rather than anecdotal "knowledge" of brand names and system gimmicks. We submit that this rigour is needed to be able to "certify" its graduates worthy of the title "engineer". In designing our curriculum, we commenced with ideas of the needed pragmatic skills required of graduates, and of the needed underlying intellectual tools. Following our engineering paradigm imposed the described structure.

CONCLUSION

A number of important issues are yet to be dealt with, such as the incorporation of an honours stream, how administrative structures would be changed to reflect the change in academic reality, and what provision remains for the education in programming of non-specialists. Regarding the last question, we affirm our belief that only persons educated as SEs following the engineering paradigm should be trusted to undertake software development tasks of any significance or critical nature.

As far as the likelihood of implementing the proposal made by this paper, we can report some encouraging movements on the local (Australian) front, such as closer institutional ties between some universities' CS and Electrical Engineering Departments, and the mounting of at least one four-year degree in "Computer Engineering". The significance of the former is that Australian CS departments are regarded as "Science" and not "Engineering" bodies, so that a CS qualification may be obtained in three (not four) years (except in the case of honours graduates, where a fourth postgraduate year is required). The more "engineering" view of CS seems essential if four-year SE degrees are to be established. The latter shows what can be achieved: even if there is a considerable hardware component in the program overall, the program begins with a functional programming course! Overall, however, there is a lot of persuading to do. Our purpose in writing this paper was to submit our ideas to the widest informed scrutiny, with the view of constructing a most compelling case to bring about the changes we seek.

ACKNOWLEDGEMENTS

We thank the referees for their helpful comments on the first version of this paper.

REFERENCES

Abelson, H., Sussman, G.J. and Sussman, J. (1985): "Structure and Interpretation of Computer Programs", M.I.T. Press, Cambridge.

ACM (1979): "Curriculum '78: Recommendations for the Undergraduate Program in Computer Science - A Report of the ACM Curriculum Committee on Computer Science", Comm. ACM, vol. 23, no. 3, pp. 147-166.

ACM (1984): "Recommended Curriculum for CS1, 1984", Comm. ACM, vol. 27, no. 10, pp. 998-1001.

ACM (1985): "Recommended Curriculum for CS2, 1984", Comm. ACM, vol. 28, no. 8, pp. 815-818.

Bentley, J. (1988): "Teaching the Tricks of the Trade", in (Ford, 1988).

Berztiss, A. and Gibbs, N.E. (1983): "Computer Science and Computer Science Education", in R.E.A. Mason (ed.), "Information Processing 83", North-Holland, Amsterdam.

Bird, R. and Wadler, P. (1988): "Introduction to Functional Programming", Prentice-Hall International, London.

Burstall, R.M., MacQueen, D.B. and Sanella, D.T. (1981): "HOPE: An Experimental Applicative Language", University of Edinburgh, Department of Computer Science, CSR-62-80 (updated).

Fairbairn, J. (1986): "A New Type-checker for a Functional Language", Science of Computer Programming, vol. 6, pp. 273-290.

DeGroot, D. and Lindstrom, G. (1986): "Logic Programming - Functions, Relations, and Equations", Prentice-Hall, Englewood Cliffs.

Dijkstra, E.W. (1972): "The Humble Programmer", CACM, vol. 15, no. 8, pp. 859-886.

Gries, D. (ed.) (1978): "Programming Methodology", Springer-Verlag, New York.

Goldschlager, L. and Lister, A. (1982): "Computer Science - A Modern Introduction", Prentice-Hall International, London.

Field, A. and Harrison, P. (1988): "Functional Programming", Addison-Wesley.

Ford, G.A. (ed.) (1988): "Software Engineering Education", LNCS vol. 327, Springer-Verlag, New York.

Hoare, C.A.R. (1983): "Programming is an Engineering Profession", in Software Engineering Developments, State of the Art Report 11:3, pp. 77-84.

Jones, C.B. (1980): "Software Development - A Rigorous Approach", Prentice Hall International, London.

Lloyd, B.E. (1980): "Professional Engineering in Australia, Antecedents and Futures", Australasian Engineering Education Conference, Preprints of Papers, Brisbane.

Mills, H. (1988): "Strategic Imperatives in Software Engineering Education", in (Ford, 1988).

Peyton Jones, S. (1987): "The Implementation of Functional Programming Languages", Prentice-Hall International, Hemel Hempstead.

Richardson, W.E. (1988): "Undergraduate Software Engineering Education", in (Ford, 1988).

Shaw, M. (ed.) (1985): "The Carnegie-Mellon Curriculum for Undergraduate Computer Science", Springer-Verlag, New York.

Sigiletto, V.G., Blum, B.I. and Loy, P.H. (1988): "Software Engineering in the Johns Hopkins University Continuing Professional Programs", in (Ford, 1988).

Turner, D.A. (1985): "Miranda - a non-strict functional language with polymorphic types", in Jouannaud (ed.), Conference of Functional Programming Languages and Computer Architecture, Lecture Notes in Computer Science, vol. 201, pp. 1-16, Springer, Berlin.

Weiss, E.A. (1987): "MIT Starts with Lisp", ABACUS, vol. 5, no. 1, pp. 45-49.

Wexelblat, R.L. (1981): "The Consequences of One's First Programming Language", Software - Practice and Experience, vol. 11, pp. 733-740.

Wirth, N. (1974): "On the Design of Programming Languages", Information Processing 74, North-Holland, Amsterdam.

HOLISTIC CASE STUDY APPROACH TO Ada BASED SOFTWARE ENGINEERING TRAINING

By
Ralph D. Page

Manager - Engineering Training

GE Aerospace
Government Electronic Systems Division (GESD)
Borton Landing Road
Moorestown, New Jersey 08057
609-866-6208

Abstract

The award of the Combat Submarine (BSY-2) contract to GE has challenged the Government Electronic Systems Division (GESD) in terms of involvement in the single largest Ada oriented project development to date in the world. The total project is faced with a development effort exceeding 2,200,000 lines of Ada code to be implemented by a community of software engineers totaling 900. The Government Electronic Systems Division at Moorestown, NJ, with its current staff of approximately 200 software engineers involved with on-going projects, is faced with significant numbers of additional engineers to hire that need to be integrated into the existing software engineering staff. The combined new staff is challenged with new methodologies, design, standards and Ada.

The training campaign is critical as a strategic element in the successful Ada software engineering effort of this fixed price contract. This paper will detail a fundamentally different approach in the training of engineers and engineering managers into a significantly new environment.

Introduction

Soon after the award of the Combat Submarine (BSY-2) Contract to GESD, the conclusion was reached that in general, Ada based software engineers would have to be "made" as opposed to being hired. This meant that the existing GESD Moorestown Software Engineering Staff needed extensive training as well as the two hundred newly hired engineers who are joining the staff in 1988, 1989 and 1990. In addition, our subcontractor, Computer Sciences Corporation (CSC) would join GESD in terms of an additional 150 engineers requiring training. The alternatives to not conducting a formal training program were considered unacceptable in terms of the project schedule, the fixed price nature of the contract, and retiring the technical risks associated with the world's largest Ada project. It was concluded that all engineers and managers on the BSY-2 project will require training, including "old hands".

Background

The Software Engineering Staff, at GESD, Moorestown is comprised of mostly long service employees with a mixture of recently hired graduates. The majority of software development projects in the past involved computer embedded real time systems for Command and Control Systems as well as radar system. A number of highly successful software driven systems, including AEGIS and a family of instrumentation radars comprise the basis of the staff projects. A number of the managers were instrumental in developing RCA's Aerospace software management development methodology as well as directing and teaching the Software Management Training Program, for managers. The major languages in use are Fortran, CMS-2, Assembly and a light assortment of some modern languages. Software control of phased array radars and instrumentation radar is complex, time critical as well as computational extensive. The software engineering staff is accustomed to operating under rigorous DoD standards, formal reviews, and developing large systems involving hundreds of people.

Approach to Training

An indepth assessment of the current staff of GESD Moorestown engineers and managers was made regarding skills and knowledge of contemporary development methods. This was followed by developing the objectives of a training program in terms of requirements, and developing a training process that would satisfy these requirements. Both in-house and contractor training establishments were interviewed that resulted in a baseline training program.

Objectives of the BSY-2 Software Engineering Training

Two Classes of Objectives

Two classes of objectives became evident, technical or subject matter objectives, and performance based objectives.

Technical or Subject Matter Objectives

Modern systems analysis, requirements and design methodology skills were considered basic and fundamental serving as a foundation to all other technical or subject matters. Acquiring Ada design, and Ada implementation knowledge and skills was followed with the necessity to develop a workstation approach to development. The contract requirement of DoD 2167 and its mapping with Ada needed understanding by all. Topics of Demonstration Test Milestones, debugging, testing, and systems integration were considered necessary subjects to be included into the total Ada orientated training.

Performance Based Objectives

1. Software Management Change

   Perhaps not obvious, but of great importance was the necessity focusing on software management change. Managing Ada is different, GESD Moorestown did not have any significant large systems Ada management experience and "old hands" need a new "mind set". In this sense, what needs to take place is a mind set change, and therefore the training could have been titled - "A Mind Set Change for engineers and managers".

2. Culture Change in the Development Cycle

   The development culture at GESD, Moorestown needed radical change, in every phase of the development cycle, and this involves the increased use of CASE tools and other new tool concepts, as well as the new Ada design culture. This was concluded in spite of our large DoD Systems experience with such success as AEGIS.

3. Minding the Gap

   A training approach that exceeds the delivery of facts is essential. The delivery of new technical facts is not enough. Skills must be acquired in a time frame less than the 18 months normally experienced in becoming proficient in Ada engineering. The gap between academic subject knowledge and real world skills needs to be bridged.

4. An Affordable Training Program

   An affordable training program that will leverage the training investment in terms of retiring the BSY-2 Ada risk, and build a level of confidence that GESD Moorestown and our subcontractors can do the job. The goal of the training program is that quality and productivity improvements will more than offset training cost resulting in a significant value added dimension to the issue of training costs.

5. Increased Product Quality

   Additionally, the training program must increase the overall product quality, to the point where it is correct the first time and the software is highly reliable. The knowledgeable use of Ada itself is expected to significantly increase product quality, but only when Ada is properly used in a design sense.

6. Increase Productivity

Lastly, the training program must result in increased productivity by no less than 15%, resulting for just one year alone in a savings of $3.4 million dollars at Moorestown, NJ. The 15% productivity improvement across all of GE's locations and subcontractors on BSY-2 on a yearly basis is in excess of 8 million dollars. Research data places a 15% productivity improvement in Ada engineering as extremely conservative.

Establishing a Training Base Line

Resulting from considerable research, interviews of Ada involved organizations and guidance of consultants, a training base line was established. This base line specified training elements, engineering and management levels to attend, hours of instruction and a general ordering of elements. It became evident that what was required was to establish a new mind set, a new culture and a simple standard off-the-shelf course of Ada, by itself would be wasteful and miss the objectives stated earlier.

Communicating the idea that Ada needed supporting elements of software analysis, requirements, design, Ada mapping into 2167, new tools and associated workstations to the software community and to others associated with BSY-2, exceeded all expectations of challenge.

Extensive effort was made in describing why managing Ada is different, and why the managers needed extensive training as well as the engineering community. Five months later than the originally proposed date, approval was granted to initiate the pilot training cycle, the first cycle of a planned nine cycle training program at Moorestown.

General Approaches in Achieving the Training

Fundamental decisions were made regarding how the delivery of training would be achieved. Concepts of in-house training, utilizing a single contractor, GE managed multiple training contractors, "train the trainers" or a combination of these approaches were explored.   The matrix (Table 2), summarizes the issues and resulting advantages and disadvantages.

After extensive explorations, a contractor was discovered that enabled GESD to reconsider, and actually establish a single contractor approach that had the option of developing into a train the trainers or seed team for long term training requirements. The Educational Department of the Systems Development Division of Telesoft Inc. was selected as the single contractor to develop a total training approach to specifically meet the unique BSY-2 requirements. Dr. Kenneth Bowles and Mr. Gene Kennon of Telesoft, and Ralph Page, GESD were the principal architects of the training program.

Training Architecture

Issues in Determining a Training Architecture

It became evident early on that a scheme needed to be developed that would interweave these elements together into a cohesive unity of thought. The training process would be holistic in the sense of a strong functional relationship between components of the course, yielding an Ada education greater than the sum of its parts. In addition, GESD was willing to invest dollars into a process that could significantly reduce the 18 month learning curve for engineers to become proficient with Ada which is typical of standard off-of-the shelf Ada courses. There was a concern, that after engineers received the Ada training via a traditional method with an "off the shelf" Ada course the engineers would revert back to their former older methods. Also, the planned intensity of a comprehensive Ada centered software engineering course, in a time frame of eleven weeks, was felt to be prone to lecture and instructional overloading.

Therefore, driving the top level training architecture were the following issues:

- o Interweaving of elements toward a cohesive unity of thought
- o Reduce the 18 month learning course experienced by the Ada community to not more than 6 months
- o Insure avoidance of engineers reverting back to old ways
- o Avoid lecture overloading of instruction

Interleaving of Elements Toward a Cohesive Unity of Thought

An Ada overview, followed by software engineering analysis, CADRE as a CASE tool set comprised the first week. Thereafter, the basic flow was to alternate, on a day by day basis, software engineering principles (modern methods of analysis, requirements, and design as planned to be used on BSY-2) with Ada engineering. The two broad subject matters were carefully synchronized in order that one subject would both support and reinforce the other. In addition, classes on 2167 (not 2167A) were held as well as a intensive one day "how to" class on mapping Ada and 2167. (Table 2), summarizes the interleaving approach.

Reduce the 18 Month Learning Curve to Not More than 6 Months

This was the most difficult objective that the GESD Moorestown Engineering Organization set for itself. A method to improve upon experience to date, across industry-wide data, needed to be explored. The Case study approach is the very heart of achieving this goal. The Case study model needs to be detailed here, as it is different and should not be confused with text book Case studies, or "off-the-shelf" training courses that utilize examples and student problems.

Case-Study Model

To understand how to develop large scale Ada software, any software engineer, system designer or manager needs to have prior experience working with projects of at least similar scale. Conventional instruction is helpful in preparing any of these people for such a project via delivery of facts. But no such instruction can substitute for the experience of working on a realistic Ada project.

This observation lead to a dilemma within GESD Moorestown - there will not be time available in organized instruction to permit students to carry out a complete project of realistic size from start to finish.

GESD decided to use a Case-Study to provide the needed project experience quickly and at limited cost. The basic strategy recognizes that large amounts of time are typically lost by students when they make simple errors. The time spent in recognizing and curing the simpler errors tends to dominate the learning activity of the inexperienced learner, and it tends to obscure and divert concentration on the main issues unique to the larger projects. But it is well known that a large majority of the effort expended over the lifecycle of a large software product is in fact spent in maintenance rather than initial development. Software maintenance usually involves making incremental changes to a software item that is already functioning. The changes either improve the functional characteristics of the product, or they correct original errors.

In general, a software maintainer must go through two distinct stages in order to accomplish assigned maintenance work. First, the software to be maintained must be well understood. The necessary learning is accomplished through some combination of reading documentation, walking through program code and making simple experiments, and (occasionally) through formal training. Second, the program changes are written and tested. For most individual maintenance changes, the aggregate amount of effort and time taken to accomplish both of these stages is vastly smaller than the effort needed to create the original system from its inception.

This is the key to understanding the GESD Case-Study strategy. Engineers are presented with a functioning program of non-trivial size and asked to make maintenance changes. When the trainees are preparing for a project large enough to require a team of 10 or more people, non-trivial size mean a program of at least 5,000 Ada source lines. Normally, the lifecycle of such a Case-Study involves three clearly recognizable stages of roughly equal duration. Even the simplest maintenance changes require a reasonably detailed knowledge of how the software to be changed is designed and how it operates.

In the first stage, trainees have to concentrate on learning how the original system (to be maintained) is written. Usually it is not practical to provide full tutorial documentation that might permit the trainees to complete this learning without assistance from the instructor. During this stage, the instructor spends several class sessions walking through the Case-Study design, and through selected passages of detailed Ada code, to assist the students in becoming familiar with the code. These class sessions are an opportunity for the instructor to learn about individual trainees and their strengths and weaknesses. Trainees should spend from 10 to 20 hours of effort outside of the class meeting, in work on this stage of the Case-Study, for every 2 hour class meeting.

In the second Case-Study stage, the trainees design, write, and test the assigned maintenance changes. Class meetings with the instructor shift to give/take sessions where various possible design approaches to solving the assigned problems are proposed by trainees, and considered in discussion by the instructor.

In the final Case-Study stage, trainees usually have reached the point where methods for solving the assigned problems are well in hand. Instead, class meeting attention turns to a design-seminar format in which discussion concentrates on the new BSY-2 system. This stage is especially effective if the class members constitute a team assigned to accomplish a particular BSY-2 CSCI (Computer Software Configuration Item). One of the concepts that troubles many trainees is how to practice effective design with Ada in the real world. Many texts and formal courses have promoted a cookbook approach to design principles. In reality, this kind of rote approach does not work. It is the third stage of a large Case-Study that trainees come to the point of understanding the design principles with Ada. The discussion provided at this stage is helpful in giving them the confidence needed to apply their design principles to new designs, while making the thousands of tradeoff decisions that normally have to be made in any such project.

The class structure for the BSY-2 classes involved a full Case-Study involving 14 class meetings of 4 hours each. Between classes, the trainees need from 10 to 20 hours, per 4 hour meeting, of non-class time for individual work, and work in small subgroupings. In addition, each team conducts a weekly project meeting with the team leader without having the instructor present. This team meeting time is especially important for assignment of distinct tasks to different team members, while recognizing the need for all such tasks to be consistent and coordinated. The instructor also met weekly with the team leader on a one-to-one basis without the class being present.

The Case-Study, in part, actually began in week one, starting with System Analysis. The thread of this Case-Study continues on through to the selection of teams where the study becomes the main event starting in week 7 and continuing until week 11. The Case study for BSY-2 was designed by Dr. Kenneth Bowles and his associates at Telesoft.

Insure Avoidance of Engineers Reverting Back to Old Ways

In a typical training environment, the engineer student, after receiving a lecture oriented course, does not apply the newly acquired knowledge in a real world situation. Reinforcement is necessary for applying the skills, and simple text book examples are not enough. Further, the students leave the training environment and considerable time in terms of weeks or months may lapse until the engineers actively apply the skills to a real work development.

In the BSY-2 course design, an immediate large Ada system is thrust upon the student giving the student the opportunity to use the new methodologies coupled with Ada. The large Ada system, known as Wind Park, in the pilot training cycle is dealt with by the student specifically over a period of five weeks. This time is intensive and the student learns. in an application sense, the new ways. New habits are immediately formed under strict supervision and this becomes the "Ada" way.

Lecture and Instructional Learning Overloading

Day after day of long lecture periods will always result in some degree of learning overloading. A design to avoid this problem was in four parts, interleaving of subject elements on a daily basis, not to exceed four hours lecture offset with a study/lab session on a daily basis, establishment of an AM and PM class, and a spiral approach to each subject matter.

Interleaving of subjects on a daily basis was designed to make each day more interesting and for each subject to support the other subject. The break of the subject matter, as a means of reducing overloading does have an adverse effect for some students who desire to have a concentration of one subject at a time.

The not to exceed four hours of lecture on a daily basis simply avoids saturation. The other four hours of a training day is spent either in the lab, or in self-study. Frequent breaks additionally aids in keeping interest high and learning overloading down.

The establishment of an AM and PM class is a scheme to maximize the instructional staff on an eight hour basis while limiting the student exposure to only four hours. Two instructors on this basis will alternate between the AM class and the PM class increasing student interest and further ensuring that more than one point of view is taught.

The spiral approach to subject matters works best in terms of student acceptance and for student retention. The spiral approach treats each design topic in summary form for orientation purposes, with successive revisits to the subject with added detail, with each increment corresponding to one coil of the spiral. Later spirals involve more detailed considerations of the topic.

Facilities

A brief comment regarding facilities; Two classrooms were designed, one for lecture, the other for lab and study. The lecture room is large, roomy, and well lighted with two screens, two projectors and a writing board between the two screens. A computer projection panel (LCD type) is used as a low cost highly visible means of viewing computer terminal or workstation information on one of the screens. The class room comfortably accommodates 22+ people.

The lab room has a general area for lab or lecture and a series of four work cubicles. The lab consists of 22 terminals, 8 of which are workstations.

Measurement of Training

The ultimate measurement of training success will be the performance of the engineers starting 6 months from the conclusion of the training cycle. Measurement, however, cannot wait until that time, for real time modifications to the course need to be taken as necessary during training delivery.

Measurement is in two directions, measurement of the students level of acquired knowledge and skills, and feedback from the students regarding the delivery of the training.

Measurement of Student Progress

Measurement of the students progress is by means of TELEQUIZES, a product of Telesoft, our training contractor, a comprehensive mid-term exam, the direct interworkings of the instructor with the students on the large Case study, and a final national standardized Ada exam developed by Dr. Francis Berger, of Phychometrics, Sherman Oaks, California.

The Telequizes are progressive in difficulty and support the corresponding lecture. Results of the Telequizes are summarized to the instructor in terms of specific scores, areas of difficulties on a per student basis and are available via the computer.

The comprehensive mid-term exam was difficult and served as a motivator for the student as well as a teaching vehicle during the review process. A final exam was designed by Dr. Francis Berger of Phychometrics. This exam has been administered on a national basis and results are available that will indicate how the Training Course engineers compared on a national basis.

The training contractor, Telesoft, prepared an indepth final written report on each student regarding a number of factors.

Measurement of Trainers

Feedback from the students occurs daily and weekly by means of the student filling out preprinted forms. Data from these forms are entered into a data base and processed on an on-going basis.

Immediate feedback is given to the instructors and to the training management. The daily feedback has proven to be most useful and serves as an instant means of making changes.

Verbal feedback occurs from the students and, from a senior group of professionals, is most useful and candid. A written report is required from each student at the completion of the eleven week course regarding how the course met their objectives.

Success of the Training Course

As this paper is being written, the Pilot Training Course has been completed and the second cycle has progressed into the fifth week. On May 24, 1989, forty-four additional engineers and managers will have completed the course, increasing the total graduates to eighty-eight.

The feedback from the Pilot Training Course had been significantly positive both in terms of formal student feedback, informal student feedback, and with supportive scores.

The scores of the daily feedback forms are, on a scale of 1 to 5, averaged at 4.3. Mid-term exam scores of the Pilot Cycle exceeded expected results and mid-term scores of the 2nd Cycle were even higher. The test scores, or the "final exam" from Phychometrics Inc. indicated that further analysis was in order regarding interpretation.

The Phychometrics test scores clearly supported the overall training approach but suggested that the administration of the 2nd Cycle would need modification. There was a direct correlation of student involvement in the lab sessions and Case Study to the Phychometrics score. Scores were as high as 99 percentile, but ranged between a low of 45 to 87 percentile of those students that were highly involved in the lab Case study.

There were lower scores for students that did not become involved in the lab and Case studies. The Phychometrics test are a proficiency test in Ada as opposed to a "final exam" test that addresses only students as its base.

There were two exceptions to the above conclusion with no current conclusive explanation to date.

Changes were made in the 2nd Cycle as a result of lessons learned, they are as follows:

o   A much more structured lab involvement with mandatory attendance, formal question and answer sessions, and formal student monitoring was implemented.

o   Mandatory Case Study involvement with early team selection and peer reviews at the conclusion of each of the phases of the Case study planned.

o   Pre-Cycle meetings with the students was held in advance of the next cycle. Discussions involved the intensity of the course, student commitment of time, student priorities of time for the next 12 weeks, course overview, handing out of text books, and advance reading assignments.

o   Inclusion of relational data base theory and specifics in the BSY-2 data base system (INGRES)

o   Additional time on Case tools, both lecture and lab

Other improvements in the 2nd Cycle were made as would be expected in terms of minor corrections to course material, mid-term exam improvements and increased connectivity of the Case Study to all parts of the training program.

In addition to the Holistic, and Case approaches,mention must be made of the depth of knowledge of the teaching staff. People who themselves have depth, who have managed and implemented real projects, written text books, and steered the direction of software engineering and Ada. This, or course, raises the question, that in later cycles, can GESD with its own staff carry on this underlying quality of depth.

Special mention must be given to the people and associates of Telesoft, first the designers - Dr. Ken Bowles and Gene Kennon, their management in the name of Ken Shumate, and their engineering instructors Keith Shillington, Barbara Rogers, Kami Olsson-Tapp, Sandra Swimmer, Shirley Heffernan, Dr. Manny Baker, and Dr. Kaye Grau.

Summary

At GESD, within the engineering organization at Moorestown, the Holistic Case study approach was what was needed. Standalone, off the shelf courses would not have done the job. This proved to be the only sensible approach to reduce the risk of this significant Ada-based system. Something less than this would have been short-sighted and investment poor.

Table I
General Approaches in Achieving Training Goals

CONSIDERATION	SINGLE CONTRACTOR	GE/A&D MANAGED MULTIPLE CONTRACTORS	TRAIN THE TRAINER (SEED TEAM)	COMBINATION
GE/A&D DIVERSION OF RESOURCES	MINIMUM DIVERSION	MODERATE DIVERSION	HIGH INVOLVEMENT	CONSIDERABLE
o MANAGERS	-SOME	-MODERATE	-EXTENSIVE	-MODERATE
o ENGINEERS	-NONE	-SOME	-MODERATE	-SOME
COORDINATION AND INTEGRATION OF TRAINING ELEMENTS	EXCELLENT	DIFFICULT BUT ACHIEVABLE	EXCELLENT	ACHIEVABLE
SHORT TERM START-UP OF TRAINING PROCESS	EXCELLENT	MODERATE	MOST DIFFICULT AND SLOWEST	MODERATE
CULTURE DEVELOPMENT AND MIND SET CHANGE	FAIR	DIFFICULT TO ACHIEVE	EXCELLENT, BEST ACHIEVED BY THIS MEANS	CAN BE ACHIEVED
TRAINING QUALITY	CAN BE VERY GOOD	DIFFICULT TO ACHIEVE CONSISTENT HIGH QUALITY	CAN BE OF EXCELLENT QUALITY BUT REQUIRES EXTENSIVE MANAGEMENT	CAN BE OF GOOD QUALITY
REMARKS	UNLIKELY TO QUALIFY A SINGLE CONTRACTOR	HIGHLY LIKELY TO QUALIFY MULTIPLE CONTRACTORS WILL ALSO NEED A&D INSTRUCTORS	HAS BEST LONG TERM PAYOFF	SEE NOTES

Second Training Cycle
3/89 - 5/89

Level Legend: 1-Sr.Mgmt. 2-Line Mgmt. M-Systems Eng. 3-Sr.SW Eng. 4-Jr.SW E

Week	Mon	Tue	Wed	Thu	Fri
3/06	MISSION O'VIEW 1,2,M,3,4	SE&SD O'VIEW 1,2,M,3,4	SE&SD I 2,M,3,4	SE&SD II 2,M,3,4	SE&SD III 2,M,3,4
3/13	Ada O'view 1,2,M,3,4	Ada I 1,2,M,3,4	Ada II 2,M,3,4	Workshop 1,2,M,3,4	Ada III 2,M,3,4
3/20	Ada IV 2,M,3,4	DTM/2167 1,2,M,3,4	Ada V 2,M,3,4	Ada VI 2,M,3,4	HOLIDAY
3/27	Workshop 2,M,3,4	DB Ingress 2,M,3,4	DB Ingress 2,M,3,4	Mid-Term 2,M,3,4	Review 2,M,3,4
4/03	Ada VII 2,M,3,4	SE&SD IV M,3,4	Ada VIII 2,M,3,4	SE&SD V M,3,4	Review 2,M,3,4
4/10	Ada IX 2,M,3,4	SE&SD VI M,3,4	Ada X 3,4	SE&SD VII M,3,4	Ada XI 3,4
4/17	Ada XII 3,4	SE&SD VIII M,3,4	Ada XIII 3,4	SE&SD IX M,3,4	Ada XIV 3,4
4/24	SM I 2,M,3,4	VADS 2,M,3,4	Workshop 2,M,3,4	SE&SD X M,3,4	SE&SD XI M,3,4
5/01	Ada XV 3,4	CS-I O'view 1,2,M,3,4	CS-I 2,M,3,4	CS-I 2,M,3,4	CS-I 2,M,3,4
5/08	CS-II 1,2,M,3,4	Team Work-Study	CS-II 2,M,3,4	Team Work-Study	CS-II 2,M,3,4
5/15	Team Mtg 2,M,3,4	Team Work-Study	Team Work-Study	Team Work-Study	Team Mtg 2,M,3,4
5/22	CS-III 2,M,3,4	CS-III Work-Study	CS-III Work-Study	Final Exam Work-Study	Awards 2,M,3,4

TABLE 2

Table 2 (cont.)
Second Training Cycle
3/89 - 5/89

Level Legend: 1-Sr.Mgmt. 2-Line Mgmt. M-Systems Eng. 3-Sr.SW Eng. 4-Jr.SW Eng.

Week	Mon	Tue	Wed	Thu	Fri

* Each day is divided into two class groups

Class A
0830.. 1000 - lecture
1000.. 1010 - morning break
1010.. 1130 - lecture
1130.. 1230 - supervised hands-on workshop
1230.. 1300 - lunch
1300.. 1700 - self-study (w/Assistant Instructor)

Class B
0830.. 1230 -self-study (w/Assistant
                                    Instructor)
1230.. 1300 - lunch
1300.. 1430 - lecture
1430.. 1440 - afternoon break
1440.. 1600 - lecture
1600.. 1700 - supervised hands-on
                              workshop

SE - Software Engineering
SD - Software Design
SM - Software Management
CS - Case Study
Proj Mtg - Project Meeting

Academic/Industrial Collaboration in Project Manager Education

Ilkka J. Haikala and Jukka Märijärvi
Tampere University of Technology
Software Systems Laboratory
P.O. Box 527
SF-33101, Tampere
Finland

Abstract

Sofko is a special education program for software project managers. The program has been planned in close cooperation with universities and local software companies, and it also receives government support. In a larger context, Sofko program is one of the efforts of the Finnish government to support the decentralization of software industry away from the capital area. This report describes the background, organization and preliminary course contents of the Sofko program.

Our long term plan is that a similar postgraduate educational program, arranged in close cooperation with the software industry, will become a standard part of the software engineering education provided by our university.

---

1. Background

In the beginning of the year 1988, the Finnish Ministry of Labor assigned a private consulting firm to explore the state of software industry in Finland. Not surprisingly, their report indicated that a vast majority (some 80%) of the software industry is concentrated to the capital (Helsinki) area in the southern part of the country. The software enterprises there suffer from constant lack of competent staff, with the usual consequences of high turnover of labor force and drift of wages. On the other hand, some 50% of all CS students graduate from educational institutes in the other parts of the country. This means a constant flow of graduates moving, often reluctantly, to the already overcrowded capital area.

The report also indicated that it is possible to decentralize software industry on an economically profitable basis. This can be done by directing the growth of the software industry (about 20% annually) away from the capital area. Software enterprises are willing to support such development, provided that sufficient labor force is available. The largest problem is the shortage of skilled staff at the project manager level.

The government has decided to support the decentralization of the enterprises in two ways: first, the government will direct its own software development projects (about $100 million annually) to software houses (or their satellite offices) outside the capital area. Second, the government will support financially special education programs for project managers in several regional centers. This report describes one of these programs, Sofko, which is the special education program for project managers in Tampere. Tampere is a city of about 180000 inhabitants, located about 100 miles north of the capital.

2. Objectives

The objective of the Sofko program is to educate project managers for software industry. The program fills the gap between the software engineering education given by the CS departments in universities, and the requirements imposed by practical work in software projects. This gap will most probably remain as a constant phenomenon, because the "standard" computer science curricula in the universities cannot be extended, and the postgraduate studies in universities are targeted rather to scientific work than to practical skills. Also, teaching certain managerial topics to students who have at best attended only "toy" projects, is difficult, if not totally useless.

Originating from the premises above, a typical participant of our Sofko program is expected to have the following qualities:

- an M.Sc. degree in computer science or equivalent,
- necessary personal capabilities, and
- 2-4 years of experience in participating in software projects.

The selection of students to the courses will be carried out by a steering committee, supervised by local government authorities.

3. Organization and general framework

To guarantee that each pertinent topic will be covered by the Sofko program to sufficient extent, a steering committee was established. The steering committee has members both from the universities and from the software industry in Tampere area. The Tampere University of Technology has the main responsibility in planning and organizing the program.

During 1989 and 1990 three courses, each with some 15-20 participants, will be arranged. Each course will consist of approximately 40 course days, with a time span of about one year. The course schedules are designed to keep the disturbance of regular work moderate: only one 3-4 day period about once a month (Saturdays are used as course days to some extent).

It turned out early in the design of the program that two different course types were needed: Two of our three courses will be targeted to management of "traditional" software system projects, and one to management of product development (e.g. embedded systems) software projects. Although both course types have much in common, some of the topics covered are totally disjoint, and some have different emphasis in each case.

Due to government support, the price for each of the courses is moderate: only about $4500 per person. However, from the point of view of the participating enterprises, the cost of the lost workdays is considerably larger.

4. Course contents

The software projects in Finnish enterprises are usually relatively small — typically only some 5-15 persons are involved. In such projects, the project manager must have skills for a wide spectrum of tasks, ranging from managerial and economical issues to software coding. Also, he/she must often act as an "interface" between the project group and the outside world; i.e. customers and higher levels of management in the software company.

The initial proposal for the contents of the course was developed at the Software Systems Laboratory in the Tampere University of Technology. It was based on the idea that the course should be composed from a much wider spectrum of topics than typical staff training: in addition to the acute problems in the companies, the course should promote long term career development.

This proposal was then discussed extensively with the members of the steering committee. Also, several consulting companies, software houses, ADP departments of large companies, and software vendors have been consulted. During this work, a plethora of additions to the proposal was suggested. The final program is a compromise between these educational needs and limiting the length of the course to an acceptable amount of lost workdays.

Each course is composed of elements from the following areas of interest:

A. A managers view of a software project: knowledge, skills and tools that are necessary in managing a software project. This part covers among other things organizational and management issues, software project economics, ADP-systems as investments, legal issues, and human aspects.

B. A software engineering view of a software project: knowledge, skills, and tools that are necessary in software development work. Examples of topics covered by this part are software development process, requirements analysis, specification, system design, testing, quality assurance, standards, documentation, and maintenance.

C. Special topics: new, fast evolving, tools and techniques that an ADP-professional should be aware of. Examples of the topics in this category include expert systems, distributed systems, reuse, object oriented methods, security, fault tolerance, and graphical user interfaces.

A more detailed list of the contents of the first Sofko course is given in the appendix. (The first course is targeted to management of "traditional" software system projects.) Instructors for the course are hired from several sources:

- consulting companies
- experts from industry and research laboratories
- experts from academic institutions

The representatives of software houses in the steering committee have stressed that in addition to theoretical knowledge, most instructors should have sufficient experience in practical software development projects. This has limited the use of academic instructors in our program: most of the instructors belong to the first two groups mentioned above. The role of the university has been more in organizing and tailoring a relatively consistent course from modules provided by different instructors.

5. Current Status and Conclusions

After receiving the final government approval for financing of the Sofko program in the beginning of January 1989, the preliminary announcement of the program was delivered to the companies. The course announcement describing the schedule and contents of the first Sofko course, starting in April 1989, was mailed to the companies in the beginning of February. Applications to the course were accepted until the end of March. The announcement resulted in some twenty applications for the first course and some applications for the later courses also. Considering the program contents, the feedback has been enthusiastic. However, the time from the preliminary announcement to beginning of the course was much too short for many of the companies, because they make their training plans (and budgets) on a yearly basis. Also, the relatively large amount of workdays lost due to the course has been a hindering factor in many cases. At the time of the SEI conference we will be able to present the first practical experiences of the course.

In the Tampere University of Technology, we consider the Sofko program as an exiting opportunity to experiment with a new form of software engineering education. No doubt, the experiences learned in the Sofko program will have influence on our regular software engineering curriculum. Also, we hope that after the Sofko project has ended, a similar postgraduate educational program will become a standard part of the software engineering education provided by our university.

Appendix: the course contents of the first Sofko course

Human factors: Management of software project team members, motivation, customer service, communication skills, salesmanship. (Approximate duration 3 *days*)

Corporate economics: corporate strategy, strategic management, basic components of investment analysis, information systems as investments, monetary management, principal applications, profitability, finance, pricing, budgeting, prospects of the information system for the economic management in the 1990's, principles of production management, production cost analysis, cash flow, flow of materials. (5 *days*)

Legal issues pertaining software: current legislation, trends, copyright and liability issues, writing contracts, implications of legislation to software system design. (2 *days*)

Software project economics: cost analysis, budget planning with follow up actions, acquisitions. (3 *days*)

Project management: project planning, project management issues, project scheduling, project staffing, resource allocation, tools. (4 *days*)

Software evolution: feasibility studies, requirements, specification, design, implementation, CASE-tools. (8 *days*)

Testing: test methods and strategies, tools. (1 *day*)

Software operational issues: training, documentation, installation, maintenance. (1 *day*)

Documentation and standards: Useful standards and their effect to documentation planning. (1 *day*)

Configuration management: configuration management methods and tools. (1 *day*)

Quality, quality assurance: the role of quality and other quality issues, methods, standards, metrics. (2 *days*)

User interfaces: human interface problems, human factors, dialog planning, tools. (2 *days*)

Information system architectures: development, strategies, methodologies, software architecture, distributed systems, data communications. (2 *days*)

New paradigms in software: reuse, components, programming environments, object oriented programming, expert systems. (3 *days*)

Security and protection: risk management, fault tolerance, protection against hackers and viruses, criminal legislation. (1 *day*)

Networking and distributed systems: latest hardware and software trends, standardization, distributed operating systems, impact of network standardization, EDI. (2 *days*)

The Rockwell Avionics Group Software Engineering Training Program

H. E. Romanowsky
L. A. Bartelme
N. W. Jensen
C. M. Knutson

Avionics Group
Rockwell International
Cedar Rapids, Iowa

Abstract. *In July of 1987, the Rockwell International Avionics Group initiated a Software Engineering Training Program to increase our personnel's knowledge of software engineering, particularly with respect to real–time, embedded systems development. The program's design and development took place from July 1987 through January 1988. The program has been offered to engineers and managers since March of 1988. During the March to September 1988 period there have been 530 participants. The program has been very successful so far and participation has been higher than anticipated. Plans are to continue the training program at a controlled pace, with periodic program evaluations used to continually steer the program in the right direction. This paper highlights some of the efforts and "lessons learned" in developing and administering the Software Engineering Training Program.*

In July of 1987, Rockwell Avionics Group started the planning and development of a Software Engineering Training Program (SETP). This program is one of many ways in which management is addressing the problem of increased demand for software engineers.

Avionics Group has always supported continuing education for its personnel. There are company supported continuing education programs through local colleges and universities, as well as through NTU. Sole reliance on formal degree programs is not feasible or desirable for the majority of Avionics Group potential participants. Seminars, both in–house and off–site, have also been used as a method of providing further training and an alternative to degree programs. However, these are often brought in as a result of demand for a specific topic and are not any part of a formal *master training plan*. Continuity of course offerings and the covering of a spectrum of related disciplines is not the prime concern under this approach.

From the start, a formal training program was selected as the best approach toward meeting the company's software engineering needs. Formal, in our case, meant that there would be a regularly scheduled set of classes being held quarterly. Potential participants would be informed of the software engineering curriculum from the beginning of the program and would be guaranteed that the courses would be given a specific number of times per year. Students would be selected for course participation by upper management.

The SETP was not and is not seen as the solution to the problem of training engineers and managers in the area of software engineering. It is only one facet of the overall training effort. This program is complementary to on-the job training and is complementary to academic courses. The SETP serves as a cornerstone for improvement of software engineering skills within Avionics Group.

In order to gain a perspective on the sequence of the SETP development discussed in this paper, the following time line is given.

July 1987	"Go-ahead" to start developing SETP
August – December 1987	Curriculum planning and program implementation
January – February 1988	Introduction of Phase I program to management
March 1988 – September 1988	Phase I classes offered
October 1988 – September 1989	Phase II classes offered

SETP DEVELOPMENT ORGANIZATION

The Engineering/Personnel Directors Committee initiated the program's development. This committee is composed of the Avionics Group Vice President for Advanced Technology and Engineering, the divisional engineering directors, and personnel directors. A first step of this committee was to establish the Software Engineering Training Planning Committee (SETPC).

The SETPC was set up to serve as the focal point and principal planning group for software engineering training. It was immediately perceived that the development of a training program of this size, and its continued administration, requires continuing cooperation from a number of areas within the Avionics Group. Because of this, members of the committee were selected from engineering, administration, and Human Resource Development, a department within personnel.

The SETP committee charter included facilitating a division wide needs analysis survey, deciding on the approach to use in acquiring a set of courses, developing the curriculum, developing the enrollment process for potential students, implementing the curriculum, and evaluating the program. In addition, the committee was to decide on delivery mechanisms for particular courses, determine how to overcome potential barriers to success, and decide how to *market* the program to the engineering population. Assessment of non-curriculum related issues, such as equipment, facilities, and recognition for participation were also addressed.

DEFINING THE SETP SCOPE

Members of the SETPC perceived that the initial step in SETP development was to define as precisely as possible the actual scope of the training problem that was to be solved. Questions, such as those shown below, were researched in order to determine the program parameters.

- What level of software engineering skills does the current engineering work force possess?

- What software engineering skill level is needed?

- What are the projected needs for the divisions' future software engineering skills?

- What curriculum should be offered to achieve the required skill level?

- What is the most effective and economical course delivery mode?

- Who should be trained?

- How should the Software Engineering Training Program be implemented?

In summarizing the answers to these and additional questions, the initial scope of the SETP development was defined to be the following:

- Address required software engineering skill level, both for the present and for the future.

- Define a curriculum which addresses the projected requirements.

- Address implementation specific details.

SOFTWARE ENGINEERING SKILLS SURVEYS

In order to address the SETP questions related to skill levels, the SETPC needed mechanisms by which to assess the skill level of the engineering population. This was accomplished by the development of two surveys. The Manager's Software Training Needs Inventory was designed to determine managers' perceived needs for software engineering expertise within their departments. The Software Development Skills Inventory was designed to assess the current software engineering skill level of engineers with respect to areas such as software project management and software design. Response to the surveys was excellent. There were some surprising results:

- Most respondents perceived that they needed to increase their software engineering skills; even computer science graduates perceived a need for additional training in software engineering skills.

- Engineers' perceived skill needs and managers' perception of needed skills were highly correlated.

- It was shown that the training program should accommodate different levels of software development expertise, for example work experience and type of software training previously received.

- A need was indicated for separate tracks of courses for engineers and managers currently involved with software development, those transitioning into software development, and those involved indirectly with software development (i.e. marketing personnel).

PROGRAM IMPLEMENTATION

The SETP program development strategy was to use a phased implementation approach over a three year period. This would allow the SETP to address immediate areas of need for coursework topics for the targeted population. The phased approach also facilitated the laying of a firm groundwork for the program which would support its continued and controlled evolution. Program implementation involved curriculum definition and program administration.

CURRICULUM DEFINITION

The curriculum was defined by taking into account the evolution of technology and business practice within the Avionics Group. The SETPC wanted to ensure that the courses would present information which was directly applicable to the company's day to day software engineering efforts. In addition, it was also important that the variation in backgrounds among the engineers and managers be addressed so that the coursework could meet their individualized needs.

Curriculum definition efforts initially focused on programs which already existed. One option was to look into current academic programs to see if the SETP could be built from one of them. For example, contacts were made with the University of Iowa to determine how much assistance could be found via a currently existing academic program. University personnel were looking at the possibility of starting up a software engineering graduate program, but the projected time frame did not meet our needs. Commercial offerings were also looked into, but there was no coherent program that could be readily adopted. Since no currently existing programs could be found that would provide us with the desired breadth of subjects, the SETPC recommended that a customized curriculum be defined.

Three key areas were to be addressed by the SETP curriculum. These areas, listed below, served as the framework for curriculum definition. This framework was developed so that an individual's unique training requirements could be accommodated. Within each area, there is always an emphasis toward practical software engineering skills. The curriculum also was required to provide for evolution of material as business and state-of-the-art changed.

- Software Engineering Methodologies and Principles

   The coursework is required to address the basics of software engineering methodologies and principles. Courses within this area were set up to provide a consistent, common foundation for the program.

- Standardized Software Engineering Processes and Procedures

   This part of the curriculum addresses the specific software development processes and procedures which are used within the Avionics Group divisions.

- Software Engineering Environment Tools

   The training program serves as a focal point to address the use of specific tools selected by the divisions.

The SETP curriculum targets topics specifically needed for the area of avionics, real-time embedded systems. There are 49 courses which range from 2 to 72 hours in length. On the average, the majority of the courses fall into the 24 to 36 hour range. Lab time is included in classes where appropriate. It should be stressed that a single individual would not be likely to take all of the courses offered. The curriculum is defined so that an individual can take those courses which are applicable to their background and career objectives. The necessity for tailorability of an individual's *program of studies* category dictated that the trap of prerequisites preventing employee participation in a course be avoided.

From the start, the SETPC worked closely with technical advisors from the divisions, as well as with the engineering directors, in the curriculum development process. Each division selected engineers and managers to serve on a facility-wide curriculum advisory committee. This group of individuals was given an ongoing charter to assist with planning and approving the curriculum, evaluating course material, and evaluating the technical quality of the program.

The SETP curriculum was based on the three key areas mentioned earlier, and provided coursework for the specific categories of manager and practitioner. A manager was defined to be an individual responsible for planning and/or control of a software development project. Examples are group heads, department managers, and project leaders. A practitioner was defined as an individual who performs work on a software project. Examples are project leaders, software designers, systems engineers, and software developers. The resultant five category curriculum organization is shown below.

- Prerequisite to Core Courses

   The prerequisite to core courses cover topics which are of importance to individuals with no prior software development experience and no prior software specific training.

- Core Courses

  The core courses address topics that are potentially beneficial to all program participants. The core courses are heavily oriented towards basic software engineering principles and concepts.

- Practitioner Emphasis Series

  The practitioner emphasis series addresses technical areas pertinent to an engineer who is developing real–time, embedded systems software. The classes in this series complement the core courses by presenting in–depth applications of the software engineering methodologies and principles, and by presenting division specific software development processes and procedures.

- Management Emphasis Series

  The management emphasis series contains courses specific to the areas of project management.

- Cross–Emphasis Series

  Courses in the cross–emphasis series are targeted toward either practitioners or managers. The courses span the gap between courses just for managers or just for practitioners.

Concurrent with the curriculum development, the SETPC prepared an estimated budget and presented it to upper management. Overhead was calculated by using all company time for class attendance. This method produced *worst case* budget figures. Experience has shown that by offering courses on a mix of company and personal time, and by realizing the efficiencies of offering courses more frequently to larger numbers of people, actual costs have been considerably lower than was originally anticipated. It is much more cost effective to offer repeated iterations of courses as the development costs are divided among a larger number of participants.

PROGRAM ADMINISTRATION

Program administration takes a spectrum of activities into account. Financial considerations, administrative policies, and course acquisition are areas of primary concern. Some of these activities were immediately recognized as needing attention, while others were *discovered* as program implementation proceeded.

SETP COURSE ACQUISITION

Once the curriculum was defined, the actual course acquisition strategy had to be determined. It was quickly decided that in–house development of the entire curriculum was not going to be feasible. The SETPC then looked into the range of options for acquisition on a per course basis. These were determined to be *acquiring* courses from outside vendors, developing some courses in–house, interdivisional procurement of courses, and use of academic coursework. It was determined that courses to meet the curriculum framework would best be acquired via a mixture of in–house developed courses, *off the shelf* courses available from professional training vendors, and vendor developed *custom* courses.

Each of the courses in the proposed curriculum was categorized as to how it should be acquired. Those that were not to be developed by in–house personnel were to undergo a competitive selection process. To ensure a wide pool of candidate courses, the SETP committee decided to offer vendors the opportunity to bid on course development. The mechanism used to define vendor requirements was a Statement of Work (SOW) which described the program curriculum and program requirements. The SOW, along with a Request for Proposal, was sent to a large list of software training vendors. The program requirements covered such areas as ownership of developed material, videotaping rights, the use of Ada in all language specific courses, the use of real–time avionics problems in class examples and exercises, quality control, course maintenance, and instructor responsibilities.

The SOW was initially sent to twenty–three vendors who had expressed an interest in bidding on the program. Proposal evaluation required quite a bit of time from the SETPC members, as well as from curriculum advisory personnel and individuals involved with our contracts department. The criteria used during the proposal evaluation process are listed below.

- Technical content of the course proposals.

- Expertise of the proposed instructor(s); experience working with real–time systems.

- Application area of company; company and instructor both needed to show experience in the real–time, avionics systems arena.

- Quality control and modifiability issues with respect to course content.

- Cost

After the evaluation process was completed, the Avionics Group awarded contracts to five different vendor companies. While it would have been nice to have been able to award one vendor a contract for all courses within the SOW, it was not found to be a practical approach considering the time requirements for course deliveries.

SETP "MARKETING"

Defining a curriculum and subsequent acquisition of courses is only part of the implementation of a program the size of the Avionics Group SETP. A very critical part of the plan is marketing the program to all levels of management and to potential participants. Strong support is needed for such a program to be successful. Managers must be convinced that it is worthwhile for them to encourage their people to participate in the training program and to be willing to release people to attend classes. Fortunately, the SETP was, and continues to be, supported by the Avionics Group President and the Vice President of Advanced Technology and Engineering, along with the engineering directors from the divisions.

As a key part of the SETPC's marketing strategy, a formal introduction of the training program was made. The introduction took the form of a one hour "kick–off" presentation during which both the "why" and the "how" of participation in the training program was addressed. All management levels received an invitation to the session directly from the Avionics Group President.

The "kick–off" included presentations by the Avionics Group President and the Vice President of AT&E in which they stressed the increasing importance of software in the company's products, and thus the importance of participation in the training program. It was also emphasized that managers should participate in the program, as well as the engineers. The SETPC chairperson explained the program curriculum in detail. A program specialist from the Human Resource Development department also described the mechanism in place to enroll students in classes. Since managers are required to actively participate in developing programs of study for their people and enrolling them in classes, it was critical that they were comfortable with the course content and sign–up procedures.

Videotapes of the "kick–off" presentation have been made available to all managers and engineers. The SETPC suggested that managers use the videotape during staff meetings as a tool for familiarizing their employees with the program. For the most part, the participants needed very little convincing to become involved in the program. Their interest in improving their software engineering skills, and thus their job effectiveness, was very high from the start of the program.

PARTICIPANT SELECTION

The SETP has proven to be a very popular program and this has impacted the methods developed to select participants for each course. The need for a controlled mechanism to select individuals for course attendance was obvious immediately. Currently, each interested individual files a program of studies with the Human Resources Development department. This document lists the courses an individual wishes to attend. The composite list of courses is used to create a curriculum wide *candidate pool*. When a class is actually offered, participants are selected from this pool based on their background, experience and education, performance level, career development plans, and present and future involvement in software product development. Upper management, knowledgeable about their departments' software engineering needs, are always involved in the selection process.

Because of the large number of individuals wishing to enroll in courses, it was felt that screening mechanisms should be available. These screening mechanisms need to give a potential participant enough information to decide whether or not they already had knowledge of a large part of the course contents. Two self-assessment tools are used to help the potential participant determine whether a specific course is appropriate to their needs, experience and academic background. The first of these is a short preview videotape which features the course instructor describing the goals and contents of the course. Second, a self–assessment test is provided by the instructor for potential participants to evaluate their level of knowledge in the subject area.

SETP COURSE SCHEDULING

Scheduling of company sponsored training programs creates additional problems. In the case of SETP, it was desirable to keep people at their jobs for a good portion of the day, while allowing them to attend classes at convenient times and locations. There was an additional request from upper management to contain overhead costs as much as possible. As a result, the SETPC has strived to reach a 50/50 ratio of personal and company time as often as possible, while taking employees away from their jobs for no more than two hours per day. For the most part, this has been possible because of the large demand for courses. Usually two or three offerings of a course are scheduled during the same time frame. For example, two offerings of an advanced software engineering course would be scheduled during a two week period — one in the morning and one in the afternoon.

TRAINING PROGRAM FACILITIES

Avionics Group facilities in Cedar Rapids include an Education and Training Center with several training rooms. One training room is equipped with VT220 terminals which access the company's VAX clusters. This room is used for all software training and laboratories associated with the SETP. Another classroom is equipped with videotaping equipment and has been dedicated for use by the SETP.

ONGOING SETP ADMINISTRATION

All program scheduling, participant tracking, budget responsibilities, and coordination of vendor contracts are handled by Human Resource Development. They track the individualized programs of study for each participant and award certificates and plaques to participants on an ongoing basis. The engineering departments within the divisions, via the SETP committee, oversee the technical content of the program.

LESSONS LEARNED

The success of a training program depends largely on having satisfied customers. An objective is to have participants feel that time spent during class has been worthwhile and the knowledge gained is useful in their work. A complementary goal is to have management feel that time their employees spend in classes away from work results in directly applicable information. The SETPC found that the gradual, steady growth of the program helped to achieve these goals. Use of a *big–bang* approach to training, where a large program is unleashed all at once, would not have been well received nor would it have been well managed by the SETPC. It is important to remember that the administrative aspects of such a program are sometimes more difficult to deal with than developing the curriculum itself.

In addition, the engineering community needs to be involved with the development of the program. This proved to be useful not only during the initial stages of the SETP's formulation, but also during its continuation. The program must be receptive to the needs of its participants to remain successful. It has also been found that quality offerings are an important consideration. Involving the engineering community in the determination and review of courses assists with insuring that quality is a major priority.

Training is costly from a resource point of view. This fact should be readily acknowledged by those involved with a program such as SETP. The way to overcome some of the negative aspects of the costs is to emphasize the resultant benefits to the participants, their managers, and to the company as a whole. Follow–up presentations describing how participants are integrating their newly acquired skills in their work assignments helps build credibility for the program.

Achieving program flexibility without compromising program quality has become a key issue in continuation of the SETP. As time passes, some of the original parameters change and the program has had to change as a result. Schedule flexibility is essential, not only for policy changes with respect to attendance on company time versus personal time, but also to react to budget changes. The SETPC has also been fortunate to have selected vendors who have been very flexible with respect to the manner in which they deliver courses. For example, we do not always follow the usual format of having a class presented from 8 to 5 on consecutive days of the week. We have stretched a class over a period of weeks by offering it 2 or 3 hours per day and sessions on Saturday. In short, whether it be scheduling, or policy changes, flexibility is a must.

Today, the SETP continues to grow and evolve as the committee, and management, strive to "provide a quality software engineering training program.

Teaching Object-Oriented Programming Using the Macintosh MPW/MacApp Environment

Laurie Honour Werth
Department of Computer Sciences
The University of Texas at Austin
Austin, Texas 78712-1188

John S. Werth
Department of Computer Sciences
The University of Texas at Austin
Austin, Texas 78712-1188

Abstract

Experience with object-oriented systems can be provided using the powerful Macintosh™ environment. Adding to and modifying the MacApp™ application framework using ObjectPascal provides a learning-by-example solution to the difficulty of teaching Object Oriented Programming and Design,

Advanced training and funding for high-end hardware, additional tools and better documentation are the prime requisites. The Mac tools need to be more efficient, user-friendly and well-documented before they can be used widely by software engineering students. These difficulties will likely be overcome, making the Macintosh environment a useful classroom tool to prepare students to meet the demands of future software technology.

Introduction

Experience in using and developing large, object-oriented, graphical interface systems is needed to prepare students to meet the challenge of modern software technology. Object-oriented programming's popularity is based on its encouragement of reusability and the building of large systems from component parts, but it is difficult to teach [O'Shea87]. Well done graphical interfaces provide friendly, easy-to-use products conducive to the object-oriented approach, but are complex and normally difficult to develop [Cox86]. Software engineering students need practice in these modern programming practices, but how do we pack it all into an already busy course?

In previous semesters, students at The University of Texas have developed, enhanced, (re)used and evaluated software tools as projects in the undergraduate software engineering course [Werth89]. Last year, for example, students used the TeamWork™ CASE tool in the design of products which, in turn, enhanced TeamWork's capabilities. These projects, written in C in a UNIX®[1] environment on the Hewlett Packard 9000 workstations, were successful in providing both quantitative productivity improvements and qualitative learning enhancements [Werth88]. Students gained experience in working within a large system, though they actually needed only to understand the ACCESS routines provided with the system.

When funding became available for the acquisition of Macintosh SEs for the undergraduate labs, MPW (Macintosh™ Programmers WorkShop) and MacApp™ (Extended Macintosh™ Application) were added as an integrated development environment for the software engineering class. The MPW tools, Apple's ObjectPascal language, and the MacApp object library and application framework, made it possible for students to develop standard Macintosh interface applications in a single semester, achieving many of the learning goals outlined above.

This paper briefly describes the course organization and Macintosh environment. Difficulties in teaching object-oriented programming and design which motivated this approach are outlined, together with the advantages and disadvantages encountered during the semester. Conclusions about the future follow.

---

[1] UNIX is a register trademark of AT&T Information Systems

Course Description

CS 373 is a typical project-based undergraduate software engineering course. Students are divided into four teams of five or six, and each team develops a software tool for future software engineering classes. In order to allow time to learn the Macintosh environment, relatively simple software costing tools were selected as projects: COCOMO [Boehm81], COPMO [Conte86], and Putnam's model [Londe87]. Two teams implemented COCOMO.

Students document and implement their systems following Fairley's [85] outline: System Definition, User's Manual, System Requirements Specification, three Design Documents, Test Plan, Test Results, Project Legacy and Project Notebook. The User's Manual is developed early as a rudimentary "prototype" which the students find the most helpful of the documents. Students use TeamWork™ to enter their data flow diagrams, data dictionary, process specifications, finite state diagrams and structure charts. Finite state diagrams are used to define the event handler and user interface, which conforms to the Apple Macintosh™ User Interface Standard.

Projects are implemented incrementally in ObjectPascal, Apple's Object-Oriented language, using MPW and MacApp™ on Macintosh™ SEs. Since one of the goals is to distribute tools though Kinko's Academic Courseware Exchange, Kinko's testing and other requirements were part of the project specification. Testing includes both black box and white box techniques as well as performance and stress testing. After preliminary testing, each team is given a handful of Software Trouble Reports and assigned to evaluate one of the other teams' project. A small maintenance phase requires that the STRs be answered and some changes implemented. Students critique the project and the Macintosh™/MPW/MacApp™ environment using forms based on [Weide87].

Walkthroughs are held weekly on Friday with each student orally presenting some aspect of the document before it is turned in for a grade on the following Monday. Teams make a final technical presentation at the end of the semester and use a LCD overhead projection system to demonstrate their programs at that time. Handouts with advice on team organization, technical writing and oral presentations are provided. Students are encouraged to make slides of major ideas and to use figures or diagrams, rather than simply reading the photocopied pages of the document on the overhead projector (their preferred mode). Teaching Assistants are encouraged to grade for content and style rather than volume and attractiveness (their preferred mode).

Documenting on the Macintosh provides early Mac experience and excellent graphic capabilities. Snapshots of the screen can be made for the User's Manual, for example. Each week a different Phase Leader is responsible for insuring document consistency and quality. Teams also e-mail progress reports and brief notes from the walkthrough with the document. The final Project Notebook includes a Project Legacy summarizing both the technical and managerial lessons learned with the as-built documentation. Students are encouraged to make use of the HP system's mail facility for communicating and recording progress throughout the semester.

Macintosh Lab Facilities

The Computer Sciences department recently converted its beginning programming laboratories to Macintosh™ SEs. One of our motivations in getting the Macs for the beginning courses was to provide students with an introduction to windowing environments early in their careers, so there would be time to gain depth to be built upon in later courses, rather than the previous arrangement of moving courses to a different computer system every semester.

Currently, there are 75 machines, seven printers, and three hard disk file servers, all networked with AppleTalk. A department network connects these machines and gives access to the campus-wide network which includes university mainframes. Software includes GENIE (Carnegie Mellon's novice programming environment), LightSpeed Pascal, C, and the Consulair 68000 assembly environment. This equipment is primarily used by the first three classes: a very large partially self-paced beginning Pascal Programming course (CS I), two large sections of Computer Science Concepts (CS II) and a large section of Computer Organization and Assembly Language Programming (CS III). Students also have access to Macs in Computation Center and dormitory laboratories.

Object Oriented Programming and Design

Object-oriented programming (OOP) includes the ideas of object, class, method and inheritance. Objects encapsulate a data type and its operations (methods) together with their operator/operand dependencies to provide greater independence, resulting in software that supports change, reusability and enhancement. Objects naturally model many problem domains, and class inheritance provides an intuitive reuse capability. Object-Oriented Programming has been seen as desirable for some time, but it has been slow to be taken up for a variety of reasons [Cox84].

Smalltalk on the Hewlett-Packard 9000 workstations is used in our Programming Languages class, but the language is difficult to teach [Diede87]. The new vocabulary and the unusual "postfix" syntax, even when explained in terms of known Ada concepts, confuse students further. The powerful environment provides too many options for beginners to master in only a few weeks. The reference manuals [Goldb83,84] are excellent, but there is still not a good teaching text. While the paradigm is conceptually easy to understand, Smalltalk presents enough obstacles that students have a hard time concentrating on the design of their programs. The primary lesson they seem to be learning at this point is that object-oriented programming is *not* something they want to do.

ObjectPascal on the Macintosh seems to offer a possible solution. Developed by Apple in collaboration with Niklaus Wirth, the language is a minimum extension of Pascal. Objects are declared in the TYPE section with record-like fields and associated procedure (method) definitions.

Declaring object types

```
TYPE
    TSimpleObject = OBJECT                {No ancestor type}
    fData: Handle;
    PROCEDURE SomeProc;
    END;

    TMyObject = OBJECT(TObject)           {Extends TObject}
    fValue: LONGINT;
    FUNCTION AFunc: INTEGER:
    END;
```

Declaring and allocating objects

```
VAR
    oneofmine: TMyObject;
BEGIN
    NEW(oneofmine);
    ...
    oneofmine.Free;
END,
```

Referencing fields and methods
```
Write(oneofmine.fValue);
Write(oneofmine.AFunc);
```

Implementing methods
```
FUNCTION TMyObject.AFunc: INTEGER;
BEGIN
    AFunc := 1;
END;
```
Inheritance
```
TAnotherObject = OBJECT(TMyObject)
    FUNCTION AFunc: INTEGER; OVERRIDE;
END;

FUNCTION TAnotherObject.AFunc: INTEGER;
    BEGIN
        AFunc := 2 + INHERITED AFunc;        {will return 3}
    END;
```

Fig 1.   Object Pascal extensions to Pascal [WEST87; p. 599]

New objects, declared in terms of a previously declared object type, inherit properties of the earlier type, but can override these or define new properties as well.   A hybrid, rather than a pure OOP language, ObjectPascal allows combining object-oriented with conventional procedural code and the use of existing libraries of Pascal code.   Thus it provides an "evolutionary" rather than a "revolutionary" introduction [Cox84], though there is still considerable overhead to learning the Macintosh environment.

The Macintosh™ Development Environment

MPW is a UNIX® -like environment which includes a line-oriented command interpreter, full-screen editor, assembler, linker/librarian, resource tools, text analysis tools and three packages: Pascal compiler (including ObjectPascal), C compiler, and the MacApp library for object-oriented development.   Unique features of MPW include an integrated command and editing language, redirection of I/O to windows, a graphical interface for each command, and user-defined menus connectable to shell commands [Meyer88].

The User Interface Toolbox implements the Macintosh™ Standard User Interface which determines how the user views and controls the Macintosh program. The Operating System controls internal functions such as allocating memory, controlling the system clock and all peripheral devices including the keyboard, display and disk I/O. Release 2.0 requires the following minimum configuration:

- 128K ROM or later (Macintosh™ Plus, SE, Macintosh™ II)
- 1 Mb of RAM
- HFS hard disk (approximately 4 Mb) [West87].

In order to purchase the software, it is necessary to be a member of the Apple Programmer's and Developer's Association (APDA)[2] , which currently costs $100. They distribute the *Macintosh Technical Notes* to supplement the five volumes *Inside Macintosh* [Apple85-87] series, required reading for programming the Mac. Other references are included in the Selected Readings. APDA distributes these as well as other technical documentation and Mac development software.

MacApp™, an object library of more than 30 different classes and over 450 methods, provides a standard Macintosh user interface together with other common application actions. It includes sample programs which are intended to be adapted to provide additional features. Students learn by example, by modifying and by adding to existing object-oriented code. They start with a rudimentary Macintosh application framework to which they add the features desired for their application. Apple requires additional licensing requirements and a small annual license fee to distribute product which use MacApp™[3].

MacApp allows students to bypass many of the details of *Inside Macintosh*, especially its rather intricate memory management scheme. MacApp provides events, interface controls, desk accessories, and printing as well as making it easier to use menus and windows. Development is faster, though it is still necessary to learn the File Manager, QuickDraw, and other MPW tools. The Resource Editor, used to design windows and dialog boxes, proved to be the biggest stumbling block.

Object-oriented programming requires object-oriented design which differs from conventional top down design [Meyer87]. Hard to describe effectively, OOD may be learned more easily by example. Booch's Ada-Oriented-Design methodology [Booch86] and other OOD

---

[2] APDA 290 S.W. 43rd Street, Renton, WA 98055

[3] Apple Computer Software Licensing, 20525 Marianni Avenue, MS: 28B, Cupertino, CA 95014

material in [Press87] were presented, but most learning came from studying and using MacApp examples.

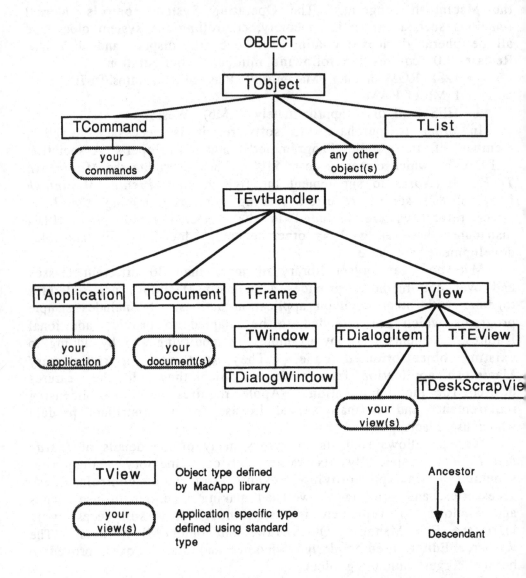

Simplified MacApp object ancestry   [West87; p 648]

It is important for students to understand MacApp before beginning to design their application. The three MPW knowledgable people were each assigned to a different team. Only one student learned MacApp sufficiently to incorporate it into his team's design.

The other two students who knew MPW designed their systems on the basis of their MPW knowledge without looking at MacApp. Their teams were dismayed to find MacApp already did much of what they had spent considerable time planning. The fourth team had no Macintosh experienced member, so designed a system with a Mac interface which they implemented by having three people "try to get something running." Interestingly, their final product compared quite favorably to the same system developed by a stronger team with an experienced, if overly ambitious, Macintosh member.

Advantages

MacApp provides a sophisticated and powerful object-oriented model which simultaneously improves learning and broadens students' programming horizons. The event handler provides an effective demonstration of the power of the finite state machine, which few students had appreciated previously. The speed with which students were able to develop complete Macintosh applications largely made up for the difficulty of mastering the complex environment.

Integrated Development Environment

Students need experience in using code developed by others and assembling programs from components, though integrated development environments are rarely available for students [Werth88]. Emphasis on the computer-human interface and the use of user interface management systems are also desirable.

Students valued MPW/MacApp as a professional integrated environment, despite the high learning curve. Several considered MPW to be better than UNIX® because of its superior editor and cleaner user interface, though they felt that UNIX® had better documentation and help features. Features such the Commando interface, more mnemonic names, and multiple window capability were other advantages. The system was large enough that naming conventions and good documentation were seen as valuable. Students also came to appreciate the treachery of global variables.

Students recognized that MacApp encouraged Object-Oriented programming, which most of them could understand even though only a few had been exposed to OOP before this class. Students who *had* used Smalltalk felt that they had learned the object-oriented approach far better than by using Smalltalk. ObjectPascal was seen as an expansion of familiar concepts, rather than a complex change of syntax, semantics and environment.

The event handler model was confusing at first, but they found it a new and interesting way to view the programming process. One student described it as "The program does not tell the user what to do; the the user tells the program what to do." While the data flow diagram was not a good representation model for the Macintosh™ Interface, students were delighted to find that state transition graphs were actually good for something! They could see that MacApp was handling much of the overhead of keeping track of the valid options for each state. There was considerable motivation once they finally got their dialog box working and realized all the power they were gaining from MacApp.

Improved Development Time

Developing code required only a month and this included the learning time as well as other course and project work. It was easy to appreciate the reusability advantages of having MacApp handle window moving, resizing and refeshing, printing, desk accessories, disk errors, and so on. Students particularly enjoyed the good debugging facilities. Even the three students with MPW experience coming into the class felt that the learning curve for MacApp was more than offset by the time gained in *not* learning the details of MPW and *Inside Macintosh*. Only one student would have preferred the familiar UNIX® and C. While the payoff was not immediate on this first small project, savings would accrue on later projects.

Students who are currently acquiring an understanding of the basic system in the introductory classes will be arriving soon. CASE, supplementary tools and documentation aids are being acquired. With testing and other software developed by later software engineering classes and revisions from Apple, there will be a marked improvement in the development time in the future as well.

Disadvantages

The major difficulties were the poor documentation and the slowness with which the software ran. A move to Mac IIs, version of 3.0 of MPW and 2.05B of MacApp next Fall will help alleviate this

problem.   Additional   memory,   dedicated   hard   disks,   on-line
documentation and an ObjectBrowser are necessities.

Lack of Documentation

The documentation provided with the system was minimal and
hard to understand.   Not an uncommon situation, but it was
especially difficult for students within tight time frames.   The
frequent references to *Inside Macintosh* and other books could be
circular or even dangling.   Many functions which were referenced
were never found.   There were a few situations in which the
students resorted to reading source code to try to figure out what
was happening!   This led to a great deal of frustration and hacked
code, described by one student as "stab-and-shoot: try something,
hope it works, then try something else."

There was little high level documentation to present object-
oriented programming strategies.   In retrospect, *Object-Oriented
Programming for the Macintosh™* by Kurt Schmucker would have
improved the situation greatly had it been available.   Tutorial
material for MacApp such as that provided to develop   MPW
programs in *Macintosh™ Revealed* [Chern85] would also have been
helpful.

The sample programs were good, but were not described in
enough detail and did not show many common situations.   It would
be nice to have code fragments of every command. MacApp contains
features appropriate for McWrite and McDraw types of applications,
but not for more general purpose applications.   One student, a
Macintosh wizard, mastered MacApp early in the semester and was
generous enough to develop additional, more complete, examples for
the class.   Future classes will have the existing, working programs as
models, so this problem will be partially alleviated.

Lack of Speed

The slowness of the system is due to several different factors.
While a Macintosh™ SE with dedicated hard disk is a legal
configuration, a Mac II is probably needed to develop code in the
time frame needed for a software engineering project course.   Two
hard disks were finally acquired so the students would not have to
contend with AppleTalk or the other students in the laboratory.
MacApp is a large system. The basic framework together with the
large $includes produce programs over 70K in size, not counting the
debugger.   Viruses were a minor problem, but one which can only
get worse in the future.

MABuild (Make) is inefficient and disk intensive. Twenty to thirty minute compiles are not reasonable. This is particularly unfortunate due to the large number of recompiles required due to naivete and lack of documentation. Slow compilation reduces all aspects from understanding the system to debugging the code. Error messages are probably not worse than other systems, but they are less than informative.

It's hard for students to differentiate between their own errors and those in the system. Because the system is relatively new, there are few MPW- and no MacApp-knowledgeable users and no vendor support. To some extent, students were disappointed because they expected the system to be as user-friendly as other Macintosh applications. As with other systems it is not truly designed for team use and lacks file sharing. This further slows development or at least encourages some students to sit on the sidelines while others do the work.

Conclusions

Using and developing software tools as class projects contributes valuable experience and motivation while supplying software engineering students with realistic projects and building up a tool library for future classes [Werth89].

The Macintosh provides a powerful programming environment which helps students gain experience in working with larger object-oriented systems. The Macintosh™ Programmers WorkShop (MPW) furnishes students with a relatively easy to use development tools, MacApp™ offers an object library for developing standard Macintosh™ Interface applications, while ObjectPascal teaches basic object-oriented programming concepts in a reasonably painless fashion.

Even for small projects, working in this complex environment encourages students to abstract, together with providing sophisticated examples upon which to model their solutions. It is not possible to develop sufficiently large applications from scratch in a single semester without these kinds of tools. Thus a major benefit is the experience in reusability and assembling code from components, many of which were written by and for other professional Macintosh developers. Experience with the event handling model was especially relevant. While the Macintosh interface was new to most students, they quickly perceived the advantages in a consistent, user-friendly graphical interface, modeled using state transition graphs.

Many of the problem areas can be rectified by advanced preparation and training, with funding for high-end hardware, supplemental tools and better documentation. Early experience on the Macintosh would be very helpful. The Macintosh environment needs to be made somewhat more efficient, well-documented and user-friendly before it is suitable for those without extensive Mac experience and the dedication shown by these students. Additional tools are needed, as are more complete, simple examples.

This semester was very rewarding and the Macintosh interchangeability offers hope for developing standardized tools to cover a wider range of the life cycle. There is considerable potential for the programming-in-the-medium and object-oriented experiences students need in order to meet the demands of future software technology.

Bibliography

[Apple85]   Apple Computer, Inc. *Inside Macintosh*, Volumes I, II, III, IV, and V. Addison-Wesley, 1985-1987.

[Boehm81]   Boehm, Barry. *Software Engineering Economics*. Prentice-Hall, 1981.

[Booch86]   Booch, Grady. Object-Oriented Development. IEEE *Transactions on Software Engineering*, Feb, 1986.†

[Chern85]   Chernicoff, Stephen. *Macintosh™ Revealed: Unlocking the Toolbox.*, Volumes One and Two, Second Edition. Hayden Books, 1985 and 1987.

[Conte86]   Conte, S., H. Dunsmore, and V. Shen. *Software Engineering Metrics and Models*. Benjamin/Cummings, 1986.

[Cox84]   Cox, Brad. Message/Object Programming: An Evolutionary Change in Programming Technology. *IEEE Software*, Jan, 1984.†

[Cox86]   Cox, Brad and B. Hunt. Objects, Icons, and Software-ICs. *Byte*, Aug, 1986.†

[Diede87]   Diederich Jim. and Jack Milton. Experimental Prototyping in Smalltalk. *IEEE Software*, May, 1987.

[Fairl85]   Fairley, Dick. *Software Engineering Concepts*. McGraw-Hill, 1985.

---

† also in Peterson, Gerald (Ed.). *Tutorial:Object-Oriented Computing*. IEEE Computer Society Press, Vol 1 and 2. 1987b.

[Goldb83]   Goldberg, Adele and Dave Robson. *Smalltalk80: The Language and its Implementation.* Addison-Wesley, 1983.

[Goldb84]   Goldberg, Adele. *Smalltalk80: The Interactive Environment.* Addison-Wesley, 1984.

[Londe87]   Londeix, Bernard. *Cost Estimation for Software Development.* Addison-Wesley, 1987.

[Meyer89]   Meyer, Bertram. Object Oriented Software Construction. Prentice-Hall, 1989.

[Meyer87]   Meyer, Bertram. Reusability: The Case for Object-Oriented Design. IEEE *Software*, March 1987.†

[Meyer88]   Meyers, Richard and Jeff Parrish. The Macintosh™ Programmer's Workshop. *Byte*, May, 1988.

[O'Shea86]   O'Shea, T., K. Beck, D. Halbert, and K. Schmucker. The Learnability of Object-Oriented Programming Systems. *Proceedings of the ACM Conference on Object-Oriented Programming Systems, Languages and Applications*, 1986.†

[Sherm88]   Sherman, M. and R. Drydale. Teaching Software Engineering in a Workstation Environment. *I E E E Software*, May, 1988.

[Schmu86a]   Schmucker, Kurt. Object-Oriented Languages for the Macintosh™. *Byte*, Aug, 1986.†

[Schmu86b]   Schmucher, Kurt. MaccApp: An Application Framework. *Byte*, Aug, 1986.†

TeamWork™   Cadre Technologies Inc., 222 Richmond Street, Providence, RI 02903.

[Weide87]   Weiderman, N. H., Habermann, A. N., Borger, M. W., and Klein, M. H. "A Methodology for Evaluating Environments." *Proceeding of the ACM SIGSOFT/SIGPLAN Software Engineering Symposium on Practical Software Development Environments*, 1987.

[West87]   West Joel. *Programming with Macintosh™ Programmer's Workshop.* Bantam Books, 1987.

[Werth87]   Werth, Laurie. Survey of Software Engineering Education. ACM SIGSOFT *Software Engineering Notes.* Vol. 12 No. 4, Oct, 1987.

[Werth88]   Werth, Laurie. Software Tools at the University: Why, What and How in G. Ford (Ed.) *Software Engineering Education*, Springer-Verlag, 1988.

[Werth89]   Preparing Students for Programming-in-the Large. *Proceedings of the Twentieth Technical Symposium, SIGCSE*, Feb, 1989.

Selected References: Macintosh, MPW and MacApp

Apple Computer, Inc. *MacApp™: The Expandable Macintosh™ Application*, Version 1.1.1, Apple Computer, Inc. Cupertino, CA. 1987.

Apple Computer, Inc. *MPW: Macintosh™ Programmer's Workshop*, Version 2.0.2, Apple Computer, Inc. Cupertino, CA. 1987.

Apple Computer, Inc. *Pascal*, Version 2.0.2, Apple Computer, Inc. Cupertino, CA. 1987.

Apple Computer, Inc. *Human Interface Guidelines: The Apple Desktop Interface*. Addison-Wesley, 1987.

Apple Computer, Inc. *Inside Macintosh*, Volumes I, II, III, IV, and V. Addison-Wesley, 1985-1987.

Apple Computer, Inc. *Macintosh Technical Notes* - extentions and updates to *Inside Macintosh*. Apple Computer, Inc. Cupertino, CA., 1985-present.

Chernicoff, Stephen. *Macintosh™ Revealed: Unlocking the Toolbox.*, Volumes One and Two, Second Edition. Hayden Books, 1985 and 1987.

Knaster, Scott. *How to Write Macintosh™ Software*. Hayden, 1986.

Knaster, Scott. Macintosh™ Programming Secrets. Addison-Wesley, 1988.

Object-Oriented Languages issue of *Byte*, August, 1986. Vol. 11, No. 8.

Poole, Lon. *MacInsights: Secrets, shortcuts, and solutions for the Apple Macintosh™*. Microsofft Press, 1986.

Price, Jonathan. *How to Write a Computer Manual: A Handbook of Software Documentation*. Benjamin Cummings, 1984.

Schmucker, Kurt. *Object-Oriented Programming for the Macintosh™*. Hayden, 1986.

West Joel. *Programming with Macintosh™ Programmer's Workshop*. Bantam Books, 1987.

A Personal Computer Environment for Realtime Programming

James D.Schoeffler
Professor of Computer Science
Cleveland State University
Cleveland, Ohio 44118

ABSTRACT

An approach to teaching realtime system design and programming is described which provides an understanding of realtime applications in terms of interacting tasks and modules sharing common resources. Emphasis is on the design and specification of the realtime system along with detailed testing and verification of the resulting concurrent programs. Programming is done on personal computers using a realtime operating system and an event tracing facility which supports both detailed execution tracing as well as "action" routines which can force occurrence of time critical events for testing.

1. Foundations of realtime programming

Realtime programming involves the design of multiple program modules which execute concurrently, share resources, interact through intertask communication of data and events, and respond to internal and external events quickly enough to affect the environment [1,2,3]. There is a major emphasis on design to meet required response times under a variety of situations.

Realtime programming requires a strong background in general operating system concepts: the various operating system functions (scheduling, memory management, file systems); concurrency control algorithms; and conventional input/output system organization including interrupt drivers, buffered I/O requests, context switching of tasks waiting for I/O request completion, and the like [1,2,4]. The design of operating systems to provide services to concurrent tasks is not the same as designing a set of concurrent tasks to carry out a realtime application.

Despite being familiar with operating system concepts and services, designers and students usually are not accustomed to thinking of system design in terms of multiple cooperating tasks and interrupt driven routines interacting with application tasks. They especially are not accustomed to performing design with stringent response time requirements and verifying that their design and implementation actually meets those requirements.

Like many other areas (data structures for instance), it has proved fruitful to introduce a student to realtime systems design by carefully considering some well understood realtime systems, the alternative designs which have been developed, and the use of these designs as building blocks for developing solutions to other realtime problems, the so called "paradigm" approach. We believe this is especially important in the realtime design area because students usually are not familiar enough with common realtime applications to critically evaluate a design even though they have finished a core program in computer science and are at the senior elective level.

The study of realtime software using examples does not imply "case studies" or the study of code associated with implementations. Rather it is the architecture or structure of the design which is studied. This includes how the application is partitioned into tasks, shared routines, interrupt driven routines, intertask communication used, and concurrency control used from the point of view of abstracting the building blocks to be used elsewhere.

This leads to two important objectives for a course:

1. an understanding of realtime applications and a facility for describing the overall software architecture of applications in terms of tasks, shared routines, interrupt routines, shared data areas, concurrent access of resources, and events which initiate tasks.

2. an understanding of constraints imposed on the program design by the overall architecture and response time needs, the use of realtime programming constructs to respond to events and solve concurrency problems, and the effects of these constructs on response time.

Studying designs is not sufficient however. The programming portion associated with implementation of designs must emphasize the use of a variety of constructs which permit programming of interrupt response routines, attaching of tasks to interrupts, and use of a variety of concurrency control techniques and must permit critical evaluation of the design experimentally.

The programming environment reported here uses readily available personal computers running a realtime operating system to allow sufficient student access time. Higher level programming languages used include Pascal and PL/M [5]. Programming assignments do not necessarily require special input/output facilities (A/D converters for example). This environment permits both the implementation of realtime software designs and also the detailed testing of the software at a level where proper solution of concurrency problems and event responses can be tested and verified.

We have oriented our course around use of a software-based realtime program monitor which is an oscilloscope-like capability to trace the detailed execution of the realtime software so that the blocking of tasks, context switching, time occurrence of events, and the like can be observed and the detailed realtime response of the designed software can be determined[6]. Since it is difficult to see how realtime software responds in a given situation simply because the situation seldom occurs, this monitor allows designer-created "action" routines which can force event occurrence which in turn forces a critical situations to occur for testing and verification purposes.

Hence the emphasis of teaching realtime systems then involves the design of software for the application, the recognition of situations under which event sequence is critical, the design of (software) experiments to force these situation to arise, and then the observing of the results. This combination forces students to concentrate on the realtime aspects of the design as opposed to the various algorithms which are the focal points of an operating system course.

In section 2, some of the realtime paradigms used are discussed. Section 3 discusses the monitor and the use of action routines. Section 4 briefly discusses the software architecture specification used. Section 5 gives three examples of realtime software designs and their use of action routines.

2. Example realtime systems paradigms

The paradigms selected to teach realtime systems must be accompanied by their motivating applications that provide the basis for response time and other constraints on the design.

We have used the data acquisition and direct digital control applications associated with industrial process control for this purpose. Discussion and readings include not only the characteristics and requirements of these applications, but also the architecture of several alternative realtime software designs used for their implementation. The software designs provide a concrete basis for comparison with other approaches already familiar to the student in order to quantify the specific problems of realtime systems. The software designs also act as paradigms which can be used as models for solving realtime design problems in the course.

The data acquisition problem is first introduced by discussion of the typical components required: sensors, multiplexors, sample/hold, and analog-to-digital converters [7,8]. Emphasis is on the function and characteristics of the devices and their impact on software rather than their design. Speed of high and low level multiplexors, A/D conversion times, and signal levels and their effects on noise provide later motivation for software architecture design. Heuristic rules for sampling rate are introduced and the need for precise periodic sampling emphasized. The direct digital control application is then added to data acquisition[9,10]. Characteristics of analog output devices are discussed along with the control loop concept. The student is introduced to small systems such as automobile engine control and large systems such as a process or manufacturing plant mainly through readings.

Various architectures of realtime software designs for data acquisition and direct digital control are introduced, including interrupt driven cyclic data acquisition triggered by interval timers, point-table oriented designs to handle a variety of sensor types and associated processing requirements, and a cyclic system with time scheduled short tasks [9]. Details of various functions assigned to tasks, the data they share, the intertask communication among them, potential concurrency problems, and effects of errors are all discussed. Each of the components of these designs is simple enough that throughput, response time, and error recovery considerations may be discussed thoroughly.

The software architectures are considered for dedicated processors and as the data acquisition and control component in a processor containing higher level tasks that both use the acquired data and also have to interact with the data acquisition and direct digital control tasks (activating/deactivating control, changing parameters, etc).

Assignments include special cases of data acquisition and control systems and other applications which involve data acquisition and control as part of the application. The intent is to use the detailed understanding of the alternative software architectures to structure a solution for the specific problem at hand.

3. PC based experimental environment

Realtime operating systems provide easy access to techniques previously studied in systems programming courses. We selected the iRMX86 operating system[4,5] which runs on IBM-PC machines because it is small, understandable, and provides access to all system above system services from high level languages. It provides all the following services:

1. preemptive-resume priority based multiprogramming with priority selection under the control of the programmer.
2. creation of subtasks under program control.
3. high level language programming of interrupt response routines and the attachment of routines to hardware interrupts.
4. flexible initiation of tasks by other tasks including the attachment of a task to an interrupt.
5. access to I/O devices, including files on secondary storage, with system services which permit control over realtime-significant aspects of I/O.
6. mailbox communication (creation, deletion, message send, and message receive)
7. semaphores and regions (creation, deletion, P and V operations).
8. interrupt handling services include routine and task attachment to interrupts, interrupt enabling, disabling, software initiation of interrupts, and interrupt response routine exit.
9. memory management services including dynamic allocation and deletion of arbitrary sized primary memory areas
10. task services including creation, suspension, priority setting, blocking, and resuming a task.

Consequently we have organized the programming around this operating system along with a general event tracing facility which records or logs significant events occurring in the execution of the concurrent processes[6]. The resulting data base is called the log file. Events traced include all calls to operating system services (task servicing, mailbox communication, semaphore and other synchronization, timer interrupt servicing, and I/O events). Events also include all defined events associated with execution of a module such as entering and leaving procedures and critical sections as well as events which are considered significant and detected in the course of execution such as occurrence of full or empty queues. Calls to operating system services are automatically traced. Defined event tracing requires the inclusion of a call to an event signalling trace routine. The selection of the significant events is part of the design of a realtime application for testing and debugging.

Event records are stored in sequence of occurrence and contain: a time stamp; identification of the routine making the system call or signalling the significant event; and a small amount of additional information related to the particular event. Event records are 8 bytes long in our implementation. Event reports are buffered in primary storage and saved to a disk file for post-experiment reporting and archival. The tracing facilities result in little interference with the timing of realtime programs and provides great insight into the interleaved execution of the concurrent program modules and hence effective feedback to the student.

Figure 1 shows the overall structure of the realtime monitor. The set of cooperating, concurrent programs under test are shown at the top of the figure along with special action routines used in testing. The realtime operating system's services constitute critical events in most systems. These are automatically traced without change to the program being tested and yield easy generation of well defined standard reports.

Intercept routines are provided which are the actual routines called in the application programs for operating system services. These intercept routines write the appropriate trace records and then call the actual system service routines. Since all system services are intercepted and traced before entering the actual system service routine, it is straightforward to provide replacement routines which provide dummy input for testing purposes. This is especially important because it obviates the need for multiple setups of expensive input/output equipment in many interesting assignments.

Logged event time resolution is usually not critical because the records are stored in their naturally occurring sequence. Hence successive records with the same event time do not cause ambiguity in reports. Time resolution need merely be sufficient for calculating reasonable time differences between events such as actual program execution time versus scheduled execution time for a periodic data acquisition task. We find a resolution of a fraction of a millisecond is adequate and easily obtained.

The event signalling routine is used to log the occurrence of some event such as queue empty, queue full, detected error, or any other condition important to understanding the sequence of events in the trace or important to the current test of the software.

Realtime programs cannot be tested simply by running them with data sources because their execution depends upon asynchronously occurring events. Hence testing and verification of some critical aspect of the design often requires forcing of time sequences of events. To this end, the realtime monitor software permits the addition of "action" routines which are triggered by event reporting routines. Action routines are used to force conditions which seldom arise to occur for testing and verification purposes: desired sequences of logical variable changes, initiation of processes, and occurrences of interrupts for example. They permit flexible forcing of concurrent tasks to synchronize in such a way that conditions for a particular test are set up and results documented in the ensuing trace report. There are no standard action routines. Rather each must be created as needed for each specific test. For example, when a critical time is signalled, an action routine might set certain variables and initiate an interrupt. Action routines contain all test specific code so that the application programs themselves have added code limited to calls to the event signal routine and the data sampling routine.

Upon completion of a run, a trace file exists which can be reported in a variety of ways. Standard reports list some or all logged events, listing the event, the routine which caused the event, and the time of occurrence in time sequence. Since reporting is offline from a standard text file, the student can write separate reporting programs in special situations.

The detailed reports available from the monitor provide great insight into the number and sequence of system service calls, timing of the program and relative timing of different task actions, dynamic effects such as queue filling, and overall operation of the design. Obviously the monitor interferes with the precise timing of the application. The amount of interference is small compared to the time required for most system service calls and did not consequently interfere with the objective of studying a realtime design.

4. Software architecture specification

The teaching of realtime control paradigms cannot be done by the direct study of code. Rather the structure or architecture must be emphasized. Modern software engineering methodology emphasizes the need for a high level design specification[1,11,12]. Realtime software design makes this even more important for it is at this level that problems with concurrency, throughput, error recovery, and response time must be recognized and solved. We introduce this specification of the design through a "system architecture diagram" [13] which displays the various program modules, interrupt routines, shared data areas and files, critical events, and their interaction as follows:

1. Program modules (rectangle) which carry out the various application functions. In data acquisition and control applications, a single task is usually associated with each program module whereas in the transaction processing application, multiple tasks are often associated with each program module. Execution of program modules occurs for one of three conditions: time scheduled, hardware interrupt triggered, or in response to a signaled event.

2. Shared subprogram modules (rectangle) which are subroutine modules shared among multiple concurrent program modules. They are included because they are common sources of concurrency problems. The prime example of such modules is an interface to data tables shared among tasks. Shared subproblem modules are executed only when they are called from a task.

3. Data stores (rectangle with one side open) which represent data areas or files stored in either primary or secondary storage which are shared among tasks. Again the inclusion in the architecture diagram is to make potential concurrency problems visible.

4. Interrupt and event routines (rectangle) which represent either hardware interrupt response routines or event triggered routines. Routines differ from program modules in that they are not scheduled by an operating system but instead run at some hardware priority level as does an actual interrupt response routine.

5. Events (circles) which represent conditions determined by programs, subprograms, or routines. They are primarily used to show triggering of program modules and routines.

The architecture diagram is used primarily to structure the realtime program design and provides an excellent vehicle for walk-through review of a design prior to programming[11,13]. This high level specification is introduced early in the course and used both for application discussed in the previous section as well as the review and documentation of the student assignments. Figure 2 shows an example of an architecture diagram for a data acquisition system which is periodically triggered from a hardware interval timer, an example developed in section 5. An alarm task is triggered to run under operating system control when certain out-of-range data conditions are detected. An operator communication task can update parameters used in data acquisition at arbitrary times chosen by a human operator. An application task uses data acquired from the shared data table. This application is rich in concurrency problems due to the shared data table and the use of both hardware interrupt initiated routines and operating system scheduled tasks. At this level of design, shared access problems, error recovery strategies, and performance evaluation can be understood, evaluated, understood, and critiqued by a class. This review of multiple designs is excellent for teaching realtime design.

The use of an event in the architecture diagram does not imply the method of implementation (eg actual event signalling or message passing). Rather it is used to clarify the conditions under which a task executes so that concurrency problems can be recognized. The design of the individual realtime program modules, shared subprogram modules, and routines then is done using whatever intertask communication and synchronization methods being studied or deemed appropriate. For example, a task designed to respond to the occurrence of a specific event might block itself using a semaphore or wait for a message at a mailbox. A task might initiate another task through a call to a realtime operating system service.

5. Application to selected concurrent situations

Process activation timing

Interrupts may be serviced directly by the interrupt response routine or by a task attached to the interrupt. The latter is necessary if either the processing takes substantial time or if it uses system services. Under iRMX86[5], such a task must run during an initialization period and attach itself to the interrupt and then suspend itself. The interrupt handler responds to the interrupt itself, when it occurs, and signals the interrupt response task. A test of such a process involves a task triggering the interrupt. Figure 3 shows the resulting trace. The interrupt response task (assigned an identification of 10) uses system calls to attach itself to the interrupt (Set Interrupt) and suspend itself (Wait Interrupt). The test task (ID 30) causes the interrupt at an opportune time. The interrupt handler (ID 5) simply signals the waiting task and exits the interrupt response routine (Signal Interrupt). The operating system starts the interrupt response task at the first available time when it is the highest priority waiting task. The first two traced events for this routine, Start and End interrupt servicing, are not system service calls but the Event Signal call of the tracing system. The interrupt service task exits servicing by again waiting for the next occurrence of the interrupt (Wait Interrupt). Elapsed time is the difference between the time stamps at the causing of the interrupt event and the finish of task interrupt processing event signal and is meaningful if greater than about 10 times the time stamp granularity. The effect of possible intervening higher priority tasks would be clearly evident in the event trace.

I/O request-I/O driver mutual exclusion testing

Consider testing a device driver for correct mutual exclusion between the interrupt driven driver and its input/output request (IOR) subroutine. For a printer driver, for example, each IOR consists of a string of characters passed to the IOR subroutine. This routine tests the printer driver status and immediately transfers the request to the driver buffer if it is idle and initiates the I/O transfer (by signalling the printer interrupt for example). If the driver is already busy, the request is added to a queue. It is the responsibility of the driver to remove the next successive request from the queue each time it finishes a request. This test should determine that the last printer interrupt associated with a request cannot occur while the IOR subroutine is in its critical section adding a request to the queue.

Figure 4 shows a test process which makes an N character output request using the IOR subroutine with a global test variable, COUNT, set at 0. For the test, the driver is assigned to an unused interrupt, I, and is initially not busy. The I/O request is passed to the IOR subroutine which initiates the I/O as usual (including signalling an initial interrupt which outputs the first character) and returns to the test process. The test process signals N-1 successive interrupts so that the driver repeatedly executes to output the next N-2 characters. The driver is left waiting for the last interrupt to output the last character. The test process then increments COUNT and performs another I/O request to the printer. The IOR subroutine this time signals an event upon entering its critical section which triggers Action 1 which simply causes interrupt I, causing the desired interrupt from the printer while the IOR subroutine is in its critical section. The resulting time sequence trace will indicate by the sequence of traces indicating entering and leaving the critical section, action initiation, and actual driver response to the interrupt whether or not mutual exclusion was correct. Figure 4 shows the two possible traces.

Periodic data acquisition and alarm testing

Testing and verification of event driven applications such as periodic data acquisition and alarming is shown in Figure 2. The point table contains one data structure per analog point to be periodically read and includes alarm limits. If the data acquisition task finds the analog point exceeding those limits, it must use interprocess communication to activate an alarm task. Among other things, the alarm task enters an acknowledgement flag into the point table to indicate that the alarm has been recognized and handled. The data acquisition task uses an alarm list to communicate with the alarm task. A point in alarm is added to this list if it is not already on the list and if it not marked as acknowledged in the point table. The data acquisition task resets the acknowledge flag when it finds the point within its alarm limits. The alarm task is lower priority than the data acquisition task. It continues processing as long as any alarms remain on its list and then suspends itself waiting for an alarm to be added.

The dashed arrows in Figure 2 indicate the Event Signal calls inserted to monitor these concurrent tasks. Data acquisition is a timer-interrupt initiated and signals its start of processing. The difference between successive events can be used to measure the average and peak "jitter" in the periodic task. The data acquisition task signals an event each time it detects a point in alarm with data flags indicating whether or not the point is marked acknowledged in the point table and whether or not it is already on the alarm list. The alarm task signals an event each time it begins execution with data corresponding to the alarm list length and another event when it suspends itself waiting for more alarms. These allow the reporting program to check for proper operation of the concurrent tasks and to determine average and peak response time to alarms.

The dummy analog input routine can be used to carry out a typical test involving a suddenly applied upset disturbance to the source of the analog signals: run for a period of time with a normal fraction of analog signals entering and leaving the alarm state; at a given time, enter an upset condition during which the rate of alarms is greatly increased; after a time corresponding to the length of the disturbance, return to the normal alarm level. The dummy analog input routine signals these times with an Event Signal. The special report routine for this test can separately report the response during the disturbance and after the disturbance including the "time to clear" the disturbance.

6. Conclusions

We have found that the teaching of realtime programming can be greatly facilitated by the use of realistic examples and assignments, a simple method for specifying the overall design for class-wide evaluation, and the provision for a support environment which permits debugging and verification of the student's design. The realtime system architecture diagram serves the review purpose well. The use of an event monitor and trace program and a realtime operating system which provides a rich variety of concurrent realtime programming constructs has provided a very useful and efficient environment. In particular, the action-routine feature of the monitor permits very detailed experimental study of an implementation of a design. The use of a personal computer environment greatly facilitates student access to the necessary hardware and software.

References

1. Stankovic, John A. and K. Ramamritham, Hard Real-Time Systems, IEEE Computer Society, No. EH0276-6, 1988.
2. Malcolm G. Lane and James D. Mooney [1988], A Practical Approach to Operating Systems, Boyd & Fraser Publishing Co, Boston,610-628.
3. Nicklaus Wirth [1983], Toward A Discipline of Real-Time Programming, in Robert L. Glass [1983], Real-Time Software, Prentice-Hall, Englewood Cliffs, NJ,128-142.
4. J.L. Peterson and A. Silberschatz [1985], Operating System Concepts, Addison-Wesley Co, Reading MA.
5. Intel Corp. [1986], The Intel iRMX86 Operating System", Document 2103301-01.
6. Schoeffler, J.D.,"A Real-Time Programming Event Monitor", IEEE Trans. Ed.,Vol 31, No 4,Nov. 1988,245-250.
7. Caxton C. Foster [1981], Real Time Programming - Neglected Topics, Addison-Wesley Publishing Co, Reding, Mass., 60-103.
8. Jules Finkel, Computer-Aided Experimentation, John Wiley, NYC, 9-86.
9. J.D.Schoeffler [1974], Minicomputer Realtime Executives, IEEE Computer Society tutorial, Compcon 74, 7-36 and 166-169.
10. J.D. Wright and J.W. White [1983], Real-Time Operating Systemss and Multitask Programming, in Duncan A. Mellichamp (editor) [1983], Real-Time Computing with Applications to Data Acquisition and Control, Van Nostrand Reinhold Co, NYC, 345-378.
11. Mellor, S.J. & P. Ward, "Structured Development for Real-Time Systems, Yourdon Prss, New York, 1986
11. Derek J. Hatley and Imtiaz A. Pirbhai, Strategies for Real-Time System Specification, Dorest House, NYC,1988.
13. W.E. Beregi, Architecture protyping in the software engineering environment, IBM Systems Journal, V23,#1, 1984, 4,18.

Figure 1
Structure of the Event Monitor

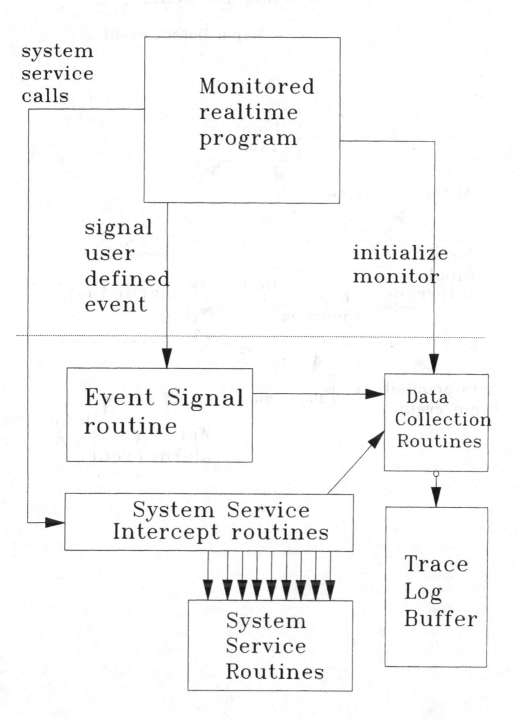

Figure 2
Monitoring of periodic data acquisition timing and events

Alarm Detect event

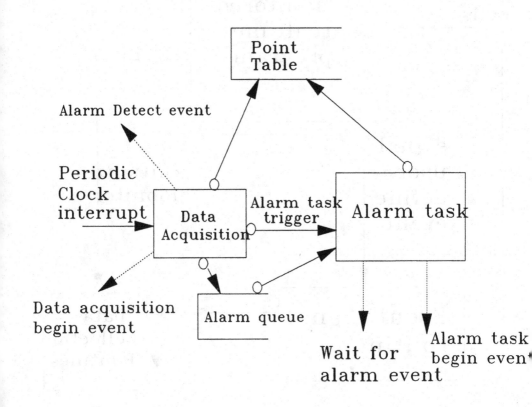

Figure 3
Test of timing of a task
Scheduled by an interrupt routine

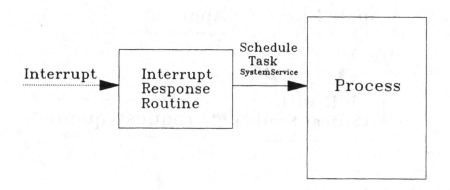

Test successful sequence:

        .....
        Enter printer IOR subroutine critical section
        Action 1 -- trigger printer ready interrupt I
        Leave printer IOR subroutine critical section
        ....
        Enter printer driver at interrupt response entry
        ....

Test fail sequence:

        .....
        Enter printer IOR subroutine critical section
        Action 1 -- trigger printer ready interrupt
        Enter printer driver at interrupt response entry
        ....
        Leave printer IOR subroutine critical section
        ....

Figure 4
Two possible traces resulting from
Mutual exclusion test

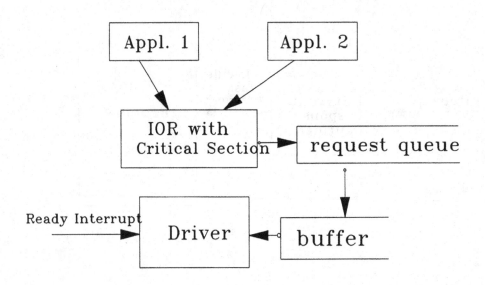

Test successful sequence:
>   .....
>   Enter printer IOR subroutine critical section
>   Action 1 −− trigger printer ready interrupt I
>   Leave printer IOR subroutine critical section
>   ....
>   Enter printer driver at interrupt response entry
>   ....

Test fail sequence:
>   .....
>   Enter printer IOR subroutine critical section
>   Action 1 −− trigger printer ready interrupt
>   ....
>   Enter printer driver at interrupt response entry
>   Leave printer IOR subroutine critical section
>   ....

Exploratory Studies of the
Software Testing Methods Used by Novice Programmers

Stuart H. Zweben[1] and Catherine Stringfellow
Ohio State University

Ruth Barton
Michigan State University

Abstract. *Computer science courses, including those at the introductory level, require students to be capable of demonstrating that the programs they write satisfy the problem specifications. This demonstration of correctness is nearly always done via testing. Yet these courses tend to offer little or no guidance to the students in selecting appropriate test data. This paper analyzes the characteristics of test data used by novice programmers in the absence of such guidance.*

Test data generated by over 100 students in introductory courses at two large public institutions were analyzed for feature, statement, and validity coverage as described in the IEEE standard for unit testing. The student test data were often found inadequate to cover all but the most high-level features described in the problem specifications. Statement coverage was frequently not achieved, and most of the students did not include invalid inputs in their test suites, even if they wrote their programs to check for such invalid inputs. Students tended to do a better job in achieving these levels of coverage when testing someone else's program than they did when testing their own program.

About 2/3 of the defective programs found in the study were tested well enough by the student to reveal a defect, but in many cases the defects were not recognized even when revealed. Simple systematic testing strategies, based only on information contained in the specifications, were found capable of revealing defects in most of the defective programs, including most of those for which the student's own data were inadequate to reveal a defect.

1. Introduction

Computer science curricula require several courses that contain a significant amount of

[1]Dr. Zweben's research is supported in part by grant CCR-8802312 from the National Science Foundation.

programming activity. Programming is traditionally an important (perhaps the most important) activity in many introductory computer science courses, and other courses are expected to build on the programming skills acquired by the earlier courses. Students in these courses are expected to debug their programs and end up with a correct solution to a given problem. This implies that the students must somehow demonstrate (to themselves and to the instructor) that they in fact have obtained a correct solution.

Though more formal methods of verifying software are taught at some institutions in the early computer science courses, the usual method of demonstrating that this student-generated software meets the problem specification is through testing. This is, of course, also the technique typically used in industry, although approaches such as the Cleanroom [9] are designed to obviate the need for programmers to test their own software. Despite this need to perform testing, undergraduate computer science curricula tend to pay little or no attention to testing as a topic for discussion in their programming courses. For the most part, textbooks for programming courses, including many of those used for introductory courses, do not even contain a section or chapter about software testing unless the book is designed for a course in software engineering. Informal discussions with instructors at the authors institutions and at other institutions confirms the inadequate attention to the subject in most programming courses, including the introductory courses.

While the subject may not be taught, students nevertheless are doing testing in these courses. What kind of testing are they doing? Are they using any kind of systematic approach? Are they developing test cases that attain criteria discussed in the literature on software testing? Does their software contain defects that are likely to be caught if only a relatively simple, systematic approach to testing had been followed? What kind of testing tools would be useful to students in the undergraduate curriculum?

The scope of the questions in the previous paragraph is much too broad to be addressed by any single study. The long-term objective of this research is to shed some light on these questions. Perhaps the most relevant research in this area that has been performed to date involves studies of the kinds of bugs present in software written by students. Examples include [3, 7, 10]. However, the variety of classification schemes used in the different studies makes it difficult to compare results and relate them to testing methods. There is also a body of research that has investigated the effectiveness of specific testing methods. Examples include [1, 4, 8]. However, none of these studies involved novice programmers.

This paper reports the results of a study of the manner in which students test software. Of particular interest in this study is the behavior of students in the introductory courses of a computer science curriculum, since this is the first place where testing must be practiced, and therefore the first place where testing methods would be of potential value.

2. Specific Objectives of the Study

The basic purpose of this study is to characterize and evaluate the quality of test data being used by the students. Unfortunately, there is no well-accepted method of determining whether or not a set of test data is qualitatively good.

Good test data should certainly be capable of revealing defects in the software if such defects are present. However, if a piece of software has a defect, a single, well-chosen, test point is all that's needed to reveal that defect. Of course, we generally don't consider a test data set consisting of one test point as a qualitatively good data set. This is because another aspect of good test data is that it should be thorough. That is, the test data must exercise the software sufficiently well that it is reasonable to conclude that the software is acceptable if it passes the test. Indicators of thoroughness abound in the testing literature. Some indicators are based on thoroughness of coverage of the software specifications, while others are based on thoroughness of coverage of the code. Therefore, it is of interest to determine the extent to which student software contains defects and, when it does, to try to assess the type(s) of testing strategies that would be capable of revealing these defects.

The ANSI/IEEE Standard for Software Unit Testing [5] gives three minimal requirements for adequate test data sets. Every feature of the unit must be covered by a test case (a feature is a characteristic such as functionality or performance that is specified or implied by requirements documentation), every reachable statement in the code must be executed by some test case, and both valid and invalid input data must be included in the test suite. The first and third of these requirements are based on the problem statements, or specifications, while the second is a function of the code. We will refer to these types of coverage as feature coverage, statement coverage, and validity coverage, respectively. They will be the primary types of coverage examined in our analysis.

In addition to developing the test data, the tester must be capable of evaluating the results of each test for conformance with specifications. We often take this task for granted, though in one study, professional programmers failed to find over 20% of the faults that were revealed by their test data [1]. Good testing procedures include a specification of the results expected from each test case, prior to execution of the test. It is of interest to see whether or not the evaluation of test results presents any problem for the students.

Testing one's own product is a process of self-examination. Individuals will often do a more critical examination of someone else's product than they will of their own product. In fact, some software development methods do not permit developers to test their own software [9]. We will therefore also investigate whether there are differences in the quality of student testing when one's own program is being tested versus when someone else's program is being tested.

The specific objectives of our study can therefore be summarized as follows.

1. Measure the extent to which the criteria of feature coverage, statement coverage, and validity coverage are achieved by test data used by students in introductory computer science courses. Do this for both test data used to test a student's own program and data used to test someone else's program.

2. Measure the extent to which students in introductory computer science courses do not properly evaluate the results of their tests for conformance with specifications. Do this for both the testing of a student's own program and the testing of someone else's program.

3. Assess the ability of simple coverage criteria to reveal observed defects in software developed in introductory computer science courses.

4. Suggest topics in the area of software testing that appear to be beneficial to incorporate into the curricula of introductory computer science courses.

3. Subjects and Environment

A total of 124 subjects participated in this study. All were students in a first course in computer science for computer science majors. Data were collected at two different universities, Ohio State University and Michigan State University, so that some potential effects due to specific course and environment might be revealed. Both universities are on the quarter system, and both courses used Pascal as the programming language in their introductory sequence. Neither course discussed the subject of software testing during the period of this study.

Though both universities conducted their introductory courses using a microcomputer environment, the specifics of the environments were different at the two institutions. Ohio State University used a Macintosh programming environment with Macintosh Pascal as the specific language. Michigan State University used an IBMPC-compatible environment with Waterloo Pascal as the specific language. Ohio State used an "open lab" system whereby students did not have scheduled lab time to do their programming assignments, though they still had a scheduled due date. Instead the labs were open for use by the computer science students for over 90 hours per week. At Michigan State, there was a scheduled lab for each section of the introductory course, and students were expected to work on their programming assignments during this scheduled time. Open lab time was also available to supplement this scheduled time. Most sections of the introductory course at Ohio State were taught by teaching associates, though the course was supervised by a faculty coordinator who worked closely with these T/As. The course was run in a "discussion" mode, rather than a "lecture/recitation" mode, with at most 35 students per section. At Michigan State, the course was run in "lecture/recitation" mode, with a large lecture taught by faculty, and small recitation sections (at most 20 students) taught by T/As.

Students in both introductory courses were required to turn in diskettes for grading purposes, and instructors (teaching associates, primarily) tested the student programs on test data that the instructors generated for this purpose. Students knew that their programs would be tested in this manner.

4. Materials

The problems used for this study were chosen from comparable parts of the courses at Ohio State and Michigan State. In each case, the problem was from the assignment immediately following the discussion of alternative constructs in Pascal. This assignment was given about 1/3 to 1/2-way through the course. Both problems involved primarily numerical input and output, and both used interactive input/output. Students in each case had one week to complete the assignment.

The Michigan State exercise was a "diskette pricing" problem, where the students were given a set of prices charged by a hypothetical diskette manufacturer. The base price depended on the quantity ordered, and an additional discount was offered for quantities that were multiples of 10. Students were asked to have the program compute the total cost and of an order and the price per diskette given the number of diskettes ordered. The Ohio State exercise was a "telephone charge" problem, where the students were given telephone rates that depended on the length of the call and the time of day that the call was initiated. The students were to have the program compute 1) the cost of a call given the length and time of initiation, and 2) the number of minutes that the caller could afford, given a budget and time of initiation.

The problem statements for both exercises are included in the appendix. Based on previous experiences with each of these problems, programs for the diskette pricing problem were expected to produce fewer defects than those for the telephone charge problem.

5. Procedure

As part of the programming assignment, students were asked to turn in the test data they used to test their programs. These test data were turned in along with the diskettes that contained the final version of their program.

A pilot study was conducted in the fall of 1987, to determine if the procedure and information being collected were reasonable for the purposes of the study. The initial set of data analyzed in this paper was collected during the winter quarter of 1988 at Ohio State, and during spring quarter 1988 at Michigan State. Only one section of the introductory course was available for study at Ohio State. Three recitation sections associated with the same lecture were used at Michigan State during this part of the study.

The study was repeated at Michigan State in the fall of 1988, and an additional experiment was conducted with the Michigan State students as a followup to the diskette pricing problem. In the scheduled lab that followed the due date for turning in the solution to the diskette pricing problem, students were given a solution to the same problem that came from a previous quarter's class. The students were asked to generate test data that they thought would adequately test this program. Students did not have access to the test data they used for their own version of the program while they were doing this part of the experiment. (These data were collected by the instructor and not returned until the conclusion of the experiment. Furthermore, the fact that the lab was scheduled made it possible for the instructor to have direct control over the materials available to the students.) A copy of the problem statement for this experiment is included in the appendix. Five recitation sections associated with the same lecture were used in the fall 1988 experiment.

Two versions of these "former solutions" were used in this part of the experiment. One of the versions correctly computed the diskette costs for all valid inputs, but crashed when invalid integer inputs were submitted. The other version did not crash for invalid integer inputs, but incorrectly computed the total costs for certain diskette quantities (namely 10, 20, 30, and 40). Students were assigned one or the other of these programs depending on the way in which they designed and tested their original program. In particular, the two cells were balanced in terms of a) number of students whose test data for their own program included invalid data, b) number of students whose test data for their own program included each base price range, and c) number of students whose own programs checked for validity of the input.

6. Analyzing Coverage

As was mentioned in an earlier section, the primary components of the analysis involve feature coverage, statement coverage, and validity coverage. We next discuss the specific features identified in each problem for analysis.

For the diskette pricing problem, two high-level features are described in the specifications, that of computing the cost of the diskettes, and that of computing the associated price per diskette. The price function can be further decomposed from the specifications into a base price function and a discount function. These will be the "features" designated for analysis in this problem.

There is clearly more than one possible interesting definition of what it means to exercise, or cover, these features. Each high-level feature (cost and price) is exercised for every input. In order to consider the possibility of different inputs exercising different features, we need to consider the features of base price function and discount function. Though the base price function is computed for every possible input, the discount function is not. A minimal definition of coverage might therefore be that there is at least one test case for which the correct computation only involved applying the base price function, and one test case for which the correct computation involved applying the discount function. Another definition of coverage would require that each of the four levels of the base price function be covered by the test suite (independent of whether or not the discount function applied), and also that each of the two levels of the discount function (i.e. discounted and non-discounted) be covered by the test suite (independent of the base price level). This type of coverage might be called "main effect" coverage, since each level of each (discrete-level) feature is included in the test suite. A third level of coverage would require that each level of each feature be covered in combination with each level of the other feature. That is, there would need to be a discounted and a non-discounted input for each base price level (except the lowest level, since there can be no discount if the number of diskettes ordered was 1-9). This type of coverage might be called "factorial" or "interaction" coverage, since it resembles the full-factorial design of a multiple-treatment experiment.

For the telephone charge problem, there are also two high-level features, that of computing the cost of a call given the length and rate, and that of computing the length of a call given the budget and rate. In each case, there are three levels of the rate function (day, evening, and night). A military time function is also hinted at in the problem statement, but the statement does not indicate how the input might divide this function into different levels. We will therefore not consider this function in our analysis, though a more in-depth investigation of the design of the programs might well reveal the details needed to incorporate this function as a feature.

Minimal coverage for the telephone charge problem will therefore consist of at least one test case in which the cost is computed and at least one test case in which the length is computed. Main effect coverage will consist of satisfying minimal coverage and also having at least one test case for each of the three levels of the rate function. Interaction coverage will consist of having each of the three rate function levels exercised for each of the two high-level features.

Minimal, main effect, and interaction coverage are each examined in the analysis. In addition, the test data were analyzed to see whether or not at least one example of invalid data was included in the student's suite. Neither of the problem statements mentioned anything about the need to worry about invalid inputs, and did not specify what was to happen in case such an input was received. The lectures in the course also did not address this issue.

The description of the specification of the input for the telephone charge problem also reveals certain "special values" that may be important for the testing of the program. These are 12 noon and 12 midnight. While the ANSI/IEEE standard does not explicitly mention the need to identify and test for special values, such a strategy is often advocated (see, e.g. [6]). No special values are identified in the diskette pricing problem.

7. Results

The results are shown in Table 1.

	OSU Wi 1988	MSU Sp 1988	MSU Fall 1988 own pgm	MSU Fall 1988 others' pgm
# subjects	28	35	54	61
# test points				
range	2-23	3-22	2-35	3-16
mean	9.0	7.6	7.7	9.8
feature coverage				
minimal	28	35	54	61
main effect	22	24	39	53
interaction	15	13	18	29
statement coverage	5	16	36	41
validity coverage	3	18	16	28
incorrect programs				
# incorrect	22	5	5	n/a
# with test sets capable of revealing defect	14	4	3	n/a

Table 1. Summary of Student Test Data Quality

Two different versions of "someone else's" program were included in the materials. An analysis is therefore possible that compares the testing of each of these two versions. A breakdown of the final column of Table 1 by version and a discussion of those results will be provided following a discussion of the overall results.

The number of test points selected was in the same general range each quarter, independent of the problem/location being studied. The fall 1988 data shows slightly less of a maximum range value when testing someone else's program. This may have been due to the form on which the data were collected, which had a maximum of 16 pre-printed spaces plus room to add more test points. Despite the smaller maximum, the mean number of test points was larger when testing someone else's data (a t-test of the difference in means was significant at the .05 level [2]). There was no significant difference between the spring and fall quarters with respect to the mean number of test points used when testing one's own version of the diskette pricing program. There was also no significant difference between the mean values for the MSU data and that for the OSU data.

All subjects in each quarter at each school had test data that achieved the minimal level of feature coverage. However, fewer than 75% of the Michigan State students had test data that covered all four levels of the base price (thereby achieving main effect coverage) when testing their own program. Only slightly more than 75% of the Ohio State students achieved main effect coverage (by covering all three levels of the rate function). These percentages were found not to be significantly different. Though 75% is a reasonable percentage of the students, over 85% of the students achieved main effect coverage when testing someone else's program. This percentage proved significantly different from that for the fall 1988 students when testing their own program. Substantially fewer students achieved interaction coverage for either their own program or someone else's. Only about 35% of the Michigan State students tested their own program this thoroughly, with no real difference from one quarter to the other. Nearly 50% of the Michigan State students tested someone else's program this thoroughly, though this percentage proved not to be significantly different from that associated with the testing of their own program. Just over 50% of the Ohio State students achieved interaction coverage, not a significantly different percentage from that for the MSU students.

The Michigan State data show a considerable difference between quarters in the percentage of students who achieved statement coverage. In spring, fewer than 50% of the students satisfied this criterion, while in fall 67% of the students achieved this level of coverage. Fewer than 20% of the OSU students achieved statement coverage, a significant difference from either MSU fraction.

There was quite a difference among the three quarters in the percentage of students who included at least one invalid input in their test set. At Michigan State, just over 50% of the students in spring did so, while fewer than 30% did so in fall. Yet nearly half of the fall quarter students tested someone else's program with at least one invalid input. Closer examination of the discrepancy between spring and fall revealed that one of the fall quarter teaching associates specifically told her class of eight students not to worry about testing for invalid inputs. Removing these eight students from the analysis still results in a higher percentage of tests during the spring (51% vs. 35%), though the difference is not statistically significant. At Ohio State, fewer than 15% of the students included invalid inputs among their test data. This is significantly different from either quarter for the MSU data.

It is interesting to note that students often failed to include invalid inputs in the test suite even though their programs included special code to process inputs that were not valid. Twelve of the MSU students in spring quarter and eight others in fall quarter fell into this category. Seven of the OSU students fell into this category.

As expected, there were very few incorrect programs in either quarter for the diskette pricing problem (though over 10% of the total number of programs were incorrect). Also as expected, there were a considerable number of incorrect programs for the telephone charge problem. At both schools, however, the test data used by students having defective programs were capable of revealing a defect in some two out of every three cases. There are several possible reasons for this phenomenon. The students might not really have used the test data they claimed to have used, and instead used test data that were incapable of revealing the defect. It is also possible that the students did not notice that the test data gave incorrect results, and thought that the output of the program was correct for these revealing test data. Finally, it is possible that the students were aware that the program was giving incorrect output on these test data, and for one reason or another did not fix the problem.

At Ohio State, students were required to turn in screen dumps for each test run at the time they turned in their program. This provided a means for auditing the set of data they claimed to have used during testing. Seven of the 28 students had discrepancies as a result of this audit. For these students, the screen dump information was used as the official set of data to construct Table 1. Only one of these students actually used non-revealing test data but claimed to have used data that would have revealed a defect.

Neither assignment required that the students pre-compute the output expected from each of their test points. However, an examination of the test data sheets turned in by the Ohio State students indicated that some of the 14 students whose test data were capable of revealing defects had actually hand-calculated, on these sheets, the expected answers for their test data. One of these students performed the hand calculations incorrectly. A second student stated that he noticed that his hand-computed results and the program's results were different, but that he didn't know how to fix the program. A third student appeared to have actually changed his hand-computed results after noticing a discrepancy!

A more careful analysis of the ten incorrect programs from Michigan State was done in order to determine the set of inputs on which the program failed, and therefore the kind of coverage that could have revealed the defects. Three of these ten programs failed to perform the discount function, and therefore failed whenever the input was a multiple of 10. Five others failed when the input was a multiple of 10 but only for a subset of the base price ranges (e.g.. it failed only on inputs 10, 20, 30, and 40). One failed whenever the input was in the last base price range (i.e. ≥ 100) whether or not it was a multiple of 10. Finally, one failed when the input was a non-multiple of 10 and was not in the first base price range. Minimal coverage is clearly enough to reveal a defect for the first three incorrect programs. Main effect coverage would have caught these three plus the one that failed for inputs that were ≥ 100. Interaction coverage is capable of revealing a defect in the other six incorrect programs. These six programs include the three for which the test data used by the student were inadequate to reveal a defect. Through an analysis of the code, statement coverage was found to be capable of revealing a defect in eight of the ten defective programs, including all three for which the student's data were incapable of revealing a defect.

A similar analysis performed for the 22 Ohio State programs that contained defects revealed that five of these programs required only minimal coverage to reveal a defect, one other reveals a defect whenever main effect coverage is achieved, and interaction coverage would have guaranteed that a defect was revealed in yet one other program. This still leaves 15 defective programs unaccounted for. Eight of these programs had defects that would be revealed by test data that included noon and midnight, since the military time conversion in these programs was done incorrectly. (The military time conversion was, in fact, also incorrect in some of the defective programs where the other feature coverage methods revealed a defect.) The other seven had defects that were only revealed by data for the length calculation feature. One of these programs failed to produce an appropriate message in case a call could not be afforded. The other six involved roundoff or truncation problems. Typically, revealing test data for these six programs required either that the entire budget be spent by the call, or that the entire budget not be spent by the call. Statement coverage was capable of revealing a defect in seven of the 22 defective OSU programs. However, neither statement coverage nor any of the feature coverage criteria could guarantee to reveal a defect in any of the eight programs for which the student's own data were inadequate to reveal a defect. Yet if coverage of the special values (i.e. noon and midnight) was included in the test data, a defect would have been revealed in six of these eight programs, and in 12 of the 22 total defective programs.

8. Further Analysis of the Testing of Others' Programs

When students in the fall 1988 experiment were given someone else's program to test, they were given one of two versions, "Even" or "Odd." The "Even" version computed an incorrect total cost when the input was 10, 20, 30, or 40. However, it checked for invalid integer input values, and wrote an appropriate error message when such an input was received. The "Odd" version gave correct answers for all valid inputs, but crashed if an invalid integer input was given to the program.

Table 2 breaks down the test data from the last column of Table 1 by version.

	Even	Odd
# subjects	30	31
# test points		
range	3-16	4-16
mean	9.4	10.2
feature coverage		
minimal	30	31
main effect	25	28
interaction	9	20
statement coverage	13	28
validity coverage	14	14
# revealing defect	26	n/a
# capable of revealing defect	28	n/a

Table 2. Breakdown for Fall 1988 Data by Program Version

The amount of testing, in terms of number of test points, is quite similar between the two subgroups. So is coverage of main effects. Recall that the two subgroups were balanced in terms of having achieved main effect coverage when testing their own program. Also recall that a greater percentage of students achieved main effect coverage when testing someone else's program than did so when testing their own program. This suggests that the specific code being tested did not influence the testing process.

Validity coverage is also similar in the two subgroups, despite the fact that one version explicitly tests for validity and the other does not. Recall that the two subgroups were balanced in terms of having checked for validity when testing their own programs and also in terms of having written programs whose code included checks for validity. This would seem to be further indicatation that the program structure (i.e. code) is not influencing the testing process, although the students had easy access to the code through the Waterloo Pascal environment. Though a substantially larger fraction of students did validity checking when testing someone else's program than did so when testing their own program, five of the 16 students who did validity checking when testing their own programs (Table 1) did not do so when testing someone else's program.

Interaction and statement coverage are quite dissimilar between the two versions. A substantially larger fraction of students who were given the correct ("Odd") version achieved these levels of coverage.

Most of the students who failed to statement cover the "Even" version only missed covering that part of the code that handled invalid data. There was no such code on the "Odd" version. No attempt was made to balance the subgroups by the achievement of statement coverage when testing their own program. It turned out, in fact, that the "Odd" subgroup contained *more* students who failed to achieve statement coverage when testing their own program. Therefore, there was no greater a priori tendency on the part of the "Odd" subgroup to achieve statement coverage. From the balancing that was done in this experiment, there was also no a priori difference between subgroups in the tendency to test invalid data. Assuming the students did not look at the code in order to construct the test cases (as hypothesized above), the difference in statement coverage is therefore explainable by the difference in actual functionality of the two versions.

The discrepancy in interaction coverage cannot be explained away as easily. The 18 subjects who achieved interaction coverage for their own program were evenly divided (9 each) between the two subgroups (though the two subgroups were not intentionally balanced this way), so there was not any a priori reason to suspect such a discrepancy in the interaction coverage of another's program. One possible explanation is that the students who tested the "Even" version were in fact able to reveal a defect without too much difficulty (26 of the 30 students did reveal a defect, and did so by the time they had used four test points, while two others had test data that were capable of revealing a defect but misinterpreted the correctness of the program's output). Once it was determined that the program was not correct, the "challenge" of the testing process may have been lost and students may not have thought very much about where to look for additional defects. Instead, a few additional test points were selected and then testing was terminated. Thus, the total number of test points used was similar, though the thoroughness was not.

Two of the 30 students who were given the incorrect ("Even") program to test did not provide test data that were capable of revealing the defect. Two others did provide data that could reveal the defect, but incorrectly interpreted the output of the program as being correct. There were also four other students who noticed that a defect existed for at least one test point, but failed to notice that a defect was being revealed when examining other test points in their test set. In none of these eight cases did the material turned in by the student show any evidence of hand computations of the expected results of the tests. Several other students did turn in material that showed such computations. While it is possible that such computations were done on scratch paper that was not turned in by the students, this analysis suggests that many students make a very cursory examination of the program's outputs for conformity with program specifications, and that such a cursory examination is often inadequate.

9. Conclusions

Students in introductory computer science courses do not seem to use any systematic procedures when testing their programs. This is not surprising, considering that they have not been taught any systematic methods. It is unfair to say, however, that they are selecting their test data completely at random. The most high-level features of the specification, at least, seem to be covered by the student test data. Nevertheless, the testing that many students do (about 25% in this study) is not even rich enough to cover the basic set of alternative input conditions described by the problem statements. Coverage of combinations of these input conditions is (predictably) much worse, even if there aren't very many possible combinations. Nearly 50-70% of the students in this study failed to test this thoroughly.

Introductory-level students do not appear to use features of the code to guide the testing process. Even a minimal level of code coverage, that of statement coverage, is frequently not achieved.

Most students in the introductory course do not seem to test using invalid input data. This is true even though these students often write their program in a defensive manner to protect against invalid input. In this study, the problem statements said nothing about the expected behavior of the program when input values were outside the normal range. Perhaps students would be more apt to use abnormal values in their test suites if the problem statements mentioned the possibility of abnormal input values and the nature of the output expected under these conditions.

A significant fraction of the defective programs produced by students at the introductory level appear to be tested well enough by the students to reveal the fact that they are defective (about 2/3 of the defective programs in this study had this property). Yet these students often fail to remove defects in their program even when their test data reveal that their software contains defects. A variety of reasons exists for this, including failure to realize that a defect is being revealed, failure to understand how to fix the defect, and unwillingness to fix the defect (perhaps due to time or other priorities and constraints). Students tend to not explicitly write down the expected outputs of the tests they have chosen prior to executing these tests. This may contribute to their failure to recognize that a defect is being revealed. More experienced programmers also fail to recognize defects that have been revealed by test data. Basili, et al [1] observed that upper division computer science majors, computer science graduate students, and professional programmers detected only 70.3% of the faults observable from the program's behavior on test data.

Simple coverage strategies, involving features, feature combinations, and special input values mentioned in the specifications, appear to be capable of revealing defects in most of the defective student programs. A simple code-based coverage strategy such as statement coverage also appears to reveal defects frequently, but to no greater extent than do simple specification-based strategies.

When students at the introductory level test someone else's program, they tend to be somewhat more thorough than when testing their own program. However, once a defect is observed, the students tend not to be as thorough when doing the rest of their testing.

10. Implications for Software Engineering Education

In this study, many of the defective student programs revealed defects from the test data supplied by the students themselves, and some of these revealed defects appear to have been observed by the students. This suggests that an important component of the problem of improving the quality of software produced by introductory level students lies outside the area of software testing. Other instructional issues, such as debugging, understanding programming concepts, and grading policies of the course, contribute to the unwillingness or inability of students to fix observed defects.

Nevertheless, one-third of the defective programs in this study did not have any defects revealed by the student test data, and in several other instances defects revealed by the test data were incorrectly interpreted as successful tests. In these cases, improved software testing practices are of potential value to introductory computer science students. Based on our study, it appears useful to teach students to analyze the problem statements so as to identify features, feature combinations and special values. Students should also be taught to cover these features and special values in their test data. Finally, students should be instructed to write down the output expected from each test prior to executing the test. This would provide a more formal basis for checking the program's output, and should reduce the frequency of misinterpretation of incorrect output as correct.

The utility of tools to assist introductory-level students in analyzing test data may be of questionable value, based on this study. Simple code-based techniques such as statement coverage were useful in revealing errors in several defective student programs, but other, specification-based methods also revealed defects in these programs. In one of the problems used in this study, data generated by the student were just as revealing as was statement coverage. A statement coverage analyzer can give the student some automated form for checking the thoroughness of test data, and may give the student an appreciation for the type of information that computer assisted software engineering tools can provide. But it may be of little value in providing insight in finding bugs that might be present in the student's software. Such test data analyzers are often capable of doing much more sophisticated code-based coverage analysis, including data flow coverage as well as control flow coverage. We did not analyze the student programs for the ability of other code-based approaches to reveal errors, so it is possible that such analyses may prove additional utility for these tools. On the other hand, it is not clear to us the extent to which one can expect the student in an introductory-level course to understand the more sophisticated approaches to covering their code. More sophisticated information will only be helpful to the student to the extent that it is understood by the student. Further research with students at varying levels of the computer science curriculum is needed to answer questions concerning the appropriate use of CASE tools in the classroom.

It is clear that a study of 124 students at two universities cannot claim to adequately sample the multitude of computer science programs in existence. Nevertheless, the results of this study provide some useful suggestive evidence of the state of affairs with respect to software testing in introductory computer science. We welcome additional research that adds to this body of evidence.

Bibliography

[1] V. Basili and R. Selby, "Comparing the Effectiveness of Software Testing Strategies," IEEE Transactions on Software Engineering, SE-13, 12, December 1987, pp. 1278-1296.

[2] W.H. Beyer (ed.) Handbook of Probability and Statistics, Chemical Rubber Co., 1968.

[3] C. Fung, "A Methodology for the Collection and Evaluation of Software Error Data," Ph.D. Thesis, Dept. of Computer and Information Science, Ohio State University, 1985.

[4] M.Girgis and M. Woodward, "An Experimental Comparison of the Error Exposing Ability of Program Testing Criteria," Proceedings of the Workshop on Software Testing, Banff, Alberta, Canada, July 1986, pp. 64-73.

[5] "IEEE Standard for Software Unit Testing," ANSI/IEEE Std. 1008-1987, IEEE, 1987.

[6] L. Morell, "Unit Testing and Analysis," SEI Curriculum Module SEI-CM-9-1.0, Software Engineering Institute, Pittsburgh, PA, October 1987.

[7] P.G. Moulton and M.E. Muller, "DITRAN - A Compiler Emphasizing Diagnostics," Communications of the ACM, 10, 1, January 1967, pp. 50-52.

[8] G. Myers, "A Controlled Experiment in Program Testing and Code Walkthroughs/Inspections," Communications of the ACM, 21, 9, September 1978, pp. 760-768.

[9] R. Selby, V. Basili and F. T. Baker, "Cleanroom Software Development: An Empirical Evaluation," IEEE Transactions on Software Engineering, SE-13, 9, September 1987, pp. 1027-1037.

[10] E.A. Young, "Human Errors in Programming," Int'l. Journal of Man-Machine Studies, 6, 3, 1974, pp. 361-376.

Appendix

Diskette Pricing Problem Statement.

A mail order computer supply house offers a discounted price structure for purchasers of flexible diskettes as follows:

amount ordered	cost per diskette
1- 9	2.95
10-49	2.75
50-99	2.45
100 or more	2.25

Diskettes are boxed at the factory in packages of 10 so the supply house offers an additional discount of 5 cents per diskette for orders that total an amount that is a multiple of 10. (Since the packages don't need to be opened and repackaged by the stockroom personnel the savings is passed along to the customer!)

Write a Pascal program that will receive as input one order at a time, calculate the total price for the number of diskettes ordered, and output the number of diskettes ordered, the price per diskette charged, and the total cost to the customer. Your program should be able to handle any number of customers.

Telephone charges problem statement.

Write an interactive Pascal program that calculates information for the user about long-distance phone charges. The program first asks the user whether a calculation from money to time or from time to money will be made; your program will then follow one of two courses of action. In the first case, prompt for the time of day of the call and the allowed budget, and then determine the maximum number of minutes that can be affordet with that budget at that time of day. In the second case, prompt for the time of day and the length of the call, and then calculate the cost of that phone call.

There are three time periods during the day for which the rates are different; a call is charged according to which period the call **starts** in. The Day period is from 5am to 5pm, meaning any call that starts at 5am, or **between** 5am and 5pm. Calls which start at 5pm or between 5pm and 11pm are charged the Evening rates. Calls at 11pm or between 11pm and 5am are charged the Night rate. Each rate period has two different rates associated with it; a rate for the first minute of the call, which is the minimum charge for any call made in that period, and a minute rate for each whole or partial minute after the first. The current rates are:

Day rate, 1st minute:	$0.50	additional mins.:	$0.30
Evening rate, 1st min.:	$0.40	additional mins.:	$0.20
Night rate, 1st min.:	$0.30	additional mins.:	$0.15

So for example, a four minute call at 7pm would cost ($0.40) + ($0.20 * 3) = $1.00

Input: For ease of input, avoid requiring the user to input military time; instead, prompt for an additional piece of information: whether the call occurs in the AM or PM half of the day. (12noon is PM and 12midnight is AM!) The user should only be required to enter the hour of the call, that is, an integer from 1 to 12, since the minutes do not affect the rate (for example, a call made at 4:59pm is charged the Day rate).

(Hint: convert to military time [24 hour clock] in your program, as it will simplify the necessary comparisons.) Budget input is to be real-valued, call length integral (in whole minutes). Make sure the information being asked for is clearly described in the prompts.

Output: In either case, neatly output the results of the calculation. When calculating the length from the budget, if the answer is 0, print a short message stating that a call cannot be afforded at all -- avoid printing "you can afford a 0 minute call."

Improving User Manuals in Software Engineering Education

By Gail Miles
Department of Computer Science
Lenoir-Rhyne College
Hickory, NC

Introduction

Applying an engineering approach to large software project development significantly reduces software problems [Pressman,87]. The software engineering method includes using standardized management techniques in conjunction with technical tools to improve development, testing, verification, and maintenance of software [Miles,88]. The documentation component of the Software Engineering process has gained in importance. Appropriate external documentation of large projects is necessary for code maintainability as well as verifiability.

Software engineering is a new subfield within Computer Science. It has only recently been offered as a course of study in colleges and universities. With any new field there is a maturational process where a strong theoretical base develops and the implementation of the theory is tested. External as well as internal documentation of software is one part of the engineering process that continues to be evaluated as it matures. This paper addresses one small part of the documentation process: the user's manual. The user's manual can be used as a development tool in software engineering education in much the same way that a prototype is now used. The manual, if developed before full specifications and previewed for customers, provides excellent feedback concerning the expectations of the customer. This approach encourages students to understand the needs of the user of the software.

This paper does not address the development of quality products. If the product is substandard, quality user documentation will not improve it. Therefore, given a well-developed product, a user's manual can enhance the use of the product.

External Documentation

Although there is by no means a standard for software system documentation, a minimum criteria is developing. First and formost, documentation must be free of errors in spelling, syntax, and content. The language must be clear enough to provide the developer a means of effectively communicating to the appropriate readers of the documentation. It must provide a clear and concise description which is effectively used to operate and maintain the software.

What constitutes effective documentation is directly related to the audience which it will serve. There are different groups of users served by any software product. For those users concerned with maintenance, there must be documentation available to maintain and modify the code. Thus, technical manuals that explain and identify the technical aspects of the product must be available. Technical manuals are often easier to create by a developer than other forms of documentation. They are written in a language familiar to the developer, and the readers of the manuals have similar backgrounds and experiences. As the software documentation migrates closer to the end user, there may be more difficulty conveying the operational narrative correctly.

The user's manual is the document which provides the interface between the software and the user of the system. Thus, it contains the instructions which will allow the user to operate the product. We have only to look at available user's manuals on our shelves to find that many developers have not mastered the techniques for writing for the end user. Even if the users are computer professionals, the user's manual must be straight-forward, readable, and free of error. At the other end of the spectrum, there are users who have little or no knowledge of computers or the software. They want an easy-to-use, menu-driven system with step-by-step fully-documented procedures. These users require even greater care given to the user's manual. It is the tool by which they can understand how to use the software.

User's Manual

There are two major issues in the development of a user's manual, one which can be addressed in a course in software engineering, while the other is left for in-the-field software developers. The second deals with the lack of importance placed on the user's manual in software development. The user's manual is often developed after the software is completed, perhaps even after major testing of the system. Little of the user's manual is written before alpha testing. Traditionally, the development organization chooses one of two methods to create user documentation. 1) The developer who is creating the software is responsible for the documentation. Often, he dislikes that part of the development process most and saves it to the very last moment. 2) A technical writer who writes well, but knows very little about the product is responsible for creating the documentation. Both approaches have serious disadvantages.

Developers assume that the user's manual will flow from the product and wait until the product is finished to begin developing the document. There are several problems with this approach. First, the user's manual is often viewed as an afterthought and thus is not considered a serious part of the project. Second, customers and end users are often not synonymous. The end user is the individual in the customer's organization which will operate the software product on the computer. The customer is that individual or organization that wishes to use the computer in some form and negotiates for the product to be written. What often results is a user's manual that is not written for the correct audience. Finally, most software products are designed with a comprehensive on-line Help facilities. Thus, developers feel that this precludes the need for a comprehensive user's manual. This is an incorrect assumption for most users. First, users cannot use the on-line help if they cannot install or start the software. Secondly, users want a narrative that gives a good overview of the software capabilities which is very difficult to get with on-line help.

The technical writers have problems in organization and content because they have no knowledge and understanding of the problem definition and functional requirements of the software. Good writing style and sophisticated presentation cannot overcome vague explanations of software tasks. Technical writers are often forced into harassing developers to provide the necessary software specifications.

The user's manual should be developed at a much earlier stage in the software life cycle and have a preview showing with the correct audience before it is commercially offered with the product. However, this problem is addressed in this paper, and is only presented to set a motivation for the approach used in the software engineering course.

In the traditional life cycle approach of software engineering education, the user's manual is written in much the same way as professional programmers now write it, i.e. it is done after the product is completed. The product determines the documentation, not the requirements and expectations of the users. The remaining part of this paper demonstrates a different method of writing the user's manual in an undergraduate software engineering course. This approach seeks to improve the overall quality of the document, upgrade its importance in the process, and improve the final product.

Students have serious misconceptions regarding the importance and use of the user's manual as a significant development tool. Myths students often have about this piece of documentation are listed below:

1. The manual should be done after the project is complete.
2. How the manual is developed has nothing to do with the end users of the product.
3. It is easy to write instructions for a novice user.
4. There is only one level of user of software products.
5. The average end-user has a certain base knowledge of computer concepts.

6. Good grammar and writing style are not that important in
   a user's manual.

The user's manual used as an undergraduate software design tool provides the students with several important lessons. First, it allows students to communicate with the user of the software before any code is written. In this case, it is used in much the same way a prototype in actual project development is used. It allows students to create on paper the user interface with the software. Thus, the users can preview how the software will work and can communicate to students whether it is adequate or needs to be modified. This process often leads to higher user satisfaction [Weiss, 85] and less stress on the developer. Secondly, students learn that they must be very careful what they take for granted concerning the computer knowledge of the user. Thirdly, although the content of the manual is extremely important, the appearance of the manual has a significant impact on the readability and acceptance of it. Finally, the students begin to understand the product from a user point of view, not only a developer's point of view.

The Software Engineering Course

Lenoir-Rhyne College offers one undergraduate software engineering course, Software Systems Design. It allows students to study and implement the software life cycle with a heavy emphasis on design. The course provides practice in creating large software projects in chief programmer teams from the problem definition phase to the final report phase, with a very limited verification section. Students taking the course are typically seniors who have completed most of their computer science courses. Thus, students can be expected to program non-trivial problems and implement complex data structures using good design techniques [Miles, 88].

Students create a software product in their teams which will provide a method to experience most major stages of a traditional life cycle. They receive a general description of a problem and a non-computer science resource person needing the work done. The programming team then creates a complete problem definition from which system specifications are devised. [Appendix-Homework Schedule]. The Homework Schedule lists the requirements necessary to complete the course.

Once the problem definition is accepted by the professor and the resource person, teams work on the preliminary user's manual. Once the User's Manual is approved in its early form, students develop the systems specifications. They use a CASE tool on microcomputers, *Excelerator*, for the requirements analysis phase. This appears to improve their productivity, their system documentation, and consistency [Index Technology Corp., 86].
The emphasis of the course is on system design. Although students do produce a prototype, they are not expected to implement their design because of time constraints.

A Case for Development of Preliminary User's Manual

Requiring students to work on the user's manual early in the system analysis phase provides important feedback to students before beginning on a design that may not meet the needs of the end user. Working on the development of the manual helps define the problem from the user's point of view, thus, often eliminating delays associated with what the analyst assumed the user wanted and what the end user actually wanted. The point at which the user's manual is required in the course is earlier than the point at which the prototype is developed, i.e. before system specifications are completed. As such, many wrong assumptions about the product are uncovered. Also, students gain a general understanding for the expertise level of the user and their perceived needs. The preliminary User's Manual must be approved before students begin on formal system specifications. Students begin to realize that writing for a certain audience is not as easy as originally expected.

Communication with the resource person is one of the first major problems which students must face. Students learn there is a general lack of basic computer concepts among many customers who want a software product written. Students use this knowledge to decide what minimum background can be reasonably assumed, i.e. what needs to be included in instructions. A second, parallel problem encountered by students occurs when the contractor of the software is not completely clear what he or she wants the software to do. This is not uncommon since many customers are unfamiliar with the limitations and abilities of a piece of software. Students learn what questions must be asked and what expectations are perceived. Thus, creating a user's manual early allows the user to provide input concerning his expectations of the software. It also allows the developer to present what he expects to offer.

Mechanics of User Manual Development

Most user's manuals fail in their mission as quality user documentation because of several factors. Many of these problems can be classified as mechanical problems.

1. They are written for the wrong audience.
2. The developer does not have a clear idea of user expectations.
3. The manual has poor organizational design (i.e. it is hard to follow).
4. There are inconsistencies in the content and presentation.
5. The quality of the presentation (i.e. print, paper, graphics) is substandard.

No two user's manuals will use the same approach since each software product has its own requirements and specifications, and end users have their own particular needs. However, there are several underlying mechanics which appear to be more successful than others. Following these mechanical rules as you would a cookbook does not guarantee an easy to read and understand user's manual. However, it often improves the quality of the instructions. First, a complete understanding of the end user is absolutely necessary. With this understanding, students can create a formal analysis of the instructional requirements necessary for the proper audience to operate the system. This formal analysis is performed in parallel with the problem definition phase of the development cycle. Once completed, students design a complete outline of the documentation to identify and define functional requirements of the documentation.

One of the most important parts of the manual, and often the most confusing, is how to install the software on the specific machine being used for specific applications. With a new user of the system, any assumptions about user knowledge is foolhardy. Each step must be clearly defined followed by explicit examples.

Mechanically, the manual must have a clear, concise, and organized table of contents, glossary, and index. The chapters of the manual should flow from the control of the product and the needs of the user. Each chapter should be dedicated to the specification of one aspect of the product. This is best accomplished by dividing the functional definitions of the product into specified tasks. For each task, all the information necessary to interact with the product should be logically organized in one section. Weiss has introduced a method to measure how well the manual is organized, the Index of Usability [Weiss,85]. By calculating the number of times the user must skip pages or back-track to find the necessary information, you can determine the index of usability. This index number provides a measure of how well organized the manual is. This is a good exercise for students to perform on existing manuals of software that they are not familiar with.

If the product is a menu-driven system, each menu selection should be explained with examples. Most often, this leads to redundancy and certainly boredom for the writer of the manual. For each menu selection, there should be a description and examples. Although conforming to a set type creates redundancy, it also improves the possibility that the user can follow the instructions correctly. There should be good graphics of menus as they appear on the screen. The screen should be divided into regions. Each screen region should be explained in detail. 1. Where will error statements appear? 2. Where does the user enter information to the system? 3. What form does the information need to be to be accepted?

The manual should be easy to read. Creating a relationship between the user and the software is fostered by using some simple techniques. First, active voice projects stronger instructions and fosters simpler language constructs. Another major factor is writing the text in second person. Using familiar vocabulary gives the user a feeling of confidence with the documentation. Language that has few computer terms as possible is easier to read. When terms are used, they must be clearly defined.

A format that is attractive to the eye has many advantages. It projects professionalism and creates easy-to-read and easy-to-follow text. Simple guidelines to improve the looks of the manual include:

1. make pages symmetric
2. use different size print and typeface to emphasize important information
3. Use graphics to show the computer interaction with the user, i.e., the screen interaction, interaction with external devices, etc.
4. provide significant white space so the user can digest the information easier.

Once the student has created the final draft, called the Preliminary User's Manual, it is tested with a specified audience. The audience, which includes the instructor, is asked to comment on mechanical errors such as syntax errors, spelling, clarity issues (Does it make sense?), presentation (How does the format present itself?), and how appropriate is the language use. Students then create a modified version and resubmit it until it is accepted.

Summary

Students are skeptical when they must create a user's manual immediately after the problem definition is completed. They express such comments as "How can we write a manual to use a system that doesn't exist yet?". Their first attempt at the document is usually discouraging. However, once students have completed the course, they have very positive evaluations and reactions to the approach. They feel that creating the user's manual early in the process helped define the scope of the project. They also felt they had learned some important interpersonal skills in dealing with the users.

Because students must develop the user's manual early in the development process, it is hoped that they see its relative importance in the entire software engineering process. Students demonstrate a significant change in their perspectives. They begin to understand the differences in writing for technical personnel and writing for an end user. They learn the
types of questions they must ask to clarify the problem both for themselves and the user. The hope is that after students enter the working environment as computer professionals, they will take with them an understanding of the importance and need of quality user documentation.

Software development is moving into an era where communication skills are becoming critical to the success of software systems. The skilled writers who have a clear understanding of the technology become the leaders of the development teams. With improved technological advances of application software in the area of drawing and publishing, the minimum requirements for quality user documentation are being raised. In the competition among software vendors the successful organizations are those who have mastered the art of creating quality user documentation. Thus, it is the responsibility of software engineering education to provide education in the development and maintenance of quality user documentation.

APPENDIX
Software Design
Homework Schedule and Grading Guidelines

Each team will submit a report on each phase of the software development project. All reports must present a professional job. No handwritten work will be accepted. Work will not be accepted for any reason 3 days beyond the due date.

% of Grade	Date Due	Homework Assignments
		CONCEPT AND DEFINITION PHASE
8	9/10	1. System Analysis Report:

Report that identifies all the system elements. This includes software interface to hardware, people, and databases.

This Report must include:
- a. Task-oriented definition of the problem (Identifies customer needs)
- b. Hardware Considerations and based on these considerations the final decision:
  1. Vendor
  2. CPU Benckmarks necessary
  3. Memory requirements and type
  4. Secondary storage medium
  5. Networking ???
- c. Software Considerations
  1. Development language (why?)
  2. Software Tools: editors, compilers, run-time libraries CASE tools.
- d. Human Considerations
  1. End-User capabilities
  2. Development team capabilities (structure and technical level)
  3. User Friendly?
  4. Consultants??
- e. Database Considerations
  1. How much data needs to be stored?
  2. Define the information to be used.
  3. Criteria for accessing in: Speed, ease of access, etc.
- f. Feasibility Study
- g. Cost Estimates (Primitive)

APPENDIX (continued)

% of Grade	Date Due	Homework Assignment
10	9/24	2. <u>User's Manual</u>

Must include:
a. Cover Page
b. Table of Contents
c. Introduction
d. A section to describe every
    task and screen.
e. Glossary
** Place it in second person.

10	10/8	3. <u>System Specifications</u>

Must Include:
a. Introduction (revised systems
    analysis report)
b. Functional Descriptions
    1. Narrative of each task
        to be performed by the
        system (in detail)
    2. Describe the input information
    3. Results of each functional task.
    4. Any interface (preliminary)
c. Databases and files described
    (include hardware and software
    specifications.)
d. Constraints
e. Cost (Use one of the Estimation
    Models in Ch. 3)
f. Schedule (Use a Gantt Chart)
    (See page 126-127)

DESIGN PHASE

1. <u>Requirements Analysis</u>
(This report is divided into two due
dates-the last date will include
the revised first part)

| 15 | 10/27 | a. Introduction |

Include system objectives and
project constraints
b. Information description
    1. Structure Chart
    2. Data Flow Diagrams
    3. Record and file definitions
c. Comprehensive Data Dictionary

B. and C. above must be done using
Excelerator. (Use the Lessons given
out in class to help you do this)

APPENDIX (continued)

% of Grade	Date Due	Homework Assignments
10	11/5	d. Functional Descriptions Each function is defined in terms of all the pseudocode necessary to perform the tasks, restrictions or limitations, performance requirements, design constraints, interface with other modules. e. Validation Criteria Performance Bounds and Classes of tests
3	11/10	2. Design Review Oral Report in Class
10	11/17	3. Final Design Phase Complete Design Document
15	12/1	**IMPLEMENTATION PHASE** The menu screens of the project must be coded with stubs for i/o and manipulation tasks in a high-level language or 4GL (prototype)
17	Day of Final	**FINAL REPORT** 1. Final User's Manual with revisions 2. All phases of project defined and a prototype developed and working 3. Technical Manual (includes all the requirements analysis material revised-DFD, IPO Charts, Data Dictionary, Code , etc) 4. Indexed program listing with cross reference to charts and dictionaries

Bibliography

[1] Browning,C. *Guide to Effective Software Technical Writing*. Prentice-Hall, Englewood Cliffs, NJ, 1984.

[2] Index Technology Corporation. *Excelerator*. Cambridge, Ma., 1986.

[3] Licker, *Fundamentals of System Analysis*. Boyd & Fraser, Boston, 1987.

[4] Meinke, J. "Augmenting a Software Engineering Projects Course with Oral and Written Communication", *Proceedings of Eighteenth SIGCSE Technical Symposium of Computer Science Education*. 19(1), Feb 87, 238-243.

[5] Miles, G. "One Approach for Teaching Software Engineering Across the Undergraduate Computer Science Curriculum". *Computer Science Education Journal*. 1(1), 1988, p 53-62.

[6] Miles, G. "Using Computer-Aided Software Engineering CASE) in the Undergraduate Project-Oriented Software Design Course". *Proceedings of Second Annual Southeastern Small College Computer Conference*. Chattanooga, TN, November 18-19, 1988, pg. 57-63.

[7] Pressman, R. *Software Engineering: A Practitioner's Approach*. McGraw-Hill Book Company, NY, 1987.

[8] Sigwart, C & Van Meer, G. "Software Engineering: The Art of the User Interview", *Proceedings of Seventeenth SIGCSE Technical Symposium on Computer Science Education*. 18(1), Feb 86, 127-130.

[9] Weiss, E. *How To Write A Useable User Manual*. isi Press, Philadelphia, 1985.

Panel on Software Engineering Ethics

Abstract. *The panel addresses practical issues and approaches for integrating the study of ethics into professional software engineering education. The three presentations summarized below assume that one goal of applied ethics in software engineering education is to equip professionals to recognize and reason about ethical issues in practical situations. All three address the question of how best to do so, from different but complementary perspectives: the case-based approach to ethics (Leslie Burkholder), practical methods for ethical reasoning (Preston Covey), and models for integrating ethics in software engineering curricula (Donald Gotterbarn).*

Cases in Software Engineering Ethics

Leslie Burkholder
Carnegie Mellon University

Applied or professional ethics courses typically include the discussion of cases or dilemmas intended to raise issues that professionals will encounter in their working lives.

There is a good reason for this, as I shall explain in my presentation. There is some evidence that case-based discussion of ethical issues has a beneficial effect on the ethical reasoning abilities of the participants. The evidence is not unequivocal and more research needs to be done.

I will also give an example of what the discussion of particular cases in software engineering ethics might involve. The case I discuss is a variant of one found in the Parker, Swope and Baker collection, *Ethical Conflicts in Information and Computer Science, Technology, and Business* (Menlo Park CA: SRI International, 1988):

A software engineering firm has been contacted by a bank to provide an automated teller service with speech-recognition and voice-response capabilities. No capability is to be included which would let a bank customer know whether a particular conversation is with the device or a person. In fact, the bank's requirements are that the automated teller should perform in such a convincing way that its customers will believe that they are dealing with a person even when they are dealing with the device.

A discussion of this case would certainly consider the following matters: (1) Is the bank planning to do anything ethically questionable? (2) Suppose someone (the bank, in this case) is doing or planning to do something wrong. Wouldn't it be wrong to help (by writing the software)? (3) Suppose several competing software firms would do the work for the bank were this one to refuse. Would that make any ethical difference in what the firm should do? My presentation will illustrate what can be learned from such discussion and how it might be conducted.

Methodology for Applied Ethics

Preston Covey
Carnegie Mellon University

Several years ago in a *Wall Street Journal* article, "When Values Are Substituted for Truth," William J. Bennett related an ironic and telling conversation from an ethics class; I paraphrase:

Student: *I don't think you can teach ethics because there really aren't any in any real sense. Each person's values are as good as anybody else's. Values are subjective.*

Teacher: *No, that's not true. Some people's values are better than others.*

Student: *No, they're subjective. No one can impose his values on somebody else.*

Teacher: *Well, what do you think of this? I say values are not subjective and, if you don't agree with me, then I'll flunk you.*

Student: *You can't do that! Are you crazy?*

Teacher: *No. And I can do that. Why not?*

Student: *Well . . . because it's . . . it's not fair!*

Philosophers, amateur and professional, have argued the rationality, reality and teachability of ethics for millenia, and will for millenia more. This vignette shows the practical irrelevance of that perennial debate, by illustrating the hard fact that we must appeal to ethical considerations even as their status is debated.

The basic practical problem is *how* to identify and deliberate ethical issues, how to negotiate ethical dilemmas and disagreements. There is no question about *whether* such things can be done. They will be, if only willy nilly, if only by default. Grappling responsibly with ethical issues does not require answers to metaphysical and meta-ethical disputes about the objectivity or subjectivity of values and ethics; nor does it require hard and fast, black or white answers to moral muddles: a dilemma, by definition, is a choice for which there *is* no happy or costless alternative, a problem of hard trade-offs. Such is life. The fact is that we confront ethical issues and dilemmas, make and argue value judgments, all the time; the question is how well we do so, and how we best learn to do better.

One goal of applied ethics education is to improve skills in reasoning about ethical issues, ethical dilemmas, and ethical disagreements. We need to define, refine, and teach practicable, generalizable, transferable methods for addressing ethical disputes.

In *Ethical Conflicts in Information and Computer Science, Technology, and Business* (Menlo Park CA: SRI International, 1988), Parker, Swope and Baker expound and illustrate "a new, experimental approach to discussing ethical issues, scenario analysis." The use of cases or scenarios, real or imaginary, to generate and test ethical hypotheses (hypotheses about what is right, wrong, decent, obligatory, good, or best to do) is itself not new. Case-based (casuistic) reasoning has enjoyed a prominent role in ethics from the days of Socrates. Its analogue is case law. The contentious history of this venerable tradition has recently been traced by Albert Johnson and Stephen Toulmin in *The Abuse of Casuistry: A History of Moral Reasoning* (University of California Press, 1988). *Casuistry* (from the Latin *casu,* case) admits of two faces: the careful study of particular cases for principled resolution; and the disingenuous, oversubtle, sophistical manipulation of cases for self-interested ends. The face validity of the general approach, the practical necessity of getting down to cases, is obvious: How, after all, could inquiry be conducted into ethics, or any practical matter, without close attention to some data: facts about cases, consequences, and constraints?

It is not obvious, however, what we are supposed to learn from scenario analysis, or how we should best conduct it. What, precisely, are its objectives? What are the norms and success criteria that govern good case analysis, either as a method of inquiry or as a learning strategy? In what sense are its methods *experimental?* What counts as *evidence* for or against an ethical hypothesis or principle? How are the results of case analysis *generalized,* if at all? If they are not generalizable, what good are they? And what recourse do we have, what methods of resolution or negotiation are available, when we encounter *disagreements* in deliberating what should be done in any particular case?

My presentation will focus on practical issues and pragmatic models for teaching a methodology for applied ethics. A *method* is a way of doing something. A *methodology* provides standards for assessing methods, an explicit rationale for why one way of doing something is good, or *better* than another. One issue for teaching applied, practical ethics is whether explicit attention to the methodology of ethics is really efficacious for improving skills of ethical reasoning. Some say: Just do a lot of it (for example, case analysis) and learn by doing. Others say: We learn better by reflecting on what we're doing and why we're doing it this way rather than another way.

Building on the example of case analysis discussed by Leslie Burkholder, I will focus on two types of reasoning problem and skill: (1) deliberating what is best to do, ethically speaking, in any particular case and (2) negotiating disagreements that arise in such deliberation. I will highlight what can be learned by attending to methodological issues. Even assuming the practical value of methodological study, two further practical questions arise: How to make any methodology accessible and useful to software engineering instructors. And how to integrate a methodology for applied ethics in the software engineering curriculum; for example, according to the models that Donald Gotterbarn discusses.

A Model for Software Engineering Ethics

Donald Gotterbarn
The Wichita State University

In my paper I shall present: a model for the study of software engineering ethics, some illustrations applying this model, and an argument for the way ethics should be handled in the curriculum.

The teaching of ethics in a software engineering curriculum ought to prepare students to understand the types of moral issues they will confront as software engineers and introduce them to the moral ideals of the profession. What is the best model for the study of software engineering ethics, given these goals?

Organizing an ethics course around a set of unethical practices develops a checklist morality. The student will not recognize new ethical issues that are not on the checklist. A better model for the study of issues as they arise in the profession is one tied to some version of the software development life cycle.

This model can be used in a stand alone ethics course. The students could work on a single small software project. At each stage of the project ethical issues develop during an examination of the technical issues. They would learn to see the issues as they arose in a real work situation. They would also learn that some concerns, such as risk management, are not unique to any one stage of a life cycle but are problems across the life cycle. This is a good way to get them to think about moral issues involved in their work life where their individual professional decisions can make a difference. The project should also be designed to be conditioned by economic, political or other factors which impact ethical issues normally faced in project development. This helps them develop new insights into the problems faced in professional practice.

Studies have shown that it is best to integrate the study of ethics throughout the curriculum. This same model can be used to distribute the examination of ethical issues over those courses which deal with the different stages of a software development life cycle.

SEI Report
on
Graduate Software Engineering Education[1,2]

Mark Ardis, Gary Ford
Software Engineering Institute

Abstract: A report on the SEI's 1988 Curriculum Design Workshop is provided, along with descriptions of the six core courses for a Master of Software Engineering degree program that were designed at that workshop. A summary of current SEI recommendations for such a degree program is also included.

1. Introduction

An ongoing activity of the SEI Education Program is the development and support of a graduate curriculum in software engineering. In such a rapidly changing discipline it is important that such a curriculum be reevaluated and revised frequently in order to ensure that it reflects the state of the art. This report describes our 1988 efforts toward that end.

To put these recent curriculum efforts in perspective, it is helpful to review the history of SEI curriculum recommendations. In 1985, the staff of the Graduate Curriculum Project developed a strawman description of the important subject areas and possible courses for a professional Master of Software Engineering (MSE) degree. This document was reviewed by the participants in the February 1986 SEI Software Engineering Education Workshop [Gibbs87], who offered numerous suggestions for improvement.

We then wrote a revised version of the document, which was widely circulated for additional comments. Those comments were sifted and analyzed over the

---

[1]This work was sponsored by the US Department of Defense.
[2]This report is an abridged version of an SEI technical report [Ardis89].

winter of 1986-87, and in May 1987 the SEI published *Software Engineering Education, An Interim Report from the Software Engineering Institute* [Ford87]. This report was our first publication of curriculum recommendations, and it addressed not only curriculum content, but also the related curriculum issues of educational objectives, prerequisites, student project work, electives, and resources needed to support the curriculum.

The interim report came to be regarded as a *specification* for an MSE curriculum, because it concentrated on the content of the curriculum rather than how that content might be organized into courses or how those courses might be taught. We expected future work to include curriculum *design* (the organization of that content into meaningful courses), *implementation* (the detailed description of each course by instructors of the course), and *execution*, the process of teaching each course. (We have not yet planned a *validation* effort, though we see the need to do so.)

Two events in 1987 made it clear that a curriculum design was needed immediately. First, the SEI established a new project, the Video Dissemination Project, through which graduate-level courses in software engineering were to be offered through cooperating universities, using the medium of videotape and the tutored video format. Second, Carnegie Mellon University committed to establishment of an MSE program within its newly proposed School of Computer Science. Both of these efforts needed a curriculum, including detailed designs for courses.

In February 1988 the SEI sponsored the Curriculum Design Workshop, whose goal was to design a curriculum for an MSE program that was consistent with the specification in the interim report. The workshop produced designs for six core courses.

During 1988 and 1989, prototype implementations of several of the core courses are being taught by the staff of the Video Dissemination Project. The experiences of both instructors and students are being collected and will be used to improve the next release of the curriculum recommendations.

Section 2 of this report describes the Curriculum Design Workshop. A summary of the SEI's current MSE recommendations appears in section 3. The descriptions of the six core courses follow this report.

2. Curriculum Design Workshop

In February 1988 we invited several software engineering educators to an MSE Curriculum Design Workshop. The participants were:

Mark Ardis, *SEI*

Jim Collofello, *Arizona State University*

Lionel Deimel, *SEI*

Dick Fairley, *George Mason University*

Gary Ford, *SEI*

Norm Gibbs, *SEI*

Bob Glass, *SEI*

Harvey Hallman, *SEI*

Tom Kraly, *IBM*

Jeff Lasky, *Rochester Institute of Technology*

Larry Morell, *College of William and Mary*

Tom Piatkowski, *SUNY at Binghamton*

Scott Stevens, *SEI*

Jim Tomayko, *The Wichita State University*

The objective of the workshop was to create descriptions of courses in "sufficient detail." Since the main task was to partition the topics (as defined in the interim report) into courses, enough detail was needed for each course to allow independent implementation of the courses. That is, instructors should be able to prepare and teach their courses in relative isolation, just as software implementors are able to produce their modules independently. Of course, awareness of and cooperation with others is important in both activities. But individuals (instructors or software developers) should feel free to make decisions about every aspect of their product that is not already specified in the design.

2.1. Workshop Organization and Procedures

Since we viewed the previous curriculum description as a specification, we viewed its recommendations as constraints that we must satisfy in our design. Therefore our first step was to review that specification. Some participants noted that other degree programs were worthy of consideration, but all agreed that the specification was a good starting point for our work.

A major constraint in the interim report was the duration of the program: 30 to 36 semester hours, or about 10 to 12 courses. Of these courses, it was suggested that six or seven would constitute the core material and that three or four would be advanced electives. The remainder of the program would be project work. Because of the limited time available during the workshop (two days), it was decided that we would concentrate exclusively on the design of the core courses.

Other constraints in the interim report included the prerequisite knowledge of entering students (a BS in computer science, or equivalent knowledge and ability), expected faculty (5 full-time for a program of 20 graduates per year), computing resources, and support staff. We assumed that the resource constraints would be met, but they rarely influenced our design decisions. Instead, we made note of these requirements when elaborating our pedagogical concerns for each course.

Our intent was to divide the participants into working groups, with each group addressing a course or courses in a broad subject area. Therefore our next step was to examine the 20 *content units* in the specification to try to identify appropriate subject areas. (The content units are summarized in section 3.3 below.) In addition, we attempted to determine the approximate size of each unit, measured by weeks of class time. A relatively coarse metric was used, having only three sizes: *small* (1-2 weeks), *medium* (3-6 weeks), and *large* (more than 6 weeks).

We found five natural subject areas of content units, whose working titles were Systems Engineering, Software Design and Specification, Implementation, Verification and Validation, and Control and Management. Although these subject areas resemble the phases of the traditional waterfall life cycle model, we did not intend to advocate any specific model for software development. We do believe, however, that the activities of requirements analysis and specification, design, implementation, verification and validation, and project management are probably elements of any reasonable model. Therefore we believe that these five subject areas are legitimate as well as convenient partitions of the curriculum content.

The five subject areas, the content units in each (numbered as in section 3.3), and the estimated size of each unit are presented below. Notice that one unit, Software Quality Assurance, appears in two subject areas. The working groups were given the task of dividing its material appropriately.

Systems Engineering
11. Software Operational Issues	small
12. Requirements Analysis	medium
14. System Design	small
18. System Integration	small
20. Human Interfaces	small

Software Design and Specification
13. Specification	large
15. Software Design	large
19. Embedded Real-time Systems	medium

Implementation
3. Software Generation   small
4. Software Maintenance   medium
16. Software Implementation   medium

Verification and Validation
7. Software Quality Issues   medium
8. Software Quality Assurance   medium
17. Software Testing   medium

Control and Management
1. The Software Engineering Process   small
2. Software Evolution   small
5. Technical Communication   medium
6. Software Configuration Management   small
8. Software Quality Assurance   small
9. Software Project Organizational and Management Issues   medium
10. Software Project Economics   small

Four of the five subject areas had an estimated size of 12 to 15 weeks each, which caused us to try to design a single core course for each. The Software Design and Specification subject area appeared to have almost 25 weeks of material, so we thought two courses were warranted.

The workshop then broke into three working groups. The first was charged with designing courses for Systems Engineering and for Software Design and Specification; the second for Implementation and for Verification and Validation, and the third for Control and Management. Each group met for two to three hours, and then we all reported our progress in a combined session. This process was iterated twice more in the hope that the boundaries between courses could be clearly drawn, without overlaps or gaps.

The product of the working groups was a set of required courses:

- Software Systems Engineering
- Specification of Software Systems
- Principles and Applications of Software Design
- Software Generation and Maintenance
- Software Verification and Validation
- Software Project Management

For each course we tried to describe the prerequisites, the major and minor topics, the relative duration of topics in the course, the educational objective for each major topic (based on an adaptation of Bloom's taxonomy of educational objectives; see [Ford87] or [Ardis89]), principal references, and other pedagogical concerns. In some cases we were able to produce relatively detailed descriptions in the first working group session. For other courses we barely managed to complete a description after all three sessions. This probably reflects the uneven maturity of topics within software engineering. Those topics that have been taught successfully for several years are easy to package into courses. Newer topics are more difficult to package.

After the workshop, a subset of the participants prepared more detailed draft descriptions of the courses. Each of the courses was reviewed for internal consistency and for its contribution to the overall integrity of the curriculum. The current versions of these course descriptions appear immediately following this report. Although the participants were given an opportunity to review intermediate forms of this report, the current authors take responsibility for any errors introduced during its preparation.

2.2 Discussion

At first glance, the required courses appear to follow a traditional waterfall life cycle model: requirements, specification, design, implementation, and testing (with project management added to complete the set of courses). However, the courses make no such assumption. Instead, the division of topics into courses emphasizes different skills required of students. For example, requirements analysis depends on communication skills (to interview users) that are not used in implementation. Software engineers may have to perform requirements analysis concurrently with implementation (e.g., as a prototyping activity), but they can best learn the skills independently.

There are no prerequisite relationships among the required courses. On the other hand, some courses depend critically on courses outside of the curriculum. For example, the Software Specification course and the Verification and Validation course require prerequisite knowledge of discrete mathematics.

Some of the skills needed by graduates of an MSE program are not easily covered in one course. Communication skills are a good example of this; we recommended that students practice these skills often in the program, and that instructors in an MSE program attempt to teach or evaluate these skills. Collaboration with faculty from English of communications departments may be helpful.

We spent very little time discussing project work, though we assumed that it would be part of the curriculum. The specification recommended that 30% of the program be devoted to this kind of activity. We noted that some of the required courses included a semester-long project, and that the equivalent of about two additional semester-long project courses were appropriate. Project work might be done in conjunction with required or elective courses, or as independent coursework.

Very little time was spent discussing elective courses. It was assumed that a variety of appropriate courses would be offered, and that students would take approximately three of these courses. In some cases we limited the amount of time allocated to a topic in a required course (in order to allow more time for other, equally important topics), noting that more advanced coverage could be given in an elective course in that area. We did, however, make some recommendations for the types of electives that should be offered:

- Electives in software engineering subjects, such as software development environments, are clearly appropriate.
- Electives in computer science topics, such as database systems, are probably appropriate, especially if they emphasize application and evaluation.
- Electives in systems engineering are probably appropriate.

3. Summary of MSE Curriculum Recommendations

This section presents a very abbreviated summary of the SEI's current MSE curriculum recommendations. The complete recommendations may be found in [Ardis89].

3.1. Objectives

The goal of the MSE degree is to produce a software engineer who can rapidly assume a position of substantial responsibility within an organization. To achieve this goal, the curriculum we propose is designed to give the student a body of knowledge that includes balanced coverage of the software engineering process activities, their various aspects, and the products they produce, and to give the student sufficient experience to bridge the gap between undergraduate programming and professional software engineering.

Detailed educational objectives may be found in [Ardis89]. They are described using a taxonomy adapted from [Bloom56]. That taxonomy has six levels of objectives (from lowest to highest): knowledge, comprehension, application, analysis, synthesis, and evaluation. These six levels are used to describe the objectives of the content units in section 3.3 and of the topics in the core courses.

3.2. Prerequisites

A detailed discussion of prerequisites may be found in [Ford87]. In summary, we assume that a student entering an MSE program will have a bachelor's degree in computer science, or the equivalent knowledge gained from professional experience. The expected mathematics background includes discrete mathematics and some calculus. Knowledge of probability and statistics is essential for some advanced topics in software engineering.

Many existing MSE programs require one or more years of professional experience as a prerequisite. We have not found the arguments for an experience prerequisite sufficiently compelling to recommend it for all MSE programs. Other engineering disciplines have successful master's level programs, and even undergraduate programs, without such a prerequisite. Most graduate professional degrees do not require it. We recognize, however, that experience can be a major factor in motivating students to learn and adopt more rigorous methods of software engineering. The lack of experience increases the burden on the instructor to motivate the students.

3.3. Curriculum Content Specification

The content units from the curriculum specification [Ford87] are summarized below. Each identifies topics, aspects of those topics (abstractions, representations, methods, tools, assessment, and communication), and educational objectives.

1. The Software Engineering Process

Topics: The software engineering process and software products. All of the software engineering activities. The concepts of software process model and software product life cycle model.

Aspects: All aspects, as appropriate for the various activities.

Objectives: Knowledge of activities and aspects. Some comprehension of the issues, especially the distinctions among the various classes of activities. The students should begin to understand the substantial differences between programming, as they have done in an undergraduate program, and software engineering, as it is practiced professionally.

2. Software Evolution

Topics: The concept of a software product life cycle. The various forms of a software product, from initial conception through development and operation to retirement. Controlling activities and disciplines to support evolution. Planned and unplanned events that affect software evolution. The role of changing technology.

Aspects: Models of software evolution, including development life cycle models such as the waterfall, iterative enhancement, phased development, spiral.

Objectives: Knowledge and comprehension of the models. Knowledge and comprehension of the controlling activities.

3. Software Generation

Topics: Various methods of software generation, including designing and coding from scratch, use of reusable components (including examples such as mathematical procedure libraries, packages designed specifically for reuse, Ada generic program units, and program concatenation as with pipes), use of program or application generators and very high level languages, role of prototyping. Factors affecting choice of a software generation method. Effects of generation method on other software development activities, such as testing and maintenance.

Aspects: Models of software generation. Representations for software generation, including design and implementation languages, very high level languages, and application generators. Tools to support generation methods, including application generators.

Objectives: Knowledge and comprehension of the various methods of software generation. Ability to apply each method when supported by appropriate tools. Ability to evaluate methods and choose the appropriate ones for each project.

4. Software Maintenance

Topics: Maintenance as a part of software evolution. Reasons for maintenance. Kinds of maintenance (perfective, adaptive, corrective). Comparison of development activities during initial product development and during maintenance. Controlling activities and disciplines that affect maintenance. Designing for maintainability. Techniques for maintenance.

Aspects: Models of maintenance. Current methods.

Objectives: Knowledge and comprehension of the issues of software maintenance and current maintenance practice.

5. Technical Communication

Topics: Fundamentals of technical communication. Oral and written communications. Preparing oral presentations and supporting materials. Software project documentation of all kinds.

Aspects: Principles of communication. Document preparation tools. Standards for presentations and documents.

Objectives: Knowledge of fundamentals of technical communication and of software documentation. Application of fundamentals to oral and written communications. Ability to analyze, synthesize, and evaluate technical communications.

6. Software Configuration Management

Topics: Concepts of configuration management. Its role in controlling software evolution. Maintaining product integrity. Change control and version control. Organizational structures for configuration management.

Aspects: Fundamental principles. Tools (such as *sccs* or *rcs*). Documentation, including configuration management plans.

Objectives: Knowledge and comprehension of the issues. Ability to apply the knowledge to develop a configuration management plan and to use appropriate tools.

7. Software Quality Issues

Topics: Definitions of quality. Factors affecting software quality. Planning for quality. Quality concerns in each phase of a software life cycle, with special emphasis on the specification of the pervasive system attributes. Quality measurement and standards. Software correctness assessment principles and methods. The role of formal verification and the role of testing.

Aspects: Assessment of software quality: appropriate measures. Tools to help perform measurement. Correctness assessment methods, including testing and formal verification. Formal models of program verification.

Objectives: Knowledge and comprehension of software quality issues and correctness methods. Ability to apply proof of correctness methods.

8. Software Quality Assurance

Topics: Software quality assurance as a controlling discipline. Organizational structures for quality assurance. Independent verification and validation teams. Test and evaluation teams. Software technical reviews. Software quality assurance plans.

Aspects: Current industrial practice for quality assurance. Documents including quality assurance plans, inspection reports, audits, and validation test reports.

Objectives: Knowledge and comprehension of quality assurance planning. Ability to analyze and synthesize quality assurance plans. Ability to perform technical reviews. Knowledge and comprehension of the fundamentals of program verification, and its role in quality assurance. Ability to apply concepts of quality assurance as part of a quality assurance team.

9. Software Project Organizational and Management Issues

Topics: Project planning: choice of process model, project scheduling and milestones. Staffing: development team organizations, quality assurance teams. Resource allocation.

Aspects: Fundamental concepts and principles. Scheduling representations and tools. Project documents.

Objectives: Knowledge and comprehension of concepts and issues. It is not expected that a student, after studying this material, will immediately be ready to manage a software project.

10. Software Project Economics

Topics: Cost estimation, cost/benefit analysis, risk analysis for software projects. Factors that affect cost.

Aspects: Models of cost estimation. Current techniques and tools for cost estimation.

Objectives: Knowledge and comprehension of models and techniques. Ability to apply the knowledge to tool use.

11. Software Operational Issues

Topics: Organizational issues related to the use of a software system in an organization. Training, system installation, system transition, operation, retirement. User documentation.

Aspects: User documentation and training materials.

Objectives: Knowledge and comprehension of the major issues.

12. Requirements Analysis

Topics: The process of interacting with the customer to determine system requirements. Defining software requirements. Identifying functional, performance, and other requirements: the pervasive system requirements. Techniques to identify requirements, including prototyping, modeling, and simulation.

Aspects: Principles and models of requirements. Techniques of requirement identification. Tools to support these techniques, if available. Assessing requirements. Communication with the customer.

Objectives: Knowledge and comprehension of the concepts of requirements analysis and the different classes of requirements. Knowledge of requirements analysis techniques. Ability to apply techniques and analyze and synthesize requirements for simple systems.

13. Specification

Topics: Objectives of the specification process. Form, content, and users of a specifications document. Specifying functional, performance, reliability, and other requirements of systems. Formal models and representations of specifications. Specification standards.

Aspects: Formal models and representations. Specification techniques and tools that support them, if available. Assessment of a specification for attributes such as consistency and completeness. Specification documents.

Objectives: Knowledge and comprehension of the fundamental concepts of specification. Knowledge of specification models, representations, and techniques, and the ability to apply or use one or more. Ability to analyze and synthesize a specification document for a simple system.

14. System Design

Topics: The role of system design and software design. How design fits into a life cycle. Software as a component of a system. Hardware vs. software trade-offs for system performance and flexibility. Subsystem definition and design. Design of high level interfaces, both hardware to software and software to software.

Aspects: System modeling techniques and representations. Methods for system design, including object oriented design, and tools to support those methods. Iterative design techniques. Performance prediction.

Objectives: Comprehension of the issues in system design, emphasizing engineering trade-offs. Ability to use appropriate system design models, methods, and tools, including those for specifying interfaces. Ability to analyze and synthesize small systems.

15. Software Design

Topics: Principles of design, including abstraction and information hiding, modularity, reuse, prototyping. Levels of design. Design representations. Design practices and techniques. Examples of design paradigms for well-understood systems.

Aspects: Principles of software design. One or more design notations or languages. One or more widely used design methods and supporting tools, if available. Assessment of the quality of a design. Design documentation.

Objectives: Knowledge and comprehension of one or more design representations, design methods, and supporting tools, if available. Ability to analyze and synthesize designs for software systems. Ability to apply methods and tools as part of a design team.

16. Software Implementation

Topics: Relationship of design and implementation. Features of modern procedural languages related to design principles. Implementation issues including reusable components and application generators. Programming support environment concepts.

Aspects: One or more modern implementation languages and supporting tools. Assessment of implementations: coding standards and metrics.

Objectives: Ability to analyze, synthesize, and evaluate the implementation of small systems.

17. Software Testing

Topics: The role of testing and its relationship to quality assurance. The nature of and limitations of testing. Levels of testing: unit, integration, acceptance, etc. Detailed study of testing at the unit level. Formal models of testing. Test planning. Black box and white box testing. Building testing environments. Test case generation. Test result analysis.

Aspects: Testing principles and models. Tools to support specific kinds of tests. Assessment of testing; testing standards. Test documentation.

Objectives: Knowledge and comprehension of the role and limitations of testing. Ability to apply test tools and techniques. Ability to analyze test plans and test results. Ability to synthesize a test plan.

18. System Integration

Topics: Testing at the software system level. Integration of software and hardware components of a system. Uses of simulation for missing hardware components. Strategies for gradual integration and testing.

Aspects: Methods and supporting tools for system testing and system integration. Assessment of test results and diagnosing system faults. Documentation: integration plans, test results.

Objectives: Comprehension of the issues and techniques of system integration. Ability to apply the techniques to do system integration and testing. Ability to develop system test and integration plans. Ability to interpret test results and diagnose system faults.

19. Embedded Real-time Systems

Topics: Characteristics of embedded real-time systems. Existence of hard timing requirements. Concurrency in systems and representing concurrency in requirements specifications, designs, and code. Issues related to complex interfaces between devices and between software and devices. Criticality of embedded systems and issues of robustness, reliability, and fault tolerance. Input and output considerations, including unusual data representations required by devices. Issues related to the cognizance of time. Issues related to the inability to test systems adequately.

Objectives: Comprehension of the significant problems in the analysis, design, and construction of embedded real-time systems. Ability to produce small systems that involve interrupt handling, low level input and output, concurrency, and hard timing requirements, preferably in a high level language.

20. Human Interfaces

Topics: Software engineering factors: applying design techniques to human interface problems, including concepts of device independence and virtual terminals. Human factors: definition and effects of screen clutter, assumptions about the class of users of a system, robustness and handling of operator input errors, uses of color in displays.

Objectives: Comprehension of the major issues. Ability to apply design techniques to produce good human interfaces. Ability to design and conduct experiments with interfaces, to analyze the results, and to improve the design as a result.

3.4. Core Courses

The six core courses in the MSE curriculum are:

> Software Systems Engineering
> Specification of Software Systems
> Principles and Applications of Software Design
> Software Generation and Maintenance
> Software Verification and Validation
> Software Project Management

Descriptions of these courses follow this report.

A significant fact about these courses is that there is no prerequisite structure among them. This is primarily a result of the overall program prerequisites. A modern undergraduate curriculum in computer science includes significant coverage of programming-in-the-small, including some simple models of software development. Therefore the MSE core courses constitute a second, substantially more detailed, pass through much of this material. Elective courses can provide a third, still more detailed study of some topics.

The primary consideration in scheduling the courses is that they and the student project work are mutually supportive. For many schools, it is likely that the courses will be offered in "waterfall-model order" since the project proceeds in that order.

3.5. Project Experience Component

Project work is essential to developing software engineering skills (see section 3.7 below). We recommend that approximately 30% of students' time be devoted to realistic project work.

This curriculum component can be structured in a number of ways, and we do not have evidence that any one of them is substantially better than the others. Some schools have a *capstone* project that follows most of the course-work, while others integrate one or more projects with individual courses. Still others have developed cooperative programs with industry. These various approaches are discussed in more detail in [Ford87].

3.6. Electives

Electives may make up 20% to 40% of a curriculum. Software engineering is already sufficiently broad that students can choose specializations (such as project management, systems engineering, real-time systems, etc.); there is no "one size fits all" MSE curriculum. The electives provide the opportunity for that specialization.

In addition, there is a rather strong perception among industrial software engineers that domain knowledge for their particular industry is essential to the development of effective software systems. Therefore we also suggest that an MSE curriculum permit electives to be chosen from the advanced courses in various application domains. Software engineers with a basic knowledge of avionics, radar systems, or robotics, for example, are likely to be in great demand. Furthermore, there is increasing evidence that better software project management can significantly influence the cost of software, so electives in management topics may be appropriate.

To summarize, there are five recommended categories of electives:

- software engineering subjects, such as software development environments;
- computer science topics, such as database systems or expert systems;
- systems engineering topics, especially topics at the boundary between hardware and software;
- application domain topics;
- engineering management topics.

3.7. Pedagogical Considerations

Software engineering is difficult to teach for a variety of reasons, including that it is a relatively new and rapidly changing discipline, and that it has aspects of an art and a craft as well as a science and an engineering discipline. Educators must develop a variety of teaching techniques and materials in order to provide effective education.

Psychologists distinguish *declarative* knowledge and *procedural* knowledge. The former is easy to write down and easy to teach; the latter is nearly impossible to write down and difficult to teach. It is largely subconscious, and it is best taught by demonstration and best learned through practice. Many of the processes of software engineering depend on procedural knowledge. It is for this reason that we recommend such a significant amount of project experience in the curriculum (see section 3.5).

There is another aspect of experience that we believe can be built into the curriculum. Software engineers, during their first several years in the profession, will likely be exposed to a large number of recurring problems for which there are accepted solutions. These problems and solutions will vary considerably from one application domain to another, but all software engineers seem to accumulate quite a few of them in their "bags of tricks." Learning these tricks is a major part of the informal apprenticeship of software engineers.

We propose that if it were possible to document these problems and solutions and include them in the curriculum in a concentrated way, then the students would receive a lot of the benefits of that apprenticeship period while still in school. For this reason, we have included large course segments titled "Paradigms" in the specification and design courses (see the descriptions of these courses following this report).

The principal definition of the word *paradigm* is "EXAMPLE, PATTERN; *esp* : an outstandingly clear or typical example or archetype" [Webster88]. The word *archetype* is defined in the same source as "the original pattern or model of which all things of the same type are representations or copies : PROTOTYPE; *also* : a perfect example." We believe that these definitions capture very well the notion of a widely accepted or demonstrably superior solution to a recurring problem.

Unfortunately, there is not a ready source of appropriate paradigms. The paradigms sections of the specification and design courses only hint at the kinds of material to be presented. Therefore the SEI Education Program has begun efforts to identify and document paradigms in a variety of important software application domains. We hope to report initial success in this endeavor in our next curriculum report.

4. Future SEI Curriculum Efforts

Several kinds of efforts are planned by the SEI to support graduate software engineering education. Among these are activities to gain experience with the courses recommended in this report, so that they may be improved.

Foremost among these is the teaching of these courses as part of the SEI Video Dissemination Project. Over the next two years all six of these courses will be taught, and the experiences of the instructors and students will be analyzed after each offering. In addition, two academic affiliates of the SEI have been designated *graduate curriculum test sites*. They will teach their own implementations of these courses and report their experiences to us.

A second major effort for us is the identification and documentation of paradigms to support the specification and design courses. We also plan to develop teaching materials to support the six core courses, including case studies, examples, and exercises. Educators interested in contributing to this effort are invited to contact us, for it is through the sharing of information throughout the software engineering education community that we can all benefit the most.

References

[Ardis89]   Ardis, M., and Ford, G. *1989 SEI Report on Graduate Software Engineering Education.* Tech. Rep. CMU/SEI-89-TR-21, Software Engineering Institute, Carnegie Mellon University, Pittsburgh, Pa., June 1989.

[Bloom56]   Bloom, B. *Taxonomy of Educational Objectives: Handbook I: Cognitive Domain.* New York: David McKay, 1956.

[Ford87]   Ford, G., Gibbs, N., and Tomayko, J. *Software Engineering Education: An Interim Report from the Software Engineering Institute.* Tech. Rep. CMU/SEI-87-TR-8, Software Engineering Institute, Carnegie Mellon University, Pittsburgh, Pa., May 1987.

[Gibbs87]   *Software Engineering Education: The Educational Needs of the Software Community.* Norman E. Gibbs; Richard E. Fairley, eds. New York: Springer-Verlag, 1987.

[Webster83]   *Webster's Ninth New Collegiate Dictionary.* Springfield, Mass.: Merriam-Webster Inc., 1983.

Software Systems Engineering

Catalog Description

This course exposes students to the development of software systems at the very highest level. It introduces the system aspect of development and the related trade-offs required when software and hardware are developed together, especially with respect to user interfaces. It exposes students to requirements analysis and techniques to develop a system from those requirements. System integration and transition into use are also covered.

Course Objectives

After completing this course students should comprehend the alternative techniques used to specify and design systems of software and hardware components. They should be able to find the data and create a requirements document, be able to develop a system specification, and understand the concepts of simulation, prototyping and modeling. They should know what is needed to prepare a system for delivery to the user and what makes a system usable.

Prerequisites

Students should have knowledge of software life cycle models, computer architectures, and basic statistics.

Syllabus

Wks	Topics and Subtopics	Objectives
1	Introduction	Knowledge

Students should see the "big picture" in this part of the course. The emphasis should be on how software is only one component of a larger system.

	Overview of topics	
1	System Specification	Comprehension
	Contents	
	Standards	
	Global issues such as safety, reliability	
2	System Design	Comprehension
	Simulation	

    Queuing theory
    Trade-offs
    Methods (levels, object-oriented, function-oriented)

| 3 | Interfaces | Comprehension |

Both human interfaces and interfaces to hardware devices should be included. These areas require different skills, but are logically combined here to emphasize the notion of encapsulation of software within larger systems.

    Human factors
    Guidelines
    Experiments
    Devices

| 1 | System Integration | Comprehension |

Students should learn how to perform integration of entire systems, not just software.

    Simulation of missing components
    System build

| 5 | Requirements Analysis | Synthesis |

This is the largest part of the course. Students should learn the interpersonal skills as well as the technical skills necessary to elicit requirements from users. Expression and analysis of requirements are often performed with CASE tools.

    Objectives
    Interview skills
    Needs and task analysis
    Prototypes
    SADT, RSL (and other specific methods)

| 1 | Operational Requirements | Comprehension |

Students should appreciate and know how to satisfy the other operational requirements of systems, such as training and documentation.

    Training
    On-line help
    User documentation

Relevant SEI Curriculum Modules

CM-6:   Software Safety, *Nancy G. Leveson*
CM-11:   Software Specification: A Framework, *H. Dieter Rombach*
CM-17:   User Interface Development, *Gary Perlman*
CM-19:   Software Requirements, *John W. Brackett*

Pedagogical Concerns

Case studies should be available as assigned readings. A requirements analysis project should be assigned to students, with topics in the lectures sequenced to match the project schedule. A user interface prototype project should be assigned, including an exercise in user documentation. The students should give a presentation on their requirements study. An instructor of this course should have experience in requirements analysis and system design.

Comments

We had a great deal of difficulty naming this course. Much of the work that students will perform as exercises and projects deals with requirements analysis. On the other hand, this course attempts to place software in perspective with other elements of systems. The theme of the course is not just requirements analysis, but total systems engineering. We noted that universities often have courses titled "systems engineering" that cover the same topics from an electrical engineering perspective.

Bibliography

The bibliography for this course is still being developed.

Specification of Software Systems

Catalog Description

Specification occurs at many levels in software engineering. High-level specifications often attempt to capture user requirements, while detailed functional specifications often describe implementation decisions. This course covers several different models of and languages for specification of software systems. The role of documents and standards and the notion of traceability between documents is also covered.

Course Objectives

After completing this course students should be able to write specifications in at least one formal language, analyze specifications for consistency and completeness, trace requirements to parts of functional specifications, and be able to recognize and apply a number of standard paradigms.

Prerequisites

Students should have a working knowledge of set theory, functions and relations, and predicate calculus. They should also have basic knowledge of state machines. A course in discrete mathematics usually satisfies this requirement.

The discussion of the role of specifications presumes some knowledge of the software life cycle. For example, traceability presumes knowledge of requirements, at least at the concept level.

Syllabus

Wks	Topics and Subtopics	Objectives
1	Types of Specification	Comprehension

Non-functional specifications are notoriously hard to describe precisely. It is important that students know about this topic, though the course will emphasize functional specifications.

Functional
Non-functional: performance, reliability, quality, usability, etc.

5.5	Models and Languages of Specification	Synthesis

It is not possible to teach (or even categorize) all of the competing models and languages. Students should be exposed to several different ways of thinking, perhaps four of the models listed below. Only one model and language can be mastered well enough to use in a semester-long project.

Axiomatic [Guttag79], [Guttag80], [Guttag85]

State-machine [Parnas72], [Bartussek78]

Abstract model [Bjørner78], [Bjørner82], [Jones86]

Operational [Zave81], [Zave82]

Concurrency [Hoare78], [Harel87], [Peterson77]

| 5.5 | Paradigms | Application |

For each specification model there are application domains or solutions well-suited to that model. Also, specialization of a language or method to a particular problem class is an important type of knowledge to impart to students. The list of paradigms below is meant to be representative, not exhaustive.

Transformational: refinement of specifications into implementations [Agresti86]

Real-time systems: problems involving the notion of time, concurrency, reliability and performance

Data processing: problems that have "batch" solutions

Expert systems: constraint-based problems

| 2 | Role of Documentation | Comprehension |

Where do specifications fit into the software life cycle? Who are the participants in the writing and reading of specifications? What restrictions are placed on the format of specifications? These are the types of issues that should be addressed in this topic.

Document classes (*e.g.*, the distinction between C-specs and D-specs)

Standards (*e.g.*, Mil Std 2167A)

Traceability to requirements

Relevant SEI Curriculum Modules

CM-8:   Formal Specification of Software, *Alfs Berztiss*
CM-11:   Software Specification: A Framework, *H. Dieter Rombach*
CM-16:   Software Development Using VDM, *Jan Storbank Pedersen*

The overview module by Rombach (CM-11) provides a good framework for concepts and terminology. The modules by Berztiss (CM-8) and Pedersen (CM-16) each cover one formal method in depth.

Pedagogical Concerns

Students should participate in a semester-long project in order to master at least one method and language. Smaller assignments should be given to reinforce understanding of other languages and models. Case studies are an effective means to show practical examples. Since the students will spend a lot of time with at least one language, tool support is important.

In teaching the paradigms topic, good examples are needed. It would be best to interleave the appropriate paradigms with the models and languages most often used. For example, the state-machine and concurrency models could be illustrated with real-time examples.

Comments

Formal specification languages and methods require appropriate motivation within a software engineering curriculum. We felt that the appropriate paradigms should be used to illustrate the formalisms, so that students would appreciate the relative merits of each. Most of the formalisms also require significant investment in technology in order to use them effectively. It is unlikely that students can master several languages and tools within one semester. On the other hand, they need to master at least one technology in order to see its benefits.

Bibliography

Agresti86   Agresti, W. W. "What Are the New Paradigms?." *Tutorial: New Paradigms for Software Development*, William W. Agresti, ed. IEEE Computer Society, 1986.

[Bartussek78]   Bartussek, W., and Parnas, D. L. "Using Assertions About Traces to Write Abstract Specifications for Software Modules." *Proc. of Second Conf. of European Cooperation in Informatics*. 1978.

[Bjørner78]   Bjørner, D. "Programming in the Meta-Language: A Tutorial." *The Vienna Development Method: The Meta-Language*, Dines Bjørner; Cliff B. Jones, eds. New York: Springer-Verlag, 1978, 24-217.

[Bjørner82]   Bjørner, D., and Jones, C. B. *Formal Specification and Software Development*. Englewood Cliffs, N.J.: Prentice-Hall, 1982.

[Guttag79]   Guttag, J. V. "Notes on Type Abstraction." *Proc. SRS Conf..* 1979.

[Guttag80]   Guttag, J. V., and Horning, J. J. "Formal Specification as a Design Tool." *Seventh Symp. Principles of Prog. Lang..* ACM, 1980.

[Guttag85]   Guttag, J. V., Horning, J. J., and Wing, J. M. "The Larch Family of Specification Languages." *IEEE Software 2*, 5 (Sept. 1985), 24-36.

[Harel87]   Harel, D. "Statecharts: A Visual Formalism for Complex Systems." *Science of Computer Programming 8* (1987), 231-274.

[Hoare78]   Hoare, C. A. R. "Communicating Sequential Processes." *Comm. ACM 21*, 8 (Aug. 1978), 666-677.

[Jones86]   Jones, C. B. "Systematic Program Development." *Proc. Symposium on Mathematics and Computer Science.* 1986.

[Parnas72]   Parnas, D. L. "A Technique for Software Module Specification with Examples." *Comm. ACM 15*, 5 (May 1972), 330-336.

[Peterson77]   Peterson, J. L. "Petri Nets." *Computing Surveys 9*, 3 (Sept. 1977), 223-252.

[Zave81]   Zave, P., and Yeh, R. T. "Executable Requirements for Embedded Systems." *Proc. Fifth Intl. Conf. Soft. Eng..* New York: IEEE, 1981, 295-304.

[Zave82]   Zave, P. "An Operational Approach to Requirements Specification for Embedded Systems." *Trans. Soft. Eng. SE-8*, 3 (May 1982), 250-269.

Principles and Applications of Software Design

Catalog Description

Design is a central activity of software development. This course covers several different methods and languages for expressing designs. The process of assessment is also covered.

Course Objectives

After completing this course students should be able to use at least one method to design large systems. They will know how to choose the appropriate method and notation for a problem class, will be able to evaluate designs created by others, and will comprehend several design paradigms.

Prerequisites

Students should have a good working knowledge of programming-in-the-small. Experience in designing small systems is helpful.

Syllabus

Wks	Topics and Subtopics	Objectives
1	Design Principles and Attributes	Comprehension

Students should learn the value of a good design and how to recognize one when they see it.

> Abstraction
> Information hiding
> Modularity
> Cohesion and coupling

5	Design Methods	Evaluation

The pedagogical objective for this topic is to reach the evaluation level for one method, and the comprehension level for the other methods. It is important that students be exposed to several different models, perhaps four out of the following list. At the minimum, students should be exposed to both top-down (decomposition) and bottom-up (composition) methods. Examples of top-down methods are iterative enhancement, SCR, Jackson, and Mills. Examples of bottom-up methods are object-oriented and data abstraction. Since dataflow methods will probably be covered in the Software Systems Engineering course, they do not have to be covered here.

Object-oriented

Data abstraction [Liskov86]

Iterative enhancement [Wirth71], [Dijkstra68]

Dataflow [Yourdon79], [Gane79]

Program design languages (PDLs)

Software Cost Reduction (SCR) [Parnas85]

Jackson (JSP and JSD) [Jackson75], [Jackson83]

Mills [Mills86]

1   Design Verification   Application

Designs should be checked for internal consistency and completeness, and for accuracy in elaborating a functional specification. This is typically done by review.

7   Paradigms   Comprehension

Some design methods work better with particular application domains or problem types. For each method the appropriate examples should be chosen to illustrate the success of that method. Some examples of these paradigms are:

User interfaces

Examples are problems that require the specification and use of windows, icons, devices, or user interface management systems (UIMS).

Real-time

Examples are problems that include timing constraints, concurrency, interrupts, etc.

Distributed systems

Examples are problems that involve reliability, synchronization, and availability of resources.

Embedded systems

Examples are problems that involve interfaces to hardware devices.

Relevant SEI Curriculum Modules

CM-2:   Introduction to Software Design, *David Budgen*
CM-3:   The Software Technical Review Process, *James S. Collofello*
CM-16:   Software Development Using VDM, *Jan Storbank Pedersen*

Modules on concurrent programming and design of real-time systems are presently under development.

Pedagogical Concerns

There is a need to compare specific methods (*e.g.*, Jackson, Yourdon, Mills), without advocating the use of one method for all purposes. Students should work on a semester-long team project using one method, but different teams might use different methods. The results of the projects should be assessed by students. Paradigms should be interspersed with lectures on specific methods. Case studies are an effective means to illustrate paradigms.

Comments

Although many design notations are currently taught in software engineering courses, the creative process of design is often neglected. We were unable to recommend an approach to teach this process, but noted that the instructor's experience and abilities play an important role.

Bibliography

[Dijkstra68]   Dijkstra, E. "The Structure of the THE-Multiprogramming System." *Comm. ACM 11*, 5 (May 1968), 341-346.

[Gane79]   Gane, C., and Sarson, T. *Structured Systems Analysis: Tools and Techniques.* Englewood Cliffs, N.J.: Prentice-Hall, 1979.

[Jackson75]   Jackson, M. *Principles of Program Design.* London: Academic Press, 1975.

[Jackson83]   Jackson, M. *System Development.* Englewood Cliffs, N.J.: Prentice-Hall, 1983.

[Liskov86]   Liskov, B., and Guttag, J. *Abstraction and Specification in Program Development.* New York: McGraw-Hill, 1986.

[Mills86]   Mills, H. D., Linger, R. C., and Hevner, A. R. *Principles of Information Systems Analysis and Design.* Academic Press, 1986.

[Parnas85]   Parnas, D. L., and Weiss, D. M. "Active Design Reviews:
               Principles and Practices." *Proc. 8th Intl. Conf. Soft. Eng..*
               IEEE Computer Society Press, 1985, 132-136.

[Wirth71]   Wirth, N. "Program Development by Stepwise Refinement."
               Comm. ACM 14, 4 (Apr. 1971).

[Yourdon79]   Yourdon, E., and Constantine, L. *Structured Design:
               Fundamentals of a Discipline of Computer Program and
               Systems Design.* Englewood Cliffs, N.J.: Prentice-Hall,
               1979.

Software Generation and Maintenance

Catalog Description

Software generation is the creation or reuse of software. Software maintenance is the revision of existing software. This course describes techniques for performing each of those activities. Topics include alternatives to coding, language concepts, the role of standards and style, the role of tools, performance analysis, regression analysis, and other maintenance-specific subjects.

Course Objectives

After completing this course students should know several alternatives for generating code, be able to identify good coding style and practices, know what features of languages assist or inhibit good coding practices, be able to improve the performance of implemented software, be familiar with tools to help coding and maintenance, and understand the trade-offs in maintaining software from specifications or from code.

Prerequisites

Students taking this course should have created and tested simple programs, and should have seen complex programs.

Syllabus

Wks	Topics and Subtopics	Objectives
6	Implementation	Application

Alternatives to conventional coding

This subtopic is intended to broaden the perspectives of students with respect to implementation strategies. There are several ways to reuse existing code, such as incorporating software packages or parts. Code can be generated through the use of fourth generation languages or compilable specifications. Finally, templates or macros can be used to reduce the cost of reproducing similar fragments of code.

Language concepts/constraints

Students need to understand the consequences of choosing a particular programming language. For example, some languages support software engineering principles (e.g., abstract data types), while others do not. If a language does not support a desired practice, then style or discipline must be used to achieve that practice. Some languages more easily support some design paradigms (e.g., Prolog supports constraint-based designs better than Pascal).

Performance analysis [Bentley82], [Bentley86]

Students should be exposed to a wide spectrum of techniques for measuring and improving the performance of programs.

Standards and style

There are several books on coding style. Coding standards are more difficult to obtain.

8   Maintenance   Comprehension

Maintenance activities [Glass81]

This subtopic provides an overview of maintenance activities. Students should appreciate the differences between maintaining and generating software.

Diagnosing and correcting problems

Introducing new Functionality

Porting to a new Environment

Reducing maintenance costs, modernizing software

Maintaining software engineered artifacts [Martin83], [Clapp81], [Parnas79]

There is a difference between maintaining a system for which the history of development (and associated documentation) is available, and maintaining a program of unknown origin. This topic addresses the former, while the next topic deals with the latter. Part of the effort of maintaining an engineered system includes preserving the structure and integrity of the system.

Life cycle model for maintenance [Boehm88], [Wegner84]

Top-down strategies for introducing change

Preserving design integrity

Code reading [Goldberg87]

Maintaining old code

When the original design is not present, it must be recreated from the code. This process of reverse engineering requires skills of code understanding that are developed in the Software Verification and Validation course.

Life cycle model for maintenance [Lehman84], [Lehman85]
Bottom-up strategies for introducing change
Reverse engineering [Linger79], [Britcher86]
Code restructuring

Code reading

Recording abstractions

Analyzing interfaces/coupling [Wilde87a]

Creating information hiding modules

Reducing coupling

Bottom-up and top-down strategies for design creation
Management of software maintenance [Lientz80], [Grady87]

Maintenance management differs from project management in that maintenance often has different objectives from development. However, there are some issues that are common to both, such as configuration management.

Developing and preserving product data [Freeman87]
Specifications and designs

Change histories

Design rationale

User's guide

Records of costs

Planning release cycles, configuration management
Making Cost Trade-offs
Increasing complexity vs. cestructuring

Evaluating user's cost of change vs. producer's cost of change

Identifying error-prone modules [Gremillion84]

Investing in tools [Shneiderman86]

Quality issues [Collofello87]

This topic overlaps with Software Verification and Validation, but provides a different perspective for the purpose of testing.

Reviews and inspections
Regression testing
Test cases for new function

Productivity issues [Holbrook87], [Wilde87b]

Maintenance-specific tools typically support reverse engineering.

Code restructurers

Code analyzers [Cleveland87], [Ince85]

Data analyzers

Constructors

Relevant SEI Curriculum Modules

CM-3:   The Software Technical Review Process, *James S. Collofello*
CM-4:   Software Configuration Management, *James E. Tomayko*
CM-7:   Assurance of Software Quality, *Bradley J. Brown*
CM-10:   Models of Software Evolution: Life Cycle and Process,
          Walt Scacchi
CM-12:   Software Metrics, *Everald E. Mills*

Pedagogical Concerns

An instructor in this course should have had experience in developing and maintaining significant software. Assignments in this course should involve pre-existing code at least as much as creating new code. Software maintenance assignments should involve working with a significant existing product, changing it according to specified requirements. A code artifact would be useful in this context.

Because of the nature of code reading, software generation assignments may be small and frequent, if desired. Because of the nature of code modification, software maintenance assignments may likely be large and perhaps last for the full length of the maintenance portion of the course.

Comments

Although generation of new code and maintenance of old code are distinctly different activities, the skills required to analyze code are common to both. Also, it is best to discuss the consequences of implementation (maintenance) soon after describing the implementation process (code generation).

There are several competing philosophies about maintenance, how it is best characterized, and how it might best be taught. Three such philosophies are:

- Maintenance is a unique activity requiring special skills.

- Maintenance is not intrinsically different from software development activities, but it has a different set of constraining factors (such as the existence of body of code).

- Maintenance activities should focus on the specification for the software rather than the code, with other activities being derived as in development.

Each implementation of this course is likely to be different from the others because of these philosophical differences. It is to be hoped that significant lessons can be learned from the first few implementations.

Bibliography

[Bentley82]   Bentley, J. L. *Writing Efficient Programs*. Englewood Cliffs, N.J.: Prentice-Hall, 1982.

[Bentley86]   Bentley, J. L. *Programming Pearls*. Reading, Mass.: Addison-Wesley, 1986.

[Boehm88]   Boehm, B. W. "A Spiral Model of Software Development and Enhancement." *Computer 21*, 5 (May 1988), 61-72.

[Britcher86]   Britcher, R. N., and Craig, J. J. "Using Modern Design Practices to Upgrade Aging Software Systems." *IEEE Software 3*, 3 (May 1986), 16-24.

[Clapp81]   Clapp, J. A. "Designing Software for Maintainability." *Computer Design 20*, 9 (Sept. 1981).

[Cleveland87]   Cleveland, L. *An Environment for Understanding Programs*. Tech. Rep. 12880, IBM, 1987.

[Collofello87]   Collofello, J. S., and Buck, J. J. "Software Quality Assurance for Maintenance." *IEEE Software 4*, 5 (Sept. 1987), 46-51.

[Freeman87]   Freeman, P. *Software Perspectives: The System is the Message*. Reading, Mass.: Addison-Wesley, 1987.

[Glass81]   Glass, R., and Noiseux, R. A. *Software Maintenance Guidebook*. Englewood Cliffs, N.J.: Prentice-Hall, 1981.

[Goldberg87]   Goldberg, A. "Programmer as Reader." *IEEE Software 4*, 5 (Sept. 1987), 62-70. Reprinted from *Information Processing 86*, H. J. Kugler, ed., North-Holland, Amsterdam, 1986.

[Grady87]   Grady, R. B. "Measuring and Managing Software Maintenance." *IEEE Software 4*, 5 (Sept. 1987), 35-45.

[Gremillion84]   Gremillion, L. L. "Determinants of Program Repair Maintenance Requirements." *Comm. ACM 27*, 8 (Aug. 1984), 826-832.

[Holbrook87]   Holbrook, H. B., and Thebaut, S. M. *A Survey of Maintenance Tools that Enhance Program Understanding.* Tech. Rep. SERC-TR-9-F, Soft. Eng. Res. Ctr., Purdue Univ.-Univ. of Florida, Sept. 1987.

[Ince85]   Ince, D. C. "A Program Design Language Based Software Maintenance Tool." *Software Practice and Experience 15*, 6 (June 1985).

[Lehman84]   Lehman, M. M. "A Further Model of Coherent Programming Processes." *Proc. Software Process Workshop*, Colin Potts, ed. IEEE Computer Society Press, Feb. 1984, 27-34.

[Lehman85]   Lehman, M. M. *Program Evolution: Processes of Software Change.* London: Academic Press, 1985.

[Lientz80]   Lientz, B. P., and Swanson, E. *Software Maintenance Management.* Reading, Mass.: Addison-Wesley, 1980.

[Linger79]   Linger, R. C., Mills, H. D., and Witt, B. I. *Structured Programming: Theory and Practice.* Reading, Mass.: Addison-Wesley, 1979.

[Martin83]   Martin, J., and McClure, C. *Software Maintenance: The Problem and Its Solutions.* Englewood Cliffs, N.J.: Prentice-Hall, 1983.

[Parnas79]   Parnas, D. L. "Designing Software for Ease of Extension and Contraction." *Trans. Soft. Eng. SE-5*, 2 (Mar. 1979).

[Shneiderman86] Shneiderman, B., Shafer, P., Simon, R., and Weldon, L. "Display Strategies for Program Browsing: Concept and Experiment." *IEEE Software 3*, 3 (May 1986), 7-15.

[Wegner84]   Wegner, P. "Capital-Intensive Software Technology." *IEEE Software 1*, 3 (July 1984), 7-45.

[Wilde87a]   Wilde, N., and Nejmeh, B. *Dependency Analysis: An Aid for Software Maintenance.* Tech. Rep. SERC-TR-13-F, Soft. Eng. Res. Ctr., Purdue Univ.-Univ. of Florida, Sept. 1987.

[Wilde87b]   Wilde, N., and Thebaut, S. M. *The Maintenance Assistant: Work in Progress.* Tech. Rep. SERC-TR-10-F, Soft. Eng. Res. Ctr., Purdue Univ.-Univ. of Florida, Sept. 1987. To be published in *Journal of Systems and Software.*

Software Verification and Validation

Catalog Description

This course addresses the theory and practice of ensuring high-quality software products. Topics covered include quality assessment, proof of correctness, testing, and limitations of verification and validation methods.

Course Objectives

After completing this course students should be able to prepare an effective test plan, analyze a test plan, apply systematic integration testing, prove a module correct, and plan and conduct a technical review.

Prerequisites

A second-semester course in computer science, such as data structures, and a discrete mathematics course.

Syllabus

Wks	Topics and Subtopics	Objectives
0.5	Verification and Validation Limitations	Knowledge

Students should be made aware of the theoretical and practical limitations of testing and program proving. Validation is limited by the informal nature of user requirements.

Review of concepts and terminology [Goodenough75]

0.5	Definition and Assessment of Product Quality	Knowledge

Quality is difficult to define, but users claim that it is easy to recognize. One quantifiable measure is the number of errors reported. Configuration management typically tracks this kind of data, providing a relationship between this course and the Software Project Management course.

Product quality factors
Assessment of product quality

3.5	Proof-of-Correctness Methods	Application

This topic ensures that students are familiar with the latest methods and problems in this area. The skills developed will help students read and analyze code for other purposes, such as maintenance.

> Functional correctness [Mills86]
> Weakest precondition [Dijkstra76]
> Procedures [Hoare71]
> Algebraic [Guttag78]

2.5   Technical Reviews   Analysis

Early reviews have been the most cost-effective means of eliminating errors in software. Students should learn how to plan, conduct and participate in several different forms of reviews (e.g., walkthroughs, inspections).

6   Testing   Comprehension

Although the educational objective for this topic is comprehension, some of the subtopics should achieve higher levels. For example, students should reach the application level for some specific module-level testing methods. (Other methods may only achieve comprehension.) It is important to cover the entire life cycle, especially those methods that apply to entire systems.

> Module-level testing methods (functional, structural, error-oriented, hybrid)
> Integration
> Test plans and documentation
> Transaction flow analysis
> Stress analysis (failure, concurrency, performance)

1   Test Environments   Comprehension

Students should recognize which tasks and aspects of testing are amenable to automation and which require human intervention. The goal should be to automate as many tasks as feasible.

> Tools
> Environments for testing

Relevant SEI Curriculum Modules

CM-3:   The Software Technical Review Process, *James S. Collofello*
CM-7:   Assurance of Software Quality, *Bradley J. Brown*
CM-9:   Unit Testing and Analysis, *Larry J. Morell*

CM-13:   Introduction to Software Verification and Validation,
                  James S. Collofello

Pedagogical Concerns

It is important to convey the applicability of the methods. For example, proof of correctness is currently applicable only to modules, while testing is more suitable for systems.

Comments

It is assumed that students will have seen some proof-of-correctness methods in their undergraduate program. For example, weakest preconditions are often taught in an early programming course. However, most students will need to review these topics in this course.

Bibliography

[Dijkstra76]   Dijkstra, E. *A Discipline of Programming*. Englewood
                      Cliffs, N.J.: Prentice-Hall, 1976.

[Goodenough75] Goodenough, J. B., and Gerhart, S. L. "Toward a Theory of
                      Test Data Selection." *Trans. Soft. Eng. SE-1*, 2 (June 1975).

[Guttag78]   Guttag, J. V., Horowitz, E., and Musser, D. R. "Abstract
                      Data Types and Software Validation." *Comm. ACM 21*, 12
                      (Dec. 1978), 1048-1064.

[Hoare71]   Hoare, C. A. R. "Procedures and Parameters - An
                      Axiomatic Approach." *Symp. Semantics of Algor. Lang.*, E.
                      Engeler, ed. 1971.

[Mills86]   Mills, H. D., Basili, V. R., Gannon, J. D., and Hamlet, R. G.
                      *Principles of Computer Programming, A Mathematical
                      Approach*. Allyn and Bacon, 1986.

Software Project Management

Catalog Description

This course deals with process considerations in software systems development. It provides advanced material in software project planning, monitoring and controlling mechanisms, and leadership and team building.

Course Objectives

After completing this course, students should know how to develop a software project management plan; how to set up monitoring and controlling mechanisms for software projects; how to allocate and reallocate project resources; and how to track schedule, budget, quality, and productivity. In addition, students should understand the relationships among quality assurance, configuration management, and project documentation. They should also gain an understanding of the key issues in motivating workers, leading project teams, intellectual property issues, contracts and licenses, and process assessments.

Prerequisites

There are no specific prerequisites beyond admission to the MSE program.

Syllabus

Wks	Topics and Subtopics	Objectives
4	Introduction	Comprehension

Students need to see the "big picture" of software development. They also need to be motivated to study the problems of management.

Software engineering process
   Process models (waterfall, incremental, spiral, rapid prototype, domain)
   Organizational structures (functional, matrix, individual roles)
Motivational case studies
   Problematical projects (Project Foul, Medinet, *Scientific American*, OS/360, Multics, *Soul of a New Machine*)
   Successful projects (RC2000 (GE), NASA space shuttle, ESS #1, Olympics message system)
   Huge systems (Air traffic control, Strategic Defense Initiative)

Project origins
    Requests for proposals (RFP), statements of work (SOW), contracts, business plans
    System requirements
    Software requirements
Legal issues
    Intellectual property rights
    Contracts
    Licensing
    Liability
    Post-employment agreements

4.5   Planning   Application

Good planning is still considered an art, rather than a science. However, students should learn how to use the best methods available. It is important to stress the importance of tailoring any method to the problem and the environment.

Standards
    External (2167A, 2168, NASA, IEEE)
    Internal (corporate, project)
    Tailoring
Work breakdown
Scheduling
    CPM, PERT, activity networks
    Milestones and work products
Resources
    Acquisition
    Allocation
    Trade-offs
Risk analysis
    Identification
    Assessment
    Contingency planning
Estimates
    Expert judgement (individual, Delphi)
    Size estimates

Models (lines-of-code-driven, function-point-driven, time-sensitive)

4.5   Monitoring and Controlling   Application

Much of this topic deals with issues of product quality. There is an overlap here with material from the Software Verification and Validation course. The subtopic on leadership may be difficult to teach, but its inclusion in the course is important, if only to stimulate awareness of the different kinds of problems found in this area.

Process metrics
    Quality
    Schedule
    Budget
    Productivity
Earned value tracking
Quality assurance
    Technical reviews (walkthroughs, inspections, acceptance testing)
    Planning
Configuration management
    Planning
    Identification
    Change control
    Auditing
    Tools
Risk management
    Tracking
    Crisis management
Leadership, training, and motivation
    Work environment
    Motivation and job satisfaction
    Leadership styles
    Team structures (hierarchical, chief programmer, democratic)
    Productivity assessment
    Performance reviews
    Small group dynamics

1   Project Assessment   Application

Students should assess one another's work. This is one of the best ways to synthesize material from several topics of the course. For example, the combined effects of poor planning and poor control are best seen through post-mortem analysis. Students should be given the opportunity to fail, since they will be unwilling to try novel approaches outside academia.

> In-process
> Final
> Project formation
>> Post-mortems and lessons learned
>> Summary data collection
>> Staff reassignments

Relevant SEI Curriculum Modules

CM-3:	The Software Technical Review Process, *James S. Collofello*
CM-4:	Software Configuration Management, *James E. Tomayko*
CM-7:	Assurance of Software Quality, *Bradley J. Brown*
CM-10:	Models of Software Evolution: Life Cycle and Process, *Walt Scacchi*
CM-12:	Software Metrics, *Everald E. Mills*

A module on software project management is presently under development.

Pedagogical Concerns

A project should be assigned. The project primarily involves planning; no implementation need be done.

It is difficult to provide motivation for many of the topics in this course without experience managing software development projects. Guest lecturers may be especially useful for this.

Many aspects of software maintenance may be considered project management issues. Instructors should coordinate the coverage of these topics between this course and the Software Generation and Maintenance course.

Bibliography

The bibliography for this course is still being developed.

SECTION II

SEI Workshop

on an

Undergraduate Software Engineering Curriculum

Programming and Its Relation to
Computer Science Education and Software Engineering Education

Lionel E. Deimel
Software Engineering Institute
Carnegie Mellon University
Pittsburgh, PA 15213

It seems odd that the educational communities of both computer science and software engineering pay scant attention to programming. (I do not wish to quibble over the definition of "programming." The reader may substitute "programming-in-the-small.") In undergraduate computer science curricula, although majors are usually introduced to the field through programming courses, teachers often go out of their way to say that computer science is *more* than programming. And although introductory programming courses have frequently served as filters for computer science majors—who continue to program during their entire undergraduate careers—programming is seldom the object of study after the freshman year.

One might expect that software engineering education would treat programming with more respect, but this seems not to be the case. For example, the curriculum recommendations made by the Software Engineering Institute (SEI) for a professional master's degree (its MSE curriculum) emphasize design, maintenance, project management, etc., apparently under the assumption that entering students already know whatever they need to know about programming. Software engineering also, it seems, is more than programming.

What is going on here? Is programming a trade-school skill that colleges and universities should not even be teaching? What is the nature of programming and how does it relate to computer science and software engineering?

Quite rightly, computer science has asserted that it is *not* merely the study of programming. For both intellectual and political reasons, computer science has emphasized the study of algorithms and models of computation. Its proper role is to build theories; programming is only an ancillary concern. The agenda of computer science may be influenced by physical machines and the installed software base, but the discipline is more akin to mathematics than physics, and it has only the vaguest resemblance to engineering. Its highest ideals are truth and elegance.

Software engineering, on the other hand, is properly an engineering discipline. Its realm

This work was sponsored by the U.S. Department of Defense.

is the application of computer science knowledge and engineering methods to the production of useful software artifacts. Programming is essential to software engineering—it is more central than it is to computer science—though it is but a part of it. Software engineering is driven by the idiosyncrasies of reality, much as is mechanical or civil engineering. Whereas computer science is concerned with mathematical objects, software engineering must deal with human problems and social organizations. Its highest ideal is the fulfillment of human needs.

The software engineering literature largely ignores programming or downplays its importance. Partly, this is so because coding, that most conspicuous marker of programming activity, is known to consume but a small fraction of the effort expended on any software product. Yet programming, however construed and however measured, continues to be done badly. If the skill is so straightforward and well-understood, why cannot programmers get their programs right the first time, without having to devote such extraordinary efforts to debugging and testing? Why is code often inscrutable to other programmers? Why is internal documentation often omitted, worthless, or—which is worse than worthless—misleading? The unreadability of code has devastating implications for its maintenance, and the unreliability of software seems as often the result of local errors as global ones. If software engineering seeks to improve software development and maintenance processes, therefore, it should not overlook the benefits of improved programming performance. The legendary productivity differences among programmers suggest there is opportunity for improvement; consideration of the effect of code quality on verification and maintenance effort suggest there may be significant opportunity for improvement over the entire life cycle. The software engineer should be concerned with this potential and must be knowledgeable about programming to achieve it. Even if he does not program, the software engineer must be able to assess code quality and must understand constraints imposed by implementation languages.

A major reason improved programming performance has not become a priority of software engineering hinges on the question of who is a programmer, who is a software engineer, and what each one does. The term "software engineer" is currently popular and prestigious, of course, and the term "programmer" is passé. (It is reported that some companies have, by fiat, converted all programmers into software engineers. Such a move sidesteps an important question!) The obvious distinction to be made is that the programmer is concerned with programming-in-the-small and the software engineer with programming-in-the-large. In an effort to increase respect for software engineering, many have tried to distance the software engineer from the activities of "mere" programmers and to elevate his position. Are there properly two professions here, or is there a need for a class of professionals (software engineers) and a class of technicians (programmers)? The engineer/technician distinction may seem attractive, based on the models of other disciplines, but, at least for now, this seems the wrong choice. The consequences of poor programming are expensive, and therefore programming needs to be done well and needs to be monitored by someone who understands what doing it well means. We do not know enough about production of large software products that we can afford not to have well-trained, intelligent programmers producing the lowest-level program specification and feeding back observations to designers. Furthermore, despite numerous predictions that the programmer's job will disappear, this has not happened. However much computers take over the code-production process, some human is required to perform the penultimate step. By convention, this person is a programmer. (One can dispute this statement, but it is difficult to imagine a world in which the programmer is not needed, at least for software designed for totally new applications.) Thus, we need both programmers and software engineers, and both should understand programming well.

There are important consequences of these observations for the education of computer professionals. Computer science education is probably justified in paying little attention to programming, at least insofar as its goal is to produce computer scientists. (This view assigns to software engineering the study of programming, *per se*.) The reality, however, is that most computer science graduates do not become computer scientists, any more than most physics graduates become physicists. Physics majors realize their study is aimed at theoretical understanding, rather than broadly marketable competence, whereas computer science majors do not. Computer science graduates, by and large, become programmers and software engineers, exactly what they intended to become in declaring themselves to be computer science majors in the first place. These students, even as computer science majors, would clearly benefit from curricula that were more forthcoming about the very existence of software engineering and about its relation to computer science. More attention paid to programming and a few lectures on the organizational environment in which it conventionally takes place would serve both fields well and have no adverse effect on the achievement of the legitimate goals of computer science departments. In fact, increasing student programming skill early in the computer science curriculum would likely facilitate learning of related material that is conventionally taught with the aid of programming exercises.

The position of programming in software engineering education is more problematic. The decision not to spend much time on programming seems a pragmatic compromise for an MSE program. After all, incoming students *can* be assumed to have some minimal programming skills, whereas they are probably not at all competent in other areas recommended by the SEI curriculum. Time is very limited in a master's-level program and compromises are unavoidable. But if programmer education is important, yet is destined to be slighted by computer science curricula generally and by graduate-level software engineering programs as well, the only place it can receive the attention it deserves is in an undergraduate software engineering curriculum. Here is the place where we can have the luxury of enough time to really get programmer education "right." We can emphasize documentation, formal techniques, style (especially through technical reviews), and debugging and testing skills. Along with programming topics, the undergraduate curriculum must teach a lot of computer science, the standard software engineering topics (design, project management, etc.), as well as communication skills, ethics, and perhaps such topics as small-group dynamics and organizational behavior.

These considerations, I believe, strongly support the idea of establishing undergraduate curricula in software engineering. The computer science/software engineering relationship is a traditional science/engineering relationship. Neither field is a subset of the other; neither discipline is properly subsumed by the other. To be sure, the content of what is now called software engineering is volatile. There is, however, especially for undergraduates, some body of principles and knowledge underlying software engineering that can be expected to be more enduring. This material is largely from computer science and the social sciences. But there is also programming, properly the concern of software engineering and an activity that can play a major role in improving software quality, that deserves to be taught more effectively to the next generation of practitioners and which is likely to be so taught nowhere else but in an undergraduate software engineering program. If for no other reason than to advance the art of programming, the initiation of undergraduate software engineering curricula should be encouraged.

Software Engineering is *Not* Computer Science

Charles B. Engle, Jr.
Software Engineering Institute
Carnegie Mellon University
Pittsburgh, PA 15213

Abstract: One of the many confusing issues in today's software world is the use of many names that describe different aspects of the software sciences, but which have widely overlapping activities. One such area is the distinction between computer science and software engineering. Undergraduate programs to teach software sciences should decide upon an area in which to concentrate, either computer science or software engineering. The distinction is more than semantics; there are practical differences in the philosophy of each of these subjects. Computer science, though beyond its infancy, is still a dynamic area, but is suitable for undergraduate curricula due to the body of knowledge which exists to support it. Software engineering, in contrast, is still in its infancy and is not yet well enough understood to warrant a separate undergraduate curriculum.

Introduction

Since the late 1960's an understanding has been developing that software for large systems must be developed in a fundamentally different manner than software for small systems. The so-called programming-in-the-large projects require teams of programmers, communicating with system designers under the control and direction of a program manager. The issues of management, coordination of effort, documentation of requirements, specifications, designs, etc., life-cycle implications of decisions, and other related items are critically important in the production of a large software project. Programming-in-the-small is more concerned with the coding aspects of the project, which, while important for a programming-in-the-large project, are not the overriding concern. Thus, a distinction has developed between the means and methods for programming-in-the-large and those employed for programming-in-the-small. This, then, is a simplistic description of the difference between software engineering and computer science.

This work was sponsored by the U.S. Department of Defense.

Definition of Terms

Programmer. This is the term for someone that writes computer programs. This is a technician job and does not really require more than a knowledge of the language syntax and some simple understanding of the canonical algorithms needed to produce results in well defined circumstances. The level of education required is on the order of a community college degree in programming, usually with a specialization in a certain language.

Computer Scientist. This is the term for someone that studies the science of computing, especially the theory of computing and its ancillary topics. This person is concerned with algorithm generation, and finding more efficient, more effective means of computation. The level of education is up to a Ph.D.

Software Engineer. This is the term for a person concerned with the development of a large scale software project. It includes an understanding of the life cycle issues involved in software generation. A software engineer applies the principles and concepts created by the computer scientist to real world projects. The software engineer is more concerned with the pragmatics of developing, using and maintaining large software projects than with computing theory; he or she is more "production oriented." The level of education is again up to the Ph.D., although often a software engineer is a computer scientist with perhaps a Master of Science degree and years of experience in the development of commercial software; education by practical experience.

Software Project Manager. This is the term for a person that manages a large software development effort. This person must be familiar with the ideas and fundamentals of all of the previous three areas, but he or she must be especially strong in the management of people. Developing a large software project requires teamwork and extraordinary leadership. Thus, the software project manager must be adept at influencing people to accomplish their assigned tasks. He or she must also be well versed in risk identification and reduction, especially as it applies to software development.

Software Engineering versus Computer Science

Similarities. Some of the confusion in the use of these terms comes from the fact that the areas of responsibility of each overlap to some degree. They both deal with computers. They both deal with software to support those computers. They both need to understand the fundamentals of systems, including hardware and software. They both need a level of sophistication which separates a profession from a trade.

Differences. However, there are several differences between the two terms. A computer scientist is interested in the theory or science of computing. The software engineer is interested in the application of the science to solve a real world problem. (This analogy is somewhat akin to the difference between a chemist and a chemical engineer. One is a scientist, concerned with knowledge acquisition and creation, the other is an engineer concerned with the application of the science to solve real world problems.) The computer scientist is a theorist; the software engineer generally is a pragmatist. The computer scientist is concerned with how things ought to be; the software engineer is concerned with applying the theory to how things are. The computer scientist is concerned with design aesthetics and has little concern for performance or efficiency, except in the academic sense. The Turing machine, computability, NP-complete world of the computer scientist is in contrast to the methodology, documentation, requirements and specifications world of the software engineer.

Software Engineering Undergraduate Curriculum

Requirements. A software engineering undergraduate curriculum requires that we understand the discipline of engineering. The American Heritage dictionary defines engineering as "the application of scientific and mathematical principles to practical ends such as the design, construction, and operation of efficient and economical structures, equipment, and systems." In using the term engineering in connection with the development of software systems, are we deliberately taking liberty with the term or do we really propose that software can be built using "scientific and mathematical principles?"

A curriculum for software engineering would *necessarily* have some, possibly large, overlap with the present computer science curriculum. Certain concepts and principles underlying software systems must be taught to *both* sets of students. Examples of these topics might include analysis of algorithms, data structures, fundamentals of operating systems, fundamentals of compilers, computer architecture, networks, numerical analysis, comparative languages, etc. The level of depth in each of the areas mentioned would, probably, be different for each type of student; in addition, a computer science student may well need a second course in some of these areas.

A curriculum for software engineering must have certain knowledge units which would either not be found in a computer science curriculum or which would be secondary concerns. Notably, a software engineering curriculum must stress life-cycle concerns. It must impart to the student an appreciation of the tradeoffs which are necessary in building real-world systems. This means that in addition to coding concerns, attention must be paid to the more important issues such as requirements definition and analysis, creation of specifications from requirements, designing from specifications, design methodologies, documentation, engineering tradeoffs, performance analysis, embedded testing, verification and validation, and the general issue of software maintenance. Also, the use of tools and environments should be addressed, as well as an understanding of available metrics, configuration management, and quality assurance.

There is also a need for the software engineer to be educated in communication and management skills. These are skills which are vital to the success of a software engineer and as such they cannot be left to be learned by "osmosis." The conduct of a design review, besides its obvious technical requirements, is rooted in "people" skills. Thus, these skills are necessary survival skills for a software engineer.

Finally, like any other engineering profession there is the whole question of professional ethics and values. Since the software engineer is more likely to sell his or her services to commercial concerns and since lives and property are dependent upon the products of those services, ethical behavior and values would probably be an issue more likely to find a place in a software engineering curriculum than in computer science.

Realities. The reality is that we do not yet know enough about what it is that software engineers do to treat it as an engineering discipline. I think that, in general, we have "ideas" or "feelings" about what is meant by the term "software engineer", but we cannot seem to arrive at a consensus as to exactly what the definition of this term ought to be. Until software economics can accurately (*i.e.*, within an order of magnitude!) predict costs or schedules for projects, or until there are sufficient useful tools to apply to the software process, we cannot call this profession an engineering discipline. Similarly, until we understand enough about the whole process of software development, or until the profession is self-governing with a standard, enforceable code of ethics, we should not call this profession an engineering discipline.

Therefore, curricula must address those items enumerated above in a subjective manner. Since we do not yet know how to develop large software projects in a repeatable, consistent manner and since we do not yet have enough experiential base to propose principles for the development of software, we are not in a position to teach this material at the undergraduate level in an objective manner. The available material is, however, suitable for discussion in seminar style classes, such as those typically found on the graduate level. This is possible because the students, having completed undergraduate training as computer scientists, have already studied the fundamentals of the science of computing and are in a position to discuss and synthesize ideas about large-scale software development.

As we gain experience in developing large software systems, we will learn certain *concepts* which seem to work. Over time these concepts will solidify into *principles* which guide future development projects. With even more experience, these principles can be worked into *models* which assist in making our development process repeatable and form the basis for metrics. Once models are iteratively developed in which there is a degree of confidence, we can develop *methodologies* which support the models. That, in turn, leads to the development of *tools* which can be created to assist in supporting the methodologies. Finally, these tools can be integrated into *environments*. But this process takes time and we have not yet had enough experience in developing such systems to be beyond the level of isolating a few principles upon which there can be general consensus.

Note that this view argues that the issues of which methodologies to use and which tools to use at this time are specious arguments. The foundations upon which those ideas are built are not yet in place! Perhaps that is why there are so few repeatable software development processes.

Another view of this approach is that when we can establish certain industry-wide *practices* upon which some consensus can be reached, these practices can evolve into *guidelines*. When the volatility of these guidelines reaches some equilibrium, amounting to general agreement, then we can establish *standards* upon which to base decisions, contracts, etc. Without this evolutionary approach, standards are less than meaningful.

In short, the realities of the situation are that we have not yet had the time or the experience to develop the level of understanding in software development on a large scale to meaningfully provide an undergraduate curriculum in this area.

However, this does *not* mean that we have nothing to offer to undergraduates interested in large scale software development. As we learn more about this area, the things that we establish as important, perhaps on the way to becoming the principles discussed above, need to be provided to the undergraduate student. This can be done by integrating this information into the present computer science curricula. When the body of knowledge becomes large enough to warrant a separate curriculum, then, and only then, should an undergraduate software engineering degree program be offered.

A decision not to support an undergraduate software engineering program at this time is not irrevocable. This issue deserves to be re-raised periodically to determine if the body of knowledge has developed to the point that warrants a separate curriculum.

Summary

The creation of an undergraduate software engineering curriculum is a desirable goal that needs to be pursued further and periodically reviewed. However, we do not yet have the necessary understanding of the discipline to be able to create a meaningful undergraduate program. We must, instead, inject the current computer science curricula with some of the ideas and principles of software engineering, such as we can identify them, so as to sow the seeds for the future development of an undergraduate software engineering curriculum.

Acknowledgments

The terms which are defined at the beginning of this paper are based upon a minor extension to distinct terms suggested by David Lamb. The definitions, however, are mine and cannot be blamed on David.

The ideas in the section on **Realities** are adapted from some ideas suggested by Charles McKay. In fact, this is an rather minor elaboration of the definition of software engineering which Dr. McKay uses in numerous talks.

Anticipating the Evolution of
Undergraduate Software Engineering Curricula[1]

Gary Ford
Software Engineering Institute
Carnegie Mellon University

Abstract: Some thoughts on initial development of undergraduate software engineering degree programs are presented. Included are trends in computer science curricula, the importance of clearly defined educational objectives, and the pragmatics of the evolution of new programs.

It seems inevitable that software engineering will evolve into a discipline distinct from computer science, and that both disciplines will have both undergraduate and graduate degree programs in universities. Because the Software Engineering Institute (SEI) charter includes the statement "It shall also influence software engineering curricula development throughout the education community," it is appropriate for us to begin examining the development of such an undergraduate curriculum.

At this early stage, I do not propose beginning to define the courses that should make up the curriculum. I believe it is essential to look at some contextual issues first. Among these are:

- Trends in computer science curricula: is software engineering being served?

- Educational objectives for undergraduate science and engineering programs in the 21st century.

- Pragmatic aspects of the development of new curricula within computer science departments.

---

[1]This work was sponsored by the US Department of Defense.

Trends in Computer Science Curricula

The most visible evidence of the trends in undergraduate computer science curricula are the recent report on the core of computer science[1] and the partial draft report of the ACM/IEEE-CS task force (not yet published). To its credit, the task force is undertaking to define the core of material that is common to all undergraduate programs in *computing* (the word used in the report to avoid trying to distinguish computer science, computer engineering, and other related program or department names). The premise is that many different kinds of curricula can build from this core.

Unfortunately, the task force report does not do a good job of identifying educational objectives for such curricula. In particular, it does not seem to acknowledge that giving students the ability to build large complex software systems is a legitimate goal of education. Neither does it acknowledge that the skills needed to build those systems do not necessarily depend on the skills needed to build small personal or academic computer programs. I believe that this means that computer science programs are not likely to produce graduates with significant software engineering skills in the near future.

The two reports divide computing into nine subject areas, whose names resemble the names of the upper division courses in current computer science programs. The descriptions of the subject areas include many of the same topics that we have been teaching for the past twenty years. Thus, my reading of the task force report gives me the impression that most computing curricula will be seen as already meeting the new recommendations, and thus there will not be an incentive to attempt to improve them. This is unfortunate, but it is a clear signal that those of us interested in the development of undergraduate software engineering programs must work very hard to explain what the new programs should be, why they are needed, and how they can be created.

Educational Objectives

A significant early step in the development of a curriculum is to identify its educational objectives. The objectives can be treated as a requirements specification, and they can be elaborated at many levels: whole curriculum, individual courses, topics within courses.

The major differences between a course in a computer science curriculum and a comparable course in a software engineering curriculum can often be found in the objectives. In computer science, that objective may be a deep under-

---

[1]Denning, Peter J., et al. "Computing as a Discipline." *Comm. ACM 32*, 1 (Jan. 1989), 9-23.

standing of a particular theory or algorithm, while in software engineering it may be the ability to apply that theory or use that algorithm in a real system.

Such differences exist in other fields as well. I remember studying differential equations as a freshman mathematics major and comparing my course with the course being taken by my friends who were electrical engineering majors. My course spent the majority of the semester proving existence and uniqueness theorems, while theirs taught them how to identify the differential equations in real problems and then how to solve them. It is easy to imagine similarly distinctive computer science and software engineering versions of courses in areas such as theory of computation, analysis of algorithms, or artificial intelligence.

Another aspect of educational objectives is related to the needs of an increasingly complex and technological society and of the individuals in that society. Undergraduate education must prepare individuals to function in society, to continue to acquire knowledge, and to use that knowledge in appropriate ways.

Therefore I believe it is important for those of us interested in an undergraduate software engineering curriculum to begin to develop clear educational objectives. We must consider not only the content and emphasis of the technical content of the curriculum, but also the global aspects of the role of education in our society.

Pragmatic Aspects

It is clear that even if an outstanding software engineering curriculum were published today, it would be quite a while before a large number of schools offered it. The enormous inertia of our higher education system does not permit rapid change. Therefore we should also consider appropriate mechanisms for the gradual evolution of software engineering programs within existing computer science departments.

Resources of all kinds are needed to bring new programs into being. Foremost among these are faculty and teaching materials. Both take time and money to develop.

Recent publicity about the relatively poor performance of United States students (at all levels) in the sciences has caused the National Science Foundation and other organizations to increase their support for the advancement of science education. The statement about education in the SEI charter (quoted above) shows an interest on the part of the Department of Defense in improved education. Therefore there is room for guarded optimism that some money can be found to support the development of undergraduate software engineering programs.

The other ingredient, time, is not under our direct control. However, to make effective use of time, we must begin as soon as possible a coordinated effort among all of us interested in undergraduate software engineering programs. This workshop is an example of that effort. The more frequently we put before the educational community cogent reasons for software engineering education and clear statements of its differences from compute science education, the sooner new programs will develop.

I hope that new programs will grow within existing departments, first by the inclusion of one or two senior-level courses in software engineering, then a large selection of upper division courses with existing lower division computer science as prerequisites, and finally entire programs.

There is the possibility, however, of more revolutionary growth. I have heard that at least two universities are developing formal proposals to their governing bodies for undergraduate software engineering degree programs. These will almost certainly include many existing computer science courses, but if they come into being, they might well serve as laboratories for many new courses, topics, and educational materials.

A Separate Undergraduate Software Engineering Curriculum Considered Harmful

Frank L. Friedman
Temple University

Increased Specialization is not the Answer

A Separate Undergraduate Software Engineering Curriculum Considered Harmful. Perhaps this is too strong a statement, one that is destined to be as misunderstood as the similar but more eloquently defended statements of Dijkstra [1] and Shaw [2]. It is also possibly a somewhat premature judgement since I have not yet seen any formal proposals on the content of such a curriculum. I therefore may misunderstand the intent of this goal. Nonetheless, the use of the term separate requires a response, regardless of the hazards.

I propose the following as arguments in defense of this thesis.

(1) In the science, math, and engineering disciplines, we have become obsessed with technical content. As a result, there is little time for a student to study and participate in meaningful discourse in other areas such as the foreign languages and cultures, social sciences and humanities even as these areas might directly relate to the student's studies in science or engineering.

We are graduating woefully under-educated students. If we are lucky, they are highly specialized; if we are less fortunate, they are rather functionally illiterate even in the major, often unable to even begin to fathom the environments of the practicing community. [People from industry (and elsewhere) have complained loudly, and in some cases even gone so far as to say that they will not hire computing science graduates because they do not have sufficient communications skills and in general have no better concept of the field than non-majors).] Adding another curricular specialty in any of these fields cannot help but aggravate this situation.

(2) This is no less the case within computing science. One need only examine recent information on CSAB accreditation requirements for computing science programs [3]. While these are admittedly flexible and open to considerable interpretation, they seem to indicate a total of between 54-60 credits of study, half in related (math/science) areas and half in computer science per se, for each student in an accredited program. This is simply too large a part of a typical 120 credit study program.

Many of our students are already suffering from over exposure to too many (often unrelated) areas of study – one course in graphics, one in AI; another in data bases and one in languages; yet another in computability and automata and one more in natural language processing (or networking and communications, distributed computing, information systems, parallel computation, etc.). The subareas of our discipline have proliferated, and the view is not a pretty one – it lacks coherency and has too many requirements in the major and related technical areas.

Aside from the rather minimal requirements of most universities, there is little emphasis within computing curricula on reading, writing, or oral communication. There is virtually no concern for professsionalism or the whole person, able to interact technically and socially, aware of his or her strengths and weaknesses and possible career paths. There is little interest shown concerning the social impact of computing, ethics, security, or the historical or economic dimensions of the field. And, I will admit, there is precious little in the way of relevant topics concerning the life cycle of computer software systems.

The emphasis has instead been on covering each and every area of technical endeavor that materializes. The rest is buried under an avalanche of new topics. In many cases, unfortunately, the "rest" includes, among other things, the study of how we build software systems. There are a variety of reasons for this, including the excuse that "system design can't be taught", or, there is no place in the undergraduate curriculum for software life-cycle technology, or "we already know how to do this – we have been doing it for years – what's there to teach"?

(3) As the areas of study in computing have proliferated, computing science faculty (and practitionner's, too, for that matter) have become highly specialized. Unless one or more of the issues of life-cycle technology happens to intersect their particular area of research interest, their work leaves little time for an investment in this area. They are not particularly interested in life-cycle issues, and will not devote much attention to them in the curricular environment that currently exists in many colleges and universities.

Some would say that our discipline has matured, and that it "is now possible to describe its intellectual substance in a new and compelling way" [4]. These computing scientists clearly have a vision of this intellectual whole and have described this vision in writing. Yet the more specialized we become the more difficult it is to identify this intellectual whole; any sense of coherency in the discipline is well hidden behind the mask of specialization.

What Might We Do Instead?

At the undergraduate level, a separate software engineering curriculum will only serve to exacerbate the proliferation problem, making it even more difficult for us to focus on the central issue: how do we provide undergraduate computer science majors with a balanced, coherent view of the field, with sufficient practice in the basic processes of theory, abstraction, and design (see [4]) as well as intensive laboratory and field experience.

Any curriculum designed to meet this goal will necessarily incorporate a subarea concerned with software engineering and methodologies It is equally as certain that such a curriculum must, from the very first course, incorporate basic methodological and engineering concepts such as those encouraging procedural/data abstraction and hierarchical design, and promoting at least an awareness of issues of correctness and style (to address these issues at any later stage in the curriculum is simply too late, as reform is virtually impossible [see 5 and 6]).

As the student progresses through the curriculum building larger and more complex systems, the basic concepts must be revisited and expanded, always as an integral part of the course work, at least in the laboratory component, involving the process of design.

SEI's Role

I strongly suggest that the time for specialization is at the Masters and Ph. D. level, not the undergraduate level. SEI should continue to direct its energies toward the development of software engineering Master's or Ph. D. options (or programs), but not toward the building of similar specialties at the undergraduate level. Where there are fundamental software engineering concepts and principles appropriate to the undergraduate curriculum, they should be identified and proposals made for integrating this material into existing, or better yet, substantially revised undergraduate curricula (but not to the extent of creating separate undergraduate programs or curricula in software engineering).

Thus, I would propose that if SEI is to become involved in the undergraduate curriculum arena (and I believe it should), it must take a more global view of computer science, especially as it relates to undergraduate instruction. In coordination with other agencies, foundations, and computing societies already involved in this arena, SEI should play a leading role in providing support and technical direction for the following activities:

- a substantial revision of the computer science curriculum based upon a balanced, coherent view of the discipline, and including
  - an area devoted to software methods and engineering concepts,
  - a detailed commentary and supporting materials encouraging the fullest possible integration of software methods into other subareas of the new curricula (including a wide variety of sample problems and solutions that reflect the application of new software engineering tools and techniques);
- the upgrade of the skills of computer science faculty;
- the creation and/or upgrade of laboratory facilities and instructional materials to support the new curriculum;

- the creation and distribution of automated tools that will encourage the application of good software engineering methods and techniques even at the earliest stages of the study of computing.

These suggestions are not new; several of them are in fact incorporated in other reports (see [4] and [7] for example). To the extent possible within its charter, SEI should endeavor to become a full participant in these activities.

Finally, as the NSF report [7] suggests, there is a wide range of students seeking a computer science degree and (later) working in the field. Any curriculum development effort that fails to acknowledge this reality or fails to effectively address the needs of the employers and employees who practice computing (in addition to those who do research in computing) will itself fail to be acknowledged by the community it most needs to serve.

BIBLIOGRAPHY

[1] Dijkstra, E., "GOTO Statement Considered Harmful," CACM (11,3), March, 1968 (one page letter to the editor).

[2] Shaw, M. and Wulf, W., "Global variables Considered Harmful," ACM SIGPLAN Notices (8,2), February, 1973, pp. 28-34.

[3] CSAB, Criteria for Accrediting Computer Science Programs in the United States, Computing Sciences Accreditation Board, 345 E. 47th St., NY, NY, 10017, January, 1987.

[4] Denning, P., et. al., "Computing as a Discipline", CACM (32,1), January, 1989, pp. 9-23.

[5] Gibbs, N. and Tucker, A., "Model Curriculum for a Liberal Arts Degree in Computer Science," (A report from workshops sponsored by the Alfred P. Sloan Foundation) 1985.

[6] Friedman, F., "A Methodology (with Examples) for Introducing Structured Design Concepts in the Early Stages of a CIS Curriculum ", Temple University Division of Computer and Information Sciences, internal document CIS-TR 84-4, September, 1984.

[7] Foley, J., Standish, T., et. al., Undergraduate Computer Science Education, NSF Workshop Report (Grant CCR-8811841), March, 1988.

Is the Time Right for an Undergraduate Software Engineering Degree?

Norman E. Gibbs
Carnegie Mellon University
Software Engineering Institute
Pittsburgh, PA 15213

The following definitions of the terms software, software engineering and software engineer were provided by Watts Humphrey, Director, SEI Process Program in [4]:

- **Software** refers to a program and all of its associated information and materials that are needed to support its installation, operation, repair, and enhancement.

- **Software Engineering** refers to the disciplined application of engineering, scientific, and mathematical principles and methods for the economical production of quality software.

- A **Software Engineer** is someone with the necessary skills, experience, and discipline to practice Software Engineering.

Unfortunately, a large number of people equate *software engineering* with *programming* and argue that software engineering is simply that part of computer science concerned with programming-in-the-large. It is clear that traditional ways of teaching undergraduates give students the impression that writing a program is an individual virtuoso performance where the product can later be discarded as "throw-away". This is due in part to the fact that professors issue grades based on individual performance and that the academic community tends to build software systems to demonstrate "proof-of-concept"—not products.

Professional software developers are concerned with building products that are generally delivered in multiple releases and take on a lifetime of decades. Fred Brooks notes: [[3], page 5], "As an engineering discipline, it [engineering] is

---

This work was sponsored by the U.S. Department of Defense.

concerned with quality, effectiveness, cost and schedule—concepts that, if not alien, are at least of little concern to the underlying science."

Since the late 1960's, Computer science majors have been much valued and sought after by the practitioner community. Practitioner friends tell me that these graduates bring new ideas, techniques and technologies into established organizations. On the other hand, the practitioner community has been trying to tell the academic community since the early 1970's that their needs are not for more "compiler writers," but professionals who are capable of developing software under practical constraints. These constraints include: working as a member of a team, completing projects on time and within budget, and producing software products that are usable, reliable and safe within an application domain. Software engineers build on and apply the body of knowledge known as computer science; they must be facile at programming-in-the-small. They also need to be educated in many of the following areas: software development processes, software project management, requirements analysis, technical communication, configuration management, quality assurance, formality, performance analysis, metrics, standards, verification and validation, testing, and human factors. Students need to know that acquiring specialized domain knowledge such as library or air traffic control systems will be required and expected after they start to work in industry.

I have been told that it takes a lot less time and corporate energy to turn undergraduate engineering graduates into productive entry-level engineers than it does to turn undergraduate computer scientists into productive contributors to software development projects. Over the past three years, the SEI Education Program has been repeatedly asked for recommended undergraduate software engineering degree requirements. We have argued that the best education for a software developer is a solid major in computer science followed by graduate professional education such as an MSE [2] (master of software engineering) program. The recent report of the ACM Task Force on the Core of Computer Science by Denning et. al. [1] states that there is a core of computer science knowledge that everyone ought to know before specializing. This report is the best attempt I have seen to put computer science on equal footing with the natural sciences by recommending that we initially teach an overview of the field and then reserve in-depth treatments of advanced topics for the upper level courses. Further, the report discusses three paradigms or cultural styles for viewing the topics in the field based on theory (what mathematicians do), abstraction (what natural scientists do), and design (what engineers do). The committee concludes that computer scientists tend to favor theory and abstraction over design while computer engineers tend to emphasize abstraction and design over theory.

The time may be right to consider building an undergraduate software engineering degree program that emphasizes design over abstraction and theory. The core of computer science can be augmented with four software engineering courses (one taken each semester in the junior and senior year). These courses would prepare students to enter industry with the skills, techniques, and knowledge necessary to work in large development teams and produce products delivered in multiple releases that have a lifetime of decades. In addition, four in-depth courses in computer science should also be required in the junior and senior years.

A Model Curriculum

	Fall	**Spring**
Freshman	Core Computer Science 1 Mathematics 1	Core Computer Science 2 Mathematics 2
Sophomore	Core Computer Science 3 Mathematics 3	Core Computer Science 4 Mathematics 4
Junior	Software Engineering 1 Computer Science 1	Software Engineering 2 Computer Science 2
Senior	Software Engineering 3 Computer Science 3	Software Engineering 4 Computer Science 4

If undergraduate software engineering programs develop, the resources will probably be taken from computer science programs just as computer science departments finally have enough staff to adequately cover their own teaching and research. On the other hand, faculty may not have the knowledge or experience necessary to teach software engineering topics. This, coupled with a strong push from industry for graduates, may result in unfortunate and premature fragmentation of the field of computer science.

References

1. Denning, Peter J., Comer, Douglas E., Gries, David, Mulder, Michael C., Tucker, Allen, Turner, A. Joe, and Young, Paul R. "Computing as a Discipline". *Communications of the ACM 32*, 1 (January 1989), 9–23.

2. Ford, Gary A., Gibbs, Norman E., and Tomayko, James E. Software Engineering Education: An Interim Report from the Software Engineering Institute. Tech. Rept. CMU/SEI-87-TR-8, Software Engineering Institute, Carnegie Mellon University, May, 1987. ESD-TR-87-109.

3. Gibbs, Norman E., and Fairley, Richard E. (editors). *Software Engineering Education: The Educational Needs of the Software Community*. Springer-Verlag, New York, 1987.

4. Humphrey, Watts S. The Software Engineering Process: Definition and Scope. Proceedings of the 4th International Process Workshop, Devon, England May 11–13, 1988, Washington, D. C., In Press, 1989.

SOFTWARE ENGINEERING AS PART OF AN UNDERGRADUATE COMPUTER SCIENCE PROGRAM

Lawrence G. Jones
William E. Richardson
United States Air Force Academy
Department of Computer Science

The need for properly educated software engineers grows every year, and, unfortunately, the subject is not addressed to any depth in most undergraduate computer science programs. However, it is our position that it is premature to create an undergraduate software engineering program separate from computer science. We are convinced, nevertheless, that certain of the most significant software engineering topics can be incorporated into the existing framework of a computer science program. At the Air Force Academy we have an approach to do this that we have been evolving over the last eight years. And because we have been accredited during this time we feel confident that the incorporation of software engineering into a computer science curriculum can be done within the guidelines of recognized computer science curricula. While we do not expect this approach to produce a fully qualified software engineer, the graduate will have a good basis for competence in large scale development and an appreciation of the major issues in software engineering.

It is clear that many people consider a preferred prerequisite for an Masters of Software Engineering program to be an undergraduate computer science degree [BRAC88, FAIR87, MILL87]. While some people have trimmed this broad requirement to more specific skills, there is obvious agreement that computer science and software engineering share much undergraduate core knowledge, including the whole area often referred to as "programming in the small" [FORD87]. It has also been noted that desirable extensions to a typical computer science program to facilitate a masters of software engineering might include knowledge of the basics of: management science, communication, engineering fundamentals, and an application area [JENS79, FREE87].

The obvious question is: what are the implications for undergraduate software engineering from what we know about the masters level software engineering curriculum? We believe the reason for software engineering programs currently existing at the masters level is one of historical evolution rather than necessity. The software engineering discipline came very late in the game and was more easily added as a masters level specialization rather than a new undergraduate discipline. When you examine a program such as the Software Engineering Institute's Masters of Software Engineering program, it becomes apparent that many topics from such a program could indeed be presented at an undergraduate level [ARDI88]. Of course, the difference between undergraduate and graduate coverage of the topics is one of depth and rigor. Our experience over the last several years has demonstrated that it is possible to migrate many of the software engineering topics into an undergraduate computer science program.

But the next question is: when should this migration stop? That is, do we opt to move everything from the masters to the undergraduate level and create a new undergraduate discipline called software engineering? Our response is "no." At this time there are too many factors weighing against the definition of software engineering as a totally separate discipline. The first concern is that the core of computer science is a necessary precursor to the understanding of software engineering. Because of this large degree of commonalty, a complete break between the disciplines seems unreasonable. But what about the prospect of having two years or three years of a computer science program which breaks into software engineering at the junior or senior level [LEHM87]? Our view is that there really are three coexisting (if not equally important) pillars of the computer science discipline: hardware aspects of computation, software development in the small, and software development in the large, and all of these should be supported by theoretical foundations. This leads us to believe that software engineering is not just an application, like database or graphics, but is central to the computer science discipline. Therefore, it is not reasonable to try to pile software engineering on top of the computer science core but rather it should be included in the computer science core--that is, software engineering is central enough to be required of all computer science students.

Other issues which influence our argument against an independent software engineering discipline include the immaturity of the software engineering discipline and the lack of appreciation among students for the problems that software engineering is trying to solve. Software engineering is only 20 years old and is lacking in principles and underlying theory of its own. Most of the principles and theory we attribute to software engineering are a carry over from computer science. Eventually it may be true that software engineering can stand on its own, but currently a software engineering program that doesn't draw on the foundations of computer science would tend to be very soft in the same sense that MIS programs tend to be soft when compared to computer science programs. Some work has been done to illustrate why software engineering topics tend to be difficult for undergraduates [RICH87]. One of the issues highlighted was the lack of understanding the younger students have of the "software crisis" because their only extensive experience is with small problems. As a result, it becomes very difficult to motivate students to study and to assimilate the many facets of software engineering. It is because of this problem that Wang Institute and others desired industrial experience for any student applying to their Masters program. This "work place maturity" will be hard to provide to the undergraduate in the normal four year academic experience.

Finally, other issues that concern us about the software engineering undergraduate degree are the difficult interdisciplinary nature of software engineering and the diverse application domain. These and the preceding concerns lead us to question the credibility of such a program. Would industry truly accept such a graduate without a significant apprenticeship? While we are unwilling to suggest that software engineering should breathe an undergraduate life of its own, we see software engineering no longer being relegated to a masters level course of study. As previously indicated, we are convinced that the substance of software engineering (at an undergraduate level) can and should be part of every computer science program. Further, we believe this migration of software engineering into the undergraduate computer science program can be done now, within the bounds of current computer science program specifications.

Our evolutionary approach to the downward migration of software engineering topics has several facets. First, we plant the seeds by introducing software engineering concepts in the first course of the computer science major. Second, we introduce tools and methods, plus reinforce the basic software engineering concepts in many of the courses along the way. Third, we draw the topics of software engineering together with the required computer science topics in a two semester capstone software engineering sequence. Finally, we require a variety of courses which are somewhat tangential to the area of computer science but which play a role in software engineering, such as management, communications, and engineering design. Of course this approach requires department software development standards be created and used across the curriculum. It also requires significant coordination of topics, concepts, and tools for consistency and complete coverage. The other issues that we have found to be significant are scale, analysis and design experience, development environments, faculty development and coordination, and methodologies [RICH88].

In conclusion, we believe that the time has come to introduce software engineering into computer science programs as one of the major themes. We feel strongly about this since our majors quite often find themselves in software engineering roles immediately after graduation and since industry-wide there is a deficit of software engineering trained individuals. Because there is already a growing shortage of trained computer scientists (much less software engineers), this deficit will not ever be satisfied by the output of Masters of Software Engineering programs. Although we feel strongly about the place of software engineering in the computer science curriculum, we are opposed to the development of a separate software engineering undergraduate program. The time may eventually come for such a program but currently many factors work against moving too quickly in this direction. Our approach will establish a cadre of software engineering literates who will be able to enhance their software engineering skill on the job or in further education. With such a computer science degree background the current software engineering masters programs could go even further in teaching advanced software engineering topics. This partial change in philosophy of undergraduate computer science programs will not be free, but an evolutionary approach will ease the process significantly and leave flexibility until the software engineering discipline matures.

REFERENCES

[ARDI88] Ardis, M.; "The Design of an MSE Curriculum;" *Working Draft for the 1988 SEI Conference on Software Engineering Education*; April 21, 1988.

[BRAC88] Brackett, J., Kincaid, T. and Vidale, R.; "The Software Engineering Graduate Program at the Boston University College of Engineering;" *Lecture Notes in Computer Science, Number 327*; Springer-Verlag, New York, 1988.

[FAIR87] Fairley, R.; "Software Engineering Education: An Idealized Scenario;" *Software Engineering Education-The Educational Needs of the Software Community*; Springer-Verlag, New York, 1987.

[FORD87] Ford, G., Gibbs, N. and Tomayko, J.; "Software Engineering Education, An Interim Report from the Software Engineering Institute;" *Technical Report CMU/SEI-87-TR-8*; May 1987.

[FREE87] Freeman, P.; "Essential Elements of Software Engineering Education Revisited;" *Software Engineering Education-The Educational Needs of the Software Community*; Springer-Verlag, New York, 1987.

[JENS79] Jensen, R. and Tonies, C.; *Software Engineering*; Prentice-Hall, Englewood Cliffs, NJ, 1979.

[LEHM87] Lehman, M.; "The Software Engineering First Degree at Imperial College London;" *Software Engineering Education-The Educational Needs of the Software Community;* Springer-Verlag, New York, 1987.

[MILL87] Mills, E.; "The Master of Software Engineering Program at Seattle University after Six Years;" *Software Engineering Education-The Educational Needs of the Software Community;* Springer-Verlag, New York, 1987.

[RICH87] Richardson, W.; "Why is Software Engineering So Difficult;" *Software Engineering Education-The Educational Needs of the Software Community;* Springer-Verlag, New York, 1987.

[RICH88] Richardson, W.; "Undergraduate Software Engineering Education;" *Lecture Notes in Computer Science, Number 327;* Springer-Verlag, New York, 1988.

Questions in Planning Undergraduate Software Engineering

David Alex Lamb
Queen's University, Kingston, CANADA K7L 3N6

Abstract. *This position paper proposes questions to consider in planning curricula for undergraduate software engineering education. We should specify the audience for such curricula, plan a process for deciding what material to incorporate and how to keep it up to date, plan for flexible packaging of curriculum materials, and begin to think about how we might deal with political issues in establishing such curricula.*

1. Introduction

The goals of the 1989 SEI Workshop on an Undergraduate Curriculum in Software Engineering are to examine the draft recommendations of the ACM/IEEE Task Force on Curriculum to determine how best to include software engineering concepts within that framework, and to examine how a separate undergraduate software engineering curriculum might better serve the needs of the software engineering community. This paper outlines other issues I believe we should consider first.

2. Audience

The first questions to ask are those that set broad goals and guidelines for the more detailed analysis that might follow. The ACM/IEEE proposal (CACM, January 1989) focuses too soon on the "content" of the discipline. I think the most important question is

1. What is the "audience" for an undergraduate software engineering degree?

Since comparisons with computer science programs are inevitable (and probably even appropriate), two closely related questions are

2. What is the "audience" for an undergraduate degree in computer science?

3. How do the needs of the two audiences differ?

By audience I mean to focus on the students themselves. It would make sense also to focus on those who might hire the students. These two possibilities each push us in a particular direction in the "education versus training" debate; at the moment I'm favoring the education side.

In the past, various people have proposed the following possible audiences for undergraduate computer-related education.

- Those who want some basic understanding of how to use a computer. At many universities this includes most students; typically we give them short courses (often taught by the computing center) or perhaps a "computer literacy" course.

- Those primarily interested in some other discipline, but who wish to be the computing specialists within that discipline. Typically these people take a major in their primary discipline with a computing minor or medial, but some take little or no computing as undergraduates and learn computing "on the job" or by getting a Master's degree in computing.

- Those people who want to become software practitioners (or programmers or "software specialists" or any of dozens of other possible career descriptions). The ones I meet who fit this category typically major in computer science but concentrate as much as we let them on "practical" courses; I believe they are most of those currently enrolled in computer science programs. However, other students who fit this description enroll in management information systems programs in business schools.

- Those people who want to go on to graduate school in computing. They typically major in computer science but are more willing to tackle "theoretical" courses.

I believe a software engineering program should emphasize the needs of the "practitioner" audience, while a computer science program should emphasize the needs of the "graduate" audience. Such programs might overlap considerably, especially at the high level of abstraction of a calendar description, but might differ considerably in emphasis and in details of course content. For example, a computer science course on algorithms and data structures might emphasize design and analysis of algorithms and data structures that support those algorithms; a software engineering course might emphasize modularity and hiding the representational details of several different implementations of an abstract data structure.

I do not want to draw too fine a distinction between "theoretical" and "practical" material. An engineer applies principles to solve problems; those principles may well take a mathematical or "theoretical" form. However, a scientist views a theory as a way of explaining or organizing a body of knowledge, while an engineer views it as a tool to help solve problems. An engineer must also tackle problems for which there is no firm theoretical basis; her education should prepare her to deal with such problems. A scientist is more likely to study a subject "for its own sake".

This leads to another way to focus on distinctions between computer science and software engineering: look for analogies with other science/engineering pairs. I have suggested elsewhere that we should try to think of the computer scientist / software engineer / programmer distinction by analogy with the physicist / electrical engineer / technician distinction. Typically we train technicians in a particular technology, and expect to retrain them every few years; such training typically takes much less time than the four years of a typical undergraduate degree. We teach engineers a collection of fundamental principles, expected to last a lifetime, and a body of current practice, representing the current implementation of those principles; we expect engineers to keep up with their field on their own. We give scientists a deeper understanding of a body of knowledge that includes some of the principles, more-or-less ignore details of current practice, and expect them to add to the body of knowledge during their careers. Of science students who do not go on to graduate school, we typically expect that their education might prepare them to learn the principles of several corresponding engineering disciplines reasonably quickly, but they would (at least initially) be less adept at solving problems in those disciplines than those with engineering education.

To refine a description of the intended audience, we should look more closely at the "practitioner" category, and contrast it with the others. For example, we might ask what different kinds of systems different classes of practitioners might work on, then ask what methods might be appropriate for each such class.

3. Curriculum Materials

Once we know the audience for a curriculum, we can start to think about what material such an audience would need to learn. At the early stages we still need to think about the needs of the audience; as we become more detailed, we can begin to focus on specific content. Thus the first question about materials should be

4. What should be the balance between computer-specific topics and a more general education?

Some advocates of traditional liberal arts degrees claim such programs teach how to think, and produce people who are more flexible and adaptable than those from more specialized programs. I occasionally see newspaper or magazine articles that say some employers prefer to hire people without computing degrees (such as mathematicians, or liberal arts graduates, depending on what the employer is looking for).

Computing changes rapidly — more rapidly than many other disciplines. Thus an important question to ask ourselves is

5. What methods should we follow to make sure curricula remain up-to-date?

It is inappropriate for some central source to bring forth new curriculum guidelines every ten years. Instead, we should try to agree on procedures that people in different places can use independently to keep their own curricula up to date. For example, we could provide an exhaustive list of topics that software engineering curricula might cover, perhaps including guidelines on what depth of coverage were appropriate for each topic (and perhaps also for each separate audience we identify). Individual schools could list the topics each of their courses cover, and to what depth, and decide for themselves if they were leaving out anything important or concentrating too much effort in one area.

I have many suggestions on specific software engineering content, but a full list would be too long for a short position paper. The most important suggestions are not particularly technically deep:

- Teach practitioners to modify existing software. Many principles of good practice are best learned by reading good examples. Also, much of good practice aims to simplify maintenance, and makes no sense to students who write only small throw-away programs.

- Expose practitioners to working in teams, through group assignments and projects. This helps drive home the need for precise communication, and helps motivate material on specifications and design documentation.

- Teach practitioners how to communicate with each other. Many schools teach writing across the curriculum, rather than in special writing courses, so students learn the forms of communication appropriate for their own disciplines.

We need to find ways to help individual instructors incorporate such suggestions into what they are currently doing. For example, we should find effective ways to share "artifacts" that students can study, maintain, and extend.

4. Packaging the Curriculum

Regardless of what any particular group of people (official or otherwise) might say, different universities will want to package the material into courses in their own way. However, many will want guidance on how to adapt to new proposals, especially if we make any radical departures from what has happened in the past.

6. How can we best meet the conflicting goals of flexibility and guidance for universities trying to set up their own curricula?

Providing "curriculum modules" might help. Such modules summarize and outline the various topics, and provide lists of possible textbooks and reading materials. Different people can package such material into different courses. However, a curriculum module the size of a two-semester course sequence isn't particularly useful; we should aim for much smaller "curriculum fragments" covering a few lectures' worth of material, which we organize into "curriculum modules" of a few weeks' duration, and perhaps even "curriculum subsystems" lasting a term (or more).

Ideally, we should also outline several ways to package the materials into full curricula. Perhaps people from several universities might outline how our curriculum descriptions fit their own existing curricula, so that people trying to adapt their current courses can have several different examples to work from. Ideally, we should provide at least one model curriculum as a guideline. Computing changes rapidly; ideally, such a model curriculum should outline a core course and prerequisite structure that we expect would not change rapidly, even if the contents of the courses evolved. Peripheral courses would cover topics whose presence is less stable. There should be a correlation between core and required courses, and between peripheral and elective courses, but the two pairs of terms might not be synonymous.

5. Politics

Introducing a software engineering curriculum will require facing several obstacles that I think it is fair to call "political". Initially, people might need to establish "software practitioner" tracks within existing programs. In many jurisdictions you cannot include the word "engineering" in the name of a degree program unless an appropriate professional engineering body accredits the program. We should be flexible about whether the program is part of the school of engineering, or the school of business, or anywhere else it might fit.

For the moment we should avoid bogging down in discussions of certification and accreditation. People who favor certification and who oppose it can still find common ground on educational matters. I think good curricula would need to become reasonably well established and accepted before we would have a sound basis for denying jobs to people who didn't have the credentials.

6. Summary of Questions

The following summarizes the questions I posed earlier in the paper.

1. What is the "audience" for an undergraduate software engineering degree?

2. What is the "audience" for an undergraduate degree in computer science?

3. How do the needs of the two audiences differ?

4. What should be the balance between computer-specific topics and a more general education?

5. What methods should we follow to make sure curricula remain up-to-date?

6. How can we best meet the conflicting goals of flexibility and guidance for universities trying to set up their own curricula?

7. Summary of Suggestions

The following summarizes my suggestions for continuing the discussion of undergraduate software engineering education.

1. Treat the computer scientist / software engineer / programmer distinction by analogy with the physicist / electrical engineer / technician distinction.

2. Refine a description of the intended audience for undergraduate software engineering education.

3. Define procedures that people in different places can use independently to keep their own curricula up to date.

4. Teach practitioners to modify existing software.

5. Expose practitioners to working in teams.

6. Teach practitioners how to communicate with each other.

7. Share "artifacts" that students can study, maintain, and extend.

8. Provide at least one model curriculum.

9. Outline a core course and prerequisite structure that we expect would not change rapidly, even if the contents of the courses evolved.

10. Avoid bogging down in discussions of certification and accreditation.

Undergraduate Software Engineering Education: Prospects and Opportunities

Jeffrey A. Lasky
Rochester Institute of Technology

Introduction.

At a recent NSF sponsored conference on undergraduate software engineering education[1], Mary Shaw, speaking as Professor of Computer Science at Carnegie Mellon University, expressed the view that, at this time, an undergraduate curriculum was premature. She argued that first principles were lacking, the field was ill-defined, and in the near and intermediate terms course content would unacceptably be based on best current practice. From the classical view of undergraduate education, one must agree with these arguments.

However, we believe that the magnitude of the software crisis, as repeatedly described by industry and by government, suggests that a timely, pragmatic response is due from the academic community. This note suggests several possible approaches for providing software engineering (SE) instruction at the undergraduate level. Incorporated is the point of view that SE in its entirety is distinct from the computer science (CS) discipline.

In the near term, we foresee SE course offerings (continue) to emerge from within existing computer science and computer engineering programs. The content and focus of these SE courses will naturally reflect the history and mission of the offering academic unit, as well as the experiences, perceptions, and biases of its faculty. Down the road, we expect separate software engineering degree programs to be developed.

Approaches discussed are:

1. A SE concentration within existing CS programs

2. A SE concentration within existing Computer Engineering programs

3. An upper division SE sequence for A.S. transfer students.

4. New undergraduate degree programs in software engineering.

---

[1]National Science Foundation Faculty Enhancement Program, *Undergraduate Instruction in Software Engineering Education*, Rochester Institute of Technology, Rochester, NY, June 18-21, 1988.

In addition, we advance a suggestion for universities to offer a common computing core, upon which degree programs in computer science, software engineering and systems engineering could be based.

Recent developments.

Pronouncements from the establishment.

Over the next few years, software engineering topics and courses will begin to become commonplace in undergraduate computer science curricula. The recent ACM Task Force Report on the Core of Computer Science [1] identified software methodology and engineering as one of nine subareas within the computer science discipline. It is then reasonable to expect that Curriculum 88 will include, to some extent, recommendations for software engineering course work. Similarly, the incorporation of software engineering in undergraduate computer science programs will probably be a future CSAB review item. Supporting these academic forces will be strong demand from industry and government for graduates with an understanding of the system development process and with system building skills.

Heightening tensions on campus between computer science and software engineering.

Since CS departments are the most likely immediate sources for SE courses, thoughts about undergraduate SE cannot ignore the sudden and dramatic four year national decline in undergraduate CS enrollments. In the near term, this state of affairs may well accelerate the appearance of new SE course offerings, since there will be slack computer science faculty resources available for SE course development. However, if this trend should continue for another three years or so, prospects for serious undergraduate work in SE within CS programs may actually be diminished. Real possibilities exist for the smaller CS programs to be absorbed into more stable academic units while the larger CS programs suffer budgetary cuts. In both cases, slack faculty resources begin to vanish.

It is not too farfetched to envision some CS faculty interested in SE becoming frustrated and renegade if the dark scenario should come true. In that case, a market-oriented, enterprising Dean might very well invest some reallocated budget in a software engineering group positioned outside of CS.[2]

---

[2]One such case is known to have already occurred.

Expectations.

1. SE concentrations offered by CS programs.

Deep in their hearts, and rightfully so, many CS faculty interests lie in the science of computing and in building interesting things, rather than in the engineering of large systems destined for use outside of the computing community. So, a question arises as to the willingness and commitment of the faculty to offer a deep SE concentration which is not disguised computer science. This is a tricky issue, one which has caused some of us much aggravation and soul-searching. Nevertheless, CS faculty, in the aggregate, will probably do more to advance undergraduate CS instruction than any other group.

2. SE concentration offered by computer engineering programs.

This option is driven by the current and anticipated future demands for systems engineers and system integration specialists. Virtually all practicing systems engineers note that they acquired their systems engineering background and skills from job experience rather than from formal course work. A view of computer engineering as an integration of both hardware engineering and software engineering should provide the right perspective and academic climate. A key problem here will be the definition of a neo-systems engineering discipline, based on the post-computer era and concerned with hardware/software systems embedded within larger concerns.

3. Upper division SE transfer program.

This approach potentially offers institutional advantages, as well as program flexibility at reduced risk. First, it could provide a net increase in computing program enrollments and so reduce institutional resource pressures. In a good outcome, enrollment loses suffered by existing programs due to internal transfers would be more than offset by attracting new students who would otherwise not pursue a four year degree. Second, it provides an attractive measure of flexibility, since the degree could be awarded by computer science, by computer engineering or by a new academic unit dedicated to software and/or systems engineering. In fact, since the risk associated with offering only upper division courses is substantially lower than offering an entirely new program, the transfer program approach may be the most reasonable way to begin to offer degrees in SE. Graduates of two year A.S. degree programs in Computer Science, Computer Information Systems, and Engineering Science are all possible candidates for a B.S. in SE.

4. New four year degree program in software engineering.

Practically speaking, this approach is likely to emerge short-term only under one of two sets of circumstances. One is where a successful SE graduate program has built an SE infrastructure which can be used to support an undergraduate SE program. The other is the transmutation of existing theory weak CS programs into SE programs. It is not entirely unreasonable to view such CS programs now as underdeveloped SE programs.

Unification.

In varying degrees, all of the above will be impeded or completely blocked by institutional conflicts and politics. As a matter of effectiveness and efficiency, we suggest the formation of some meta-academic unit which would offer a common, university-wide two year computing core. Students would then specialize and pursue degree programs in either computer science, software engineering or systems engineering. The one time institutional costs to form such a unit would be very high, but the interacting forces of institutional pressures for instructional efficiency, advantages of faculty synergism, and market demands, all support this type of approach. At the risk of personal peril, it is suggested that the university's School of Engineering appears to be the most sensible host.

References.

1. P. J. Denning et al., "Computing As A Discipline", *CACM*, (24,3), Jan, 89, pp. 9-23.

POSITION STATEMENT

SOFTWARE ENGINEERING UNDERGRADUATE EDUCATION

James R. Lyall, J. G. Agrawal

Embry-Riddle Aeronautical University

William Thomson (1824-1907) is considered by many to be the father of modern Engineering as a discipline. It was practiced under the names of Natural Philosophy, later Applied Physics, and still later as Engineering, with a continually expanding array of sub-disciplines. One may look upon the emergence of Electrical Engineering from the "purer" study of Applied Physics, the study of "things physical", much in the same way that we now observe the discipline of "Software Engineering" emerging from Computer Science, the study of "things logical". It is important, many feel it is crucial, that academia quickly address this emerging discipline in its own right if there are to be competent practitioners of what will, in all likelihood, be the dominant technology of the twenty first century.

Aerospace Industry Involvement

The Radio Technical Commission for Aeronautics (RTCA, a U. S. organization with representation from government and industry, dedicated to the advancement of aeronautics) and the European Organisation for Civil Aviation Electronics (EUROCAE) have concerned themselves with seeking sound technical solutions to problems involving the applications of electronics and telecommunications to aeronautics. They have been largely successful in resolving such problems through the publication of a comprehensive library of specifications and guidelines, reflecting mutual agreement among effected parties.

On March 22, 1985, RTCA published its report number RTCA/DO-178A [1]: Software Considerations in Airborne Systems and Equipment Certification, prepared by RTCA's Special Committee 152, after coordination with EUROCAE. The document describes techniques and methods that may be used for orderly development and management of software for airborne digital computer-based equipment and systems. Software produced using the described techniques and methods is assured to have the important characteristics necessary for meeting the users' and regulatory agencies' requirements for airworthiness -- that software be traceable, testable, and maintainable. Specific areas covered in the report are:

1. Overview of Software-Based System Development and Approval.

2. Guidelines for Software Development, Verification and Validation.

3. Software Configuration Management and Quality Assurance Disciplines.

4. Documentation.

5. Residual Software Error Probabilities.

The details in the report cover subjects such as:

- Software Life Cycle
- Software Requirements Analysis and Specification
- Software Design
- Software Implementation
- Verification and Validation
- Testing
- Quality Assurance
- Configuration Management

Industry Needs Identified

The RTCA report mentioned above [1] clearly raises the need for a rigorous educational program for the workforce that will teach techniques and methods, such as those recommended by RTCA, which constitute general requirements for the production of reliable, maintainable software. These techniques and methods form the basis of the discipline which has come to be known as "software engineering". None of the undergraduate computer science programs in the nation include software engineering topics to adequate depth. Some computer science programs, like ERAU's CS (With Aviation Applications) program, have a three credit hour course on software engineering. Three credit hours provides an opportunity for students to be superficially exposed to most of the relevant topic areas, but it is not sufficient to cover all the techniques and methods implied by the RTCA report.

Current undergraduate curricula for degrees in computer science do lip service, at best, to the above mentioned topic areas. A joint task force of the Association for Computing Machinery (ACM) and Institute for Electrical and Electronics Engineers (IEEE) has recently issued a draft recommendation that advocates a strong software engineering component (which will address some of the above mentioned topic areas discussed in the RTCA report) in the undergraduate computer science degree. The difficulty is that the current undergraduate degrees in the nation require over 128 semester credit hours which have already been defined. A strong component in software engineering will require between 30 and 45 semester credit hours of courses not presently in those curricula.

Is "Software Engineering" a Misnomer?

An issue which begs for a quick resolution is the use of the word "Engineering" in the discipline name. The American College Dictionary defines "Engineering" in terms of the "...application of the knowledge of pure science such as physics, chemistry, biology, etc..."; whereas Webster speaks more generally: "1. The putting of scientific knowledge in various branches to practical uses." Webster would entertain a [software] engineering curriculum which included the required semester hours in software engineering topics at the expense of many of the natural sciences: physics, chemistry, statics, dynamics, thermodynamics, materials science. The American College dictionary and, one might fear, ABET would not. This paper will take the broader perspective:

(1) The "scientific knowledge" appropriate to a software engineering degree includes the abstract sciences of discrete mathematics, systems theory, and operations research.

(2) The broad foundation in the basic physical sciences, including the much of the higher mathematics attendant thereunto, found in every other accredited engineering curriculum, would be largely superfluous and therefore negotiable.

University Involvement

Embry-Riddle Aeronautical University has placed a high priority on an undergraduate curriculum project: "Evaluate the Feasibility of an Undergraduate Software Engineering Program," as a strategic goal within the five year plan of ERAU, Prescott. The study will collect data from industry and government, collect data from other universities about what they are doing or planning to do in the software engineering area, design a draft document for the curriculum, develop a list of support lab equipment and software, support staff needed, and a training program for faculty who wish to participate in the software engineering degree program.

(1) This study will produce an outline of an undergraduate curriculum which, by virtue of the methodology used in its formulation, will produce graduates who are prepared to fill a vitally important and currently unanswered need in the aerospace industry. The requirements on airworthy software are generally as stringent or more stringent than the requirements of other software applications areas; therefore, the curriculum outlined, or a downscaled version thereof will, be appropriate for development and delivery at institutions which do not necessarily have the aerospace orientation of ERAU.

(2) The resulting economic evaluations will provide a basis for academic administrators to make the necessary decisions with regard to the development of the course of study and offering of the degree.

(3) The curriculum outline produced will provide a starting point for discussion and further refinement resulting from its circulation in the academic and professional communities.

(4) The results will be polarized due to the assumptions outlined above with regard to the meaning of "Engineering". This polarization will undoubtedly incite serious debate over the validity of these assumptions, hopefully leading to the resolution of the pressing questions:

   a. Is "Software Engineering" an appropriate appellation for the emerging discipline which has assumed the name, and which the proposed curriculum is intended to serve?

b.   What accrediting agency should be responsible for a curriculum such as the one which will be proposed?

c.   Is the discipline of **Engineering** to remain parochially defined as being concerned with only the application of the physical sciences, or formally broadened to include the application of the increasing body of knowledge referred to as the "logical sciences"?

REFERENCES

1.   SC-152 (Chaired by Frank C. Fickeisen, Boeing Commercial Airplane Company), Software Considerations in Airborne Systems and Equipment Certification, RTCA/DO-178A, Radio Technical Commission for Aeronautics, Washington, DC 20005, March 22, 1985.

2.   Allison Brunvand, "Call for Participation, Software Engineering Education and Training Week," Software Engineering Institute, Carnegie-Mellon Institute, Pittsburgh, PA 15213.

3.   Peter G. Neumann et al, "Risks to the Public in Computers and Related Systems," Software Engineering Notes, ACM, 11 West 42nd St., New York, NY 10036, Volume 13, No. 4, October 1988.

4.   Peter J. Banning (Chairman), Douglas E. Comey, David Gries, Michael C. Mulder, Allen Tucker, A. Joe Turner, Paul R. Young, "Computing as a Discipline: Preliminary Report", ACM Task Force on the Core of Computer Science, ACM SICGSE Bulletin, Vol. 120, #1, Feb. '88, pp 41-43.

Developing
an Undergraduate Software Engineering Curriculum within an Existing Computer Science Program

Frances L. Van Scoy
West Virginia University

Abstract. *This paper proposes an evolutionary approach for developing an undergraduate software engineering program within an existing computer science program. The proposed approach is evolutionary because of the fairly common university requirement that a new program must already have some identifiable courses, students, faculty, and other resources before it is formally approved. The approach consists of five steps and has two main goals: a gradual establishment of an undergraduate software engineering program and the introduction of key software engineering concepts within an undergraduate computer science program which now exists and will continue to exist.*

1. Change the programming language taught to entering students.

The Nature of the First Course. Before automatically deciding to change the programming language taught in the first course, we first need to decide whether the first college-level computer science course should emphasize a language.

The report of the Denning committee (1988) recommends that the introductory computing course span three semesters and be a survey with depth and rigor of the principal areas of computing. The report, however, indicates an assumption that beginning college students have secondary school work in computing, a remedial computing course, or a pre- or co-requisite course in "programming and computer tools" before taking this three-semester sequence.

I argue that the first college-level course should have a strong base in a programming language.

First, surprisingly many of our freshman students have no experience with computers whatsoever. (In spring semester, 1987, fully one half of my CS1 students said they had never used a computer for any purpose, including word processing or playing games.) For these students to appreciate the abstract concepts we'd like to present even at the freshman level they need some concrete experience. This is common in other disciplines. In physics, for example, an instructor teaching about acceleration and friction can draw on the students' experiences in driving cars (such as using the accelerator and brake and driving in mud or on ice). Also, college students enrolled in a physics course generally have already taken a year-long physics course in high school and so have already seen a presentation of some of the abstract principles of physics. Computer science deals with the world at an initially higher level of abstraction than does physics and requires some practical experience with computing before the abstract ideas of the field make sense.

Secondly, of course, many freshman students have some previous programming experience. This experience is often in a somewhat primitive language by computer science standards, such as Basic. Even if students have programmed in Pascal or a similar language they may have learned inappropriate ways of developing software. If we do not teach a language and make significant programming assignments in the first course, these students may map the concepts we present in lecture onto their faulty understanding, and it may be harder for us to encourage them to modify their ways of developing software later on.

The Benefits of Changing Languages. I suggest that if we wish to introduce software engineering concepts into the undergraduate curriculum that the language of CS1 be changed. Changing language has several benefits. If CS1 is taught in a language which students are unlikely to have used in high school, we are more likely to challenge the mindset of students with previous computing experience and also to prevent boredom. Secondly, the choice of a new language encourages faculty who teach the introductory course to update their lecture notes, handouts, assignments, and tests. Thirdly, and most importantly, a newer language such as Ada or Modula-2 has features which facilitate the teaching of certain software engineering principles, methods, and tools. This makes it desirable to modify the general content of the new course to include these new ideas.

New Concepts to be Taught. Koffman (1984) includes in the objectives for CS1'84, "to introduce procedural and data abstraction."

Brooks (1987) writes that the hard part of building software is in the specification, design, and testing of the conceptual construct of interlocking concepts of data sets, relationships among the data items, algorithms, and invocations of functions. He advocates buying rather than building software, that is, reusing already written and tested software rather than building new systems from scratch. He also advocates adoption of the metaphor of growing software rather building it and promotes prototyping and incremental development as ways of growing software.

Ford (1987) suggests the need to include programming-in-the-large with team programming in the first course.

The Denning committee (1988) recommends that "in a substantial number of labs dealing with program development, the assignment should be to modify or complete an existing program supplied by the instructor."

Bach (1989) argues that the object-oriented development method has wide acceptance in part because the method is close to the way we think.

Combining these statements, a new CS1 which serves the needs of software engineering students as well as computer science students should include:

> reusing existing software components, modifying existing components for reuse, and designing new software components for reuse

> the object-oriented development paradigm, including data abstraction and information hiding

> the incremental development paradigm

Comments on the Choice of Language. Koffman (1988) makes a strong case for Modula-2, and many of his arguments for Modula-2 also appy to Ada.

Many of his arguments against Ada are losing strength as compilers become more available, more affordable, and more efficient and as Ada-oriented textbooks are published.

Both languages lack direct support for classes with inheritance and dynamic binding of messages to objects, two principles common to object-oriented programming languages along with information hiding and data abstraction (Bach).

Smalltalk, C++, and Simula provide strong support for object-oriented programming but appear weak in other areas.

At the present time, Ada and Modula-2 seem to the be best candidate languages for CS1. While there are differences between the two languages, an individual department's choice of Modula-2 or Ada may be a financial one based primarily on availability and price of compilers. For example, at West Virginia University, an Ada compiler was already installed on a cluster of computers used by undergraduates, so Ada was the more affordable choice.

Additional Topics Suggested by Ada. The use of Ada as a first language motivates the introduction of certain concepts.

For example, Ada provides the concept of a package. Students need to be taught not only the syntax and semantics of the Ada package but also why and how to use a package in building a software system. Booch (1987a) suggests that there are four applications of Ada packages. These are named collections of declarations, groups of related program units, abstract data types, and abstract state machines.

Ada also provides tasks, essentially subprograms which can execute concurrently. Software developers need guidance in knowing why and how to use tasks in their implementations. In describing PAMELA2, his software development method, Cherry (1988) lists fifteen predefined task idioms from which he claims most concurrent systems can be built. These are the binary semaphore, bounded buffer, bounded pushdown-automaton, cyclic activity, device driver, forwarder, hybrid, monitor, parallel processor, prioritized activity, pump, state machine, service queue, unbounded buffer, and unbounded pushdown-automaton.

As a result, in order for our students to understand why to use packages and tasks, we must teach them about abstract data types, abstract state automata and machines, and so forth.

In fact, in order to use Ada properly, students must learn an appropriate software design/development method. (As Ed Berard has said so often, "Ada without a methodology is trash.") Two strong candidate methods are OOD (Object-Oriented Development), refined by Grady Booch(1987b) and Ed Berard(1985), and PAMELA2 (Pictorial Ada Method for Every Large Application) by George Cherry(1988). By learning to use a software development method, students will learn that software is something about which they can reason, and the concepts of assertions and correctness will seem more natural to them.

While it may not be appropriate to teach a formal software development method in CS1, students should be taught in an atmosphere that assumes that all nontrivial software will be developed using these or similar methods and should be exposed to many examples of software whose structure reflects the use of one of these methods.

A proposed CS1 in Ada. At WVU we are now developing an entirely new CS1 course based on the Ada language. This section of this paper reflects one proposed version of the course.

The paradigm for the course design comes from the language department. There students learning a new language first listen to and read many dialogs in the language. They are told the general meaning of the dialogs and some basic vocabulary and grammatical concepts but not enough to understand completely the exact meaning of each sentence. Their early use of the new language often consists of modifying phrases according to carefully chosen patterns. For most of the first course students are able to understand (from listening or reading) more examples of the language than they are able to construct (by speaking or writing).

In a similar fashion, this new course is based heavily on use of a locally developed collection of Ada subprograms and packages.

To exploit some of the language features found in Ada but not in PL/I (and also to facilitate the teaching of some software engineering ideas subtly and early) the course begins with using packages containing subprograms. By the third week of the proposed course, students will be using generic packages.

The current proposed sequence of topics is:

Unit 1 -- Using Packages

1. Using Packages and Procedures
2. Using Parameters
3. Using Declarations of Objects
4. Using Loops (loop...exit when...end loop;)
5. Using Generic Packages
6. Expressions and Assignments
7. TEXT_IO
8. Conditionals
9. Loops
10. Writing Subprograms

Unit 2 -- Designing and Implementing Packages

11. Designing Packages
12. Writing Package Specifications
13. Private and Limited Private Types
14. Scalar Types and Their Attributes
15. Arrays, Records, and Access Types and Their Attributes
16. Subtypes and Derived Types
17. Using Exceptions
18. Writing Package Bodies
19. Writing Generic Units
20. Order of Compilation

Unit 3 -- Using Concurrency

21. Observing Tasks
22. Using Tasks
23. Writing Tasks

A relatively small unit on tasking is included in the first course in the belief that students bring to CS1 a view of the world that is essentially concurrent. We need to reinforce that view from the beginning of their formal study rather than force CS1 students to adopt a totally sequential mindset which we will painfully force them to change to a concurrent one in later courses.

In this course students are not expected to become proficient in the use of all Ada features presented. Rather they are exposed to many Ada features (and shown appropriate examples of their use) in preparation for more advanced courses.

This course emphasizes using Ada units before writing them and includes practice in modifying Ada packages for reuse.

Students will also, however, be given some practice in writing complete small software systems to give them an understanding of what comprises a complete system, to give them skill which can transfer to their use of languages such as Pascal and C in other courses and on part-time jobs on campus, and to give them a sense of accomplishment.

Finally, at least one large project is planned in which each student in a section will contribute a different software component to the project.

2. Revise the sequence of courses taken by all freshman and sophomore computer science majors.

The C1, C2, and C3 courses suggested by the Denning report (1988) appears to be a reasonable overview of the field of computer science. The laboratory experiments for modules 1 (fundamental algorithmic concepts), 4 (data structures and abstraction), and 6 (operating systems and security) require students to develop software from specifications, use existing software components in building a software system, modify software to obtain slightly different functionality, and use software tools to measure performance of sample programs.

However, the only explicit mention in the entire document of the software life cycle is in the description of subarea 6 (software methodology and engineering). I suggest that a lecture on software engineering paradigms including the classic waterfall life cycle, prototyping, and 4th generation techniques similar to the content of chapter one of Pressman's book (1987) be added early in module 1 of C1. In addition, constant reference should be made throughout all three courses of how material currently being presented in lecture or studied in laboratory relates to these software engineering paradigms.

3.   Add software engineering electives to the computer science major at the junior and senior levels.

Three of the first software engineering electives to add to the computer science major are: formal software development methods, a software projects course, and a survey of the topics in the core of an MSE program. These courses should be developed with two goals in mind: to give students skills which will be useful on the job and to prepare students for graduate work in an MSE program.

The course in formal software development methods should emphasize Object-Oriented Development and PAMELA2 and should build on the concepts introduced in the freshman and sophomore years that software can be reasoned about and that software is built from well-understood components.

A software projects course similar to the one developed by James Tomayko (1987) should be offered. This course gives students practice in working with a software system which is too large for one person to build.

After the students have gained some experience with a large project and teams, they then can enroll in a survey course, The Software Life Cycle. This course will provide an overview of the topics in the six required courses for a Master of Software Engineering program developed at the SEI (Ardis, 1989). The course will begin with lectures on software operational issues and an overview of the software life cycle and then proceed through the topics of the MSE curriculum.   The goals of the course are (1) to give students familiarity with the major concerns, terminology, and concepts of software engineering and (2) to illustrate the relevance of material learned in the computer science curriculum to software engineering.

Other electives can be developed according to faculty interest.

4. Split the current computer science major into two tracks.

When sufficiently many upper division courses have been developed, enough faculty are available to support the program, and enough students are interested in the program, the computer science major can be split into two tracks, one emphasizing traditional computer science and one emphasizing software engineering. Depending on local administrative policies, these two tracks could become two majors, sharing the introduction to software development using Ada course for first semester freshmen and a modified version of the 3 semester survey advocated by the Denning committee for the remainder of the freshman and sophomore years and diverging (except for electives taken from the other track or major) in the junior and senior years.

The software engineering track or major will require several junior or senior level software engineering courses. Recommended electives include upper division computer science courses as well as oral speech communication, technical writing, business (organizational theory and management, business law), and political science (U.S. federal government).

5. Develop distinct BS CS and BS SE programs.

With the experience gained from the years spent in implementing the previous steps and with increasing knowledge and consensus in the software engineering community, an entirely separate degree program in software engineering can then be proposed and justified.

It may be appropriate at this time to introduce a new three semester survey for software engineering freshmen and sophomores to provide an overview of the field of software engineering.

Bibliography

Ardis, Mark A.*The Design of an MSE Curriculum.*working draft for SEI Faculty Development Workshop, January 1989.

Bach, William W. *Is Ada Really an Object-Oriented Programming Language?* Journal of Pascal, Ada & Modula-2, March-April, 1989, Volume 8, Number 2, pages 18-25.

Berard, E. V. *An Object Oriented Design Handbook for Ada Software.* 1985, EVB Software Engineering, Inc.

Booch, Grady *Software Engineering with Ada, second edition.*1987a, Benjamin/Cummings.

Booch, Grady *Software Components with Ada: Structures, Tools, and Subsystems.* 1987b, Benjamin/Cummings.

Brooks, Frederick P. *No Silver Bullet: Essence and Accidents of Software Engineering.* Computer, April 1987, pages 10-19.

Cherry, George W. *PAMELA2: An Ada-Based, Object-Oriented, 2167A Compliant Design Method.* 1988, Thought**Tools, Inc.

Denning, Peter J., Douglas E. Comer, David Gries, Michael C. Mulder, Allen Tucker, A. Joe Turner, Paul R. Young *Computing as a Discipline: Final Report of the ACM Task Force on the Core of Computer Science.* 1988, ACM Press.

Ford, Gary A., editor *Report on the SEI Workshop on Ada in Freshman Courses.* Carnegie-Mellon University Software Engineering Institute Technical Report CMU/SEI-87-TR-44, ESD-TR-87-207, December 1987.

Koffman, Elliot B., Philip L. Miller, and Caroline E. Wardle *Recommended Curriculum for CS1, 1984: A Report of the ACM Curriculum Committee Task Force for CS1.* Communications of the ACM, October 1984, Volume 27, Number 10, pages 998-1001.

Koffman, Elliot B. *The Case for Modula-2 in CS1 and CS2.* 19th SIGCSE Technical Symposium on Computer Science Eduation SIGCSE Bulletin, volume 20, Number 1, February 1988.

Pressman, Roger S. *Software Engineering: A Practitioner's Approach, second edition.* 1987, McGraw-Hill.

Tomayko, James E. *Teaching a Project Intensive Introduction to Software Engineering.* Carnegie-Mellon University Software Engineering Institute Technical Report CMU/SEI-87-TR-20.

Acknowledgement

PAMELA2 is a trademark of George W. Cherry, Thought**Tools, Inc.

SOFTWARE ENGINEERING IN A BS IN COMPUTER SCIENCE

Richard Louis Weis

University of Hawaii at Hilo

Abstract

This position paper outlines the rationale for and the approach used at the University of Hawaii at Hilo to further augment the ACM/IEEE computer science curriculum for software engineering considerations.

Introduction

In 1986 the author had two events coincide that provided the desire for and the opportunity to modify the ACM/IEEE computer science curriculum. First, after hearing comments of managers and key technical professionals that this curriculum fell short of meeting their needs/expectations of entry level computer programmers during a period of several years, IBM conducted a survey of opinions on specific deficiencies and a task force to analyze potential corrective measures. Second, the author had an opportunity to retire and take a position as Assistant Professor of Computer Science and Engineering in a large state university on a campus with the small, liberal arts environment.

The University of Hawaii at Hilo, in fact, would graduate its first BS in Computer Science students in 1987. The curriculum was very like the University Level Computer Science Series curriculum the author had designed and offered for IBM to its "older", non-CS programmers for the prior seven years that had elicited the comments noted earlier. Both were patterned after the ACM/IEEE recommended standard. UHH, thus, seemed a good place to design and develop some augmentation and put it into practice. IBM supported this effort financially as long as one major component was used as pilot for their own planned internal supplementation to be used with new hire CS employees.

IBM Study Results

Without all the supporting data, the author consulted (while still at IBM) with Dr. David Soldan (then at OSU) and found the IEEE function he was involved with had found similar conclusions outside of IBM. Thus, the following seemed to be reasonable considerations for augmentation:

A large, team-oriented project
Technical communications...written and verbal
Experience with a total product life cycle
More emphasis on analysis and design
Design for maintenance...and actual maintenance
Programming design, development and implementation process...ie software
  engineering and tools
Work ethics and professionalism

It was clear to the writer that this would be more than a single semester course on campus and, certainly, would be a multi-week program at IBM. On campus, in fact, this would require a willingness and an ability to alter the entire course offering philosophy while maintaining standards and commitments to the institution and declared CS major students.

UHH Actions

The following paragraphs provide some detail on the specific things which we did. Clearly, in a paper of this magnitude, we cannot cover all in complete detail. There should be an ordering by priority, I suppose, but it keeps shifting each iteration on the list.

Large Project

In the fall of 1986 we implemented a large, team-oriented project with the compiler theory course. The goals were to teach all the compiler technical materials via a project organized in a simulated corporate environment. The Chair elected to audit the course and his presence, plus the fact that the course had never been offered on campus before, eased the problem of requiring drastically different class practices. The students were required to apply for the corporate positions (resume, application and interview) and carry through all planning, implementation and support aspects to and including a final product demonstration and formal documentation.

The course was a success and has been repeated twice. The same approach has been used in two other courses (one in data base and the other in system analysis/design). The one real problem we had, of course, was teaching software engineering concepts and tools in addition to the course subject matter.

System Analysis/Design

In the UHH curriculum this course was very business data processing in flavor (nothing much on structured design methodologies........data flow diagrams, data dictionary, evaluation of module cohesion/coupling/etc) and, as a 400 level course, offered too late in the curriculum to teach about tools/techniques that would later be applied. We have since shifted to a 300 level course and made it prerequisite for compiler theory, data base and software engineering at the same time as shifting the emphasis to more contemporary software engineering considerations.

We are now able to have the students get at least one (and usually two) large project courses no matter what their concentration within the CS degree (straight CS, hardware, or software engineering). In effect, since the 300 level course does include a smaller project, they get theory reinforced with extensive application experience in multiple potential user domains.

Analysis/Design Emphasis

Whether the students enter our program via a course in Basic (offered to non-CS majors but some convert as a result) or in Pascal, we place the emphasis on analysis of problems and the structured design to the refined algorithm level. No problem is treated as too trivial to do a documented analysis and a stepwise refinement to a verifiable, pseudocode algorithm. The practice is reflected in our grading.

Laboratory Problems

We give more and larger problems and sacrifice lecture and classroom hours when/where necessary. This, too, is reflected in grading. While we give as many quizzes, the final grading is weighed to emphasize the problems solved and run on the hardware (in the introductory Pascal course, for example, we have a full problem on the average of once a week and, in total, this accounts for over 60% of the final grade). No "A" is granted unless all problems are at least designed and documented and the clear majority running correctly.

Maintenance Design

There is a bulletin board on the laboratory door and the faculty maintains the right to change program requirements up to 48 hours before any laboratory problem is due. It does not take many such changes for the students to learn to design for ease of reading and maintenance. Once a semester, and the timing is not predictable, a problem is to make changes to another's program. We tried doing this on a peer basis but that was not too good so we use one from another semester.

Big Problem Quiz

We try to have one quiz be a single problem requiring going from requirements statement to coding at least part of the modules. All quizzes emphasize thinking rather than memory. It has been a terrible faculty burden to write and grade quizzes. We have found adequate sources for the laboratory problems but, especially at lower level courses, the source materials for quizzes is inadequate for the type program and student attainment we strive for.

Co–Op Education Alternative

In 1988 we started to offer the option of delaying the CS degree by taking co-op job semester(s) in the workplace. It has enabled us to get into the curriculum a one-credit preparatory course that covers resumes, interviews, technical presentations, professionalism and related topics to anyone even considering the co-op possibility. We get most CS students to take this since it provides more in-depth experience than we get into the other courses. In 1989 we have augmented this with two more one-credit courses to treat ethics, social issues, and also, problems like security, reliability, ergonomics, etc. Taking these in smaller pieces seems less threatening to the university and students alike.

Brown–Bag Seminars

We have instituted a program of optional lunchtime seminars that attract students. The subjects and subject matter draw very heavily from the SEI modules and materials. The students get a lot out of the series and it encourages the faculty to prepare from the bibliographies provided.

Technical Communications

While this emphasis is in the project courses mainly, we do cover both written and verbal communications more often. No graduating student has left UHH without:

> Making a rehearsed, formal presentation
> Making a formal product demonstration
> Preparing a refereed technical report
> Making many peer presentations

We have used materials from other schools' programs (namely, Clemson and Vanderbilt). Teaching technical presentations by using the approaches being taught is a challenge but worth the effort. It also motivates using same for more classroom lectures.

Refereed papers is a challenge, too. We have elected as the prescribed referees: 2 CS faculty, 1 student peer, and 1 English Department faculty (this last should be negotiated ahead for the students). A real motivator for the students is having the final reports printed with some quality and available for them to take to prospective employers (we have had interviewers ask to get copies to take away).

Individual Project

In the above regard, we have each student, in at least one course, define a project of personal interest for research and implementation. They spend a lot of their own time on these, of course, and the resultant burden on faculty to advise and support and evaluate these is worth it.

Seek Opportunities

The university received a grant of money to research and propose a university-wide information/database system. We bid for the job of doing the analysis and design and made it the joint project of the system analysis/design class and the database class. The students got to interact with real customers and produce a substantial product design that is now out for procurement. This meant, of course, the two faculty had to be willing to work together and, very often, attend each other's classes and the student work sessions outside of class schedules. Both agreed, in the end, they would do so again with the next opportunity.

One compiler theory class elected to take the product of the prior class and enhance it (it was not at full function level and not very reliable....the students that built it learned more than if they had fully succeeded!). This was too good to be true and would never have been asked of them, but, having so elected, we decided to let them learn about maintenance the hard way. They did. It was.

So far we have never had two classes use "the same" project under the same circumstances. That means that every project is wholly new in major ways and the faculty must be willing and able to teach, lead and support in an environment that is unpredictable.

Results

In 1988 we had all our junior and senior level students participate in an outside achievement test and they tested well above the national averages. We had our program given a pre-accreditation review and were found deficient only in the size of the faculty and the lack of a separate discrete math course. Our university information system design was evaluated by an outside consultant on behalf of the university and was applauded.

Every graduating student has obtained suitable employment that has elected to do so. Every student who elected graduate school has been accepted to the school of his/her choice with any needed financial support.

We are a new program in a school "off the beaten path" and will have our first on-campus recruiter in CS as a result, per that employer (Hewlett-Packard), of the student we sent them that demonstrated so fully attainment of the same points listed under the IBM study noted above (IBM also offered this student a position).

Conclusion

The ACM/IEEE curriculum can be augmented with software engineering concepts, tools, and their application without degrading the CS attainment measures. It is not easy. It takes faculty effort and a team approach. The students seem to not only survive the rigor (we are rated by students as the "hard degree" on campus) but a substantial number seem to thrive on it.

Integrating Software Engineering
into an Undergraduate Computer Science Curriculum

Stuart H. Zweben
Ohio State University

Software engineering is an area that must receive prominent treatment within a computer science curriculum. A large percentage of the graduates of undergraduate computer science programs take jobs that involve software development and/or maintenance. These jobs require that the individual practice good software engineering. While the precise methods and procedures used to achieve good software products will vary from one organization to the next, there will be basic principles of software engineering on which these methods and procedures are based. An undergraduate computer science curriculum must be sure to teach these principles and, as much as is practical in the host environment, some reasonable set of methods and procedures.

Several courses in a typical undergraduate computer science program have assignments that require some form of software development. In each of these course, and for each of these assignments, there should be an enforcement of a certain amount of good software engineering discipline. Even in the first courses of the typical curriculum, there is room to improve the student's appreciation and practice of good software development skills. For example, most first courses in computer science are concerned mainly with programming, and the use of a high-level, structured computer language. Students typically have several (small) programming assignments during the term. In order to successfully complete such assignments, the student must be able to show that the program satisfies the problem statement, and this is typically done by testing the program. Yet the early courses in many computer science programs give little or no instruction to the student on the subject of software testing. While it would be unreasonable to expect the student to learn the details of sophisticated software testing methods at this stage of the curriculum, and to apply such methods to the kind of programs being developed, it is reasonable to expect students at this level to get in the habit of using some kind of systematic approach to testing their software.

There are simple, systematic testing methods that can be taught in the first courses, and built upon as the student gains more maturity in computer science.

Another feature of a modern computer science curriculum must be an appreciation for the role of design in software development, and the need to practice design prior to writing code. In order to appreciate design, a large enough project must be assigned, so that the entire project cannot easily be solved by immediately writing code. It is also useful if the student works in a team environment on such a project, thereby giving exposure to the communications and other logistics problems that will likely be encountered on the job after graduation. Most computer science programs have appropriate projects for the practice of good design and team development somewhere in their existing curricula, even if they don't have a course entitled "software engineering." A systems software course in which the students are required to write a compiler or assembler is good enough to illustrate these ideas. The design instruction must include the basic principles of good design and the major elements of one method of practicing design (e.g. structured design and analysis, object-oriented design, Jackson design, etc.). It is important that the student receive feedback on the quality of the design produced, and this requires very diligent grading of designs by the instructor and preferably the use of design reviews. The design review also has the benefit of being a major milestone in the project that takes place before the student will likely be able to write a lot of code. That is, the organization of the project assignment must include intermediate milestones where something other than the final product is turned in during the project period.

Each course that involves programming need not, and I dare say cannot, cater to all aspects of software development. The major principles of software engineering should be incorporated as they naturally fit into the kind of assignments that would be used in particular courses. Alternative methods and procedures that embody these principles should be taught to the extent that the application area is well served by a method that is different from that which was learned in another course. It would be desirable if the curriculum included some kind of capstone sequence, which would serve to broaden the student's background with respect to alternative methods, and would also serve to bring together the skills and methods (probably introduced piecemeal in earlier courses) that apply to different phases in the development lifecycle.

The use of tools to aid the student in practicing the software engineering methods that are being taught is very important. Unfortunately, these tools are not as readily available as one would like, and the discipline still suffers greatly from the lack of an integrated set of tools for use in software development. The variety of host computer systems in use exacerbates the ability to provide useful CASE software for the masses. It is expected that "tool technology" will improve over the next few years on hardware running operating systems (such as Unix) commonly used by computer science students, and computer science programs must be prepared to evolve in order to effectively utilize these emerging CASE environments. In the meantime, institutions should take whatever steps they can afford to expose their students to tools that enforce at least some aspects of the discipline of software engineering on the equipment that they are using.

At this time, I do not believe that a separate undergraduate curriculum for software engineering is the right way to proceed. A real software engineering curriculum is very interdisciplinary, and I do not think that many institutions have the talent or other resources to properly implement such a curriculum. I also think that we can make significant improvements to existing undergraduate curricula by properly incorporating good, modern software engineering skills into the courses. We will likely have a greater impact if we provide assistance and materials to our colleagues so that they can better incorporate useful projects and principles into existing environments than we will by asking them to totally redo their curricula. I am hopeful that the framework offered by the ACM curriculum task forces will allow us to proceed in an evolutionary, rather than a revolutionary, fashion.

Vol. 324: M.P. Chytil, L. Janiga, V. Koubek (Eds.), Mathematical Foundations of Computer Science 1988. Proceedings. IX, 562 pages. 1988.

Vol. 325: G. Brassard, Modern Cryptology. VI, 107 pages. 1988.

Vol. 326: M. Gyssens, J. Paredaens, D. Van Gucht (Eds.), ICDT '88. 2nd International Conference on Database Theory. Proceedings, 1988. VI, 409 pages. 1988.

Vol. 327: G.A. Ford (Ed.), Software Engineering Education. Proceedings, 1988. V, 207 pages. 1988.

Vol. 328: R. Bloomfield, L. Marshall, R. Jones (Eds.), VDM '88. VDM – The Way Ahead. Proceedings, 1988. IX, 499 pages. 1988.

Vol. 329: E. Börger, H. Kleine Büning, M.M. Richter (Eds.), CSL '87. 1st Workshop on Computer Science Logic. Proceedings, 1987. VI, 346 pages. 1988.

Vol. 330: C.G. Günther (Ed.), Advances in Cryptology – EURO-CRYPT '88. Proceedings, 1988. XI, 473 pages. 1988.

Vol. 331: M. Joseph (Ed.), Formal Techniques in Real-Time and Fault-Tolerant Systems. Proceedings, 1988. VI, 229 pages. 1988.

Vol. 332: D. Sannella, A. Tarlecki (Eds.), Recent Trends in Data Type Specification. V, 259 pages. 1988.

Vol. 333: H. Noltemeier (Ed.), Computational Geometry and its Applications. Proceedings, 1988. VI, 252 pages. 1988.

Vol. 334: K.R. Dittrich (Ed.), Advances in Object-Oriented Database Systems. Proceedings, 1988. VII, 373 pages. 1988.

Vol. 335: F.A. Vogt (Ed.), CONCURRENCY 88. Proceedings, 1988. VI, 401 pages. 1988.

Vol. 336: B.R. Donald, Error Detection and Recovery in Robotics. XXIV, 314 pages. 1989.

Vol. 337: O. Günther, Efficient Structures for Geometric Data Management. XI, 135 pages. 1988.

Vol. 338: K.V. Nori, S. Kumar (Eds.), Foundations of Software Technology and Theoretical Computer Science. Proceedings, 1988. IX, 520 pages. 1988.

Vol. 339: M. Rafanelli, J.C. Klensin, P. Svensson (Eds.), Statistical and Scientific Database Management. Proceedings, 1988. IX, 454 pages. 1989.

Vol. 340: G. Rozenberg (Ed.), Advances in Petri Nets 1988. VI, 439 pages. 1988.

Vol. 341: S. Bittanti (Ed.), Software Reliability Modelling and Identification. VII, 209 pages. 1988.

Vol. 342: G. Wolf, T. Legendi, U. Schendel (Eds.), Parcella '88. Proceedings, 1988. 380 pages. 1989.

Vol. 343: J. Grabowski, P. Lescanne, W. Wechler (Eds.), Algebraic and Logic Programming. Proceedings, 1988. 278 pages. 1988.

Vol. 344: J. van Leeuwen, Graph-Theoretic Concepts in Computer Science. Proceedings, 1988. VII, 459 pages. 1989.

Vol. 345: R.T. Nossum (Ed.), Advanced Topics in Artificial Intelligence. VII, 233 pages. 1988 (Subseries LNAI).

Vol. 346: M. Reinfrank, J. de Kleer, M.L. Ginsberg, E. Sandewall (Eds.), Non-Monotonic Reasoning. Proceedings, 1988. XIV, 237 pages. 1989 (Subseries LNAI).

Vol. 347: K. Morik (Ed.), Knowledge Representation and Organization in Machine Learning. XV, 319 pages. 1989 (Subseries LNAI).

Vol. 348: P. Deransart, B. Lorho, J. Maluszyński (Eds.), Programming Languages Implementation and Logic Programming. Proceedings, 1988. VI, 299 pages. 1989.

Vol. 349: B. Monien, R. Cori (Eds.), STACS 89. Proceedings, 1989. VIII, 544 pages. 1989.

Vol. 350: A. Törn, A. Žilinskas, Global Optimization. X, 255 pages. 1989.

Vol. 351: J. Díaz, F. Orejas (Eds.), TAPSOFT '89. Volume 1. Proceedings, 1989. X, 383 pages. 1989.

Vol. 352: J. Díaz, F. Orejas (Eds.), TAPSOFT '89. Volume 2. Proceedings, 1989. X, 389 pages. 1989.

Vol. 354: J.W. de Bakker, W.-P. de Roever, G. Rozenberg (Eds.), Linear Time, Branching Time and Partial Order in Logics and Models for Concurrency. VIII, 713 pages. 1989.

Vol. 355: N. Dershowitz (Ed.), Rewriting Techniques and Applications. Proceedings, 1989. VII, 579 pages. 1989.

Vol. 356: L. Huguet, A. Poli (Eds.), Applied Algebra, Algebraic Algorithms and Error-Correcting Codes. Proceedings, 1987. VI, 417 pages. 1989.

Vol. 357: T. Mora (Ed.), Applied Algebra, Algebraic Algorithms and Error-Correcting Codes. Proceedings, 1988. IX, 481 pages. 1989.

Vol. 358: P. Gianni (Ed.), Symbolic and Algebraic Computation. Proceedings, 1988. XI, 545 pages. 1989.

Vol. 359: D. Gawlick, M. Haynie, A. Reuter (Eds.), High Performance Transaction Systems. Proceedings, 1987. XII, 329 pages. 1989.

Vol. 360: H. Maurer (Ed.), Computer Assisted Learning – ICCAL '89. Proceedings, 1989. VII, 642 pages. 1989.

Vol. 361: S. Abiteboul, P.C. Fischer, H.-J. Schek (Eds.), Nested Relations and Complex Objects in Databases. VI, 323 pages. 1989.

Vol. 362: B. Lisper, Synthesizing Synchronous Systems by Static Scheduling in Space-Time. VI, 263 pages. 1989.

Vol. 363: A.R. Meyer, M.A. Taitslin (Eds.), Logic at Botik '89. Proceedings, 1989. X, 289 pages. 1989.

Vol. 364: J. Demetrovics, B. Thalheim (Eds.), MFDBS 89. Proceedings, 1989. VI, 428 pages. 1989.

Vol. 365: E. Odijk, M. Rem, J.-C. Syre (Eds.), PARLE '89. Parallel Architectures and Languages Europe. Volume I. Proceedings, 1989. XIII, 478 pages. 1989.

Vol. 366: E. Odijk, M. Rem, J.-C. Syre (Eds.), PARLE '89. Parallel Architectures and Languages Europe. Volume II. Proceedings, 1989. XIII, 442 pages. 1989.

Vol. 367: W. Litwin, H.-J. Schek (Eds.), Foundations of Data Organization and Algorithms. Proceedings, 1989. VIII, 531 pages. 1989.

Vol. 368: H. Boral, P. Faudemay (Eds.), IWDM '89, Database Machines. Proceedings, 1989. VI, 387 pages. 1989.

Vol. 370: Ch. Meinel, Modified Branching Programs and Their Computational Power. VI, 132 pages. 1989.

Vol. 372: G. Ausiello, M. Dezani-Ciancaglini, S. Ronchi Della Rocca (Eds.), Automata, Languages and Programming. Proceedings. XI, 788 pages. 1989.

Vol. 375: J.L.A. van de Snepscheut (Ed.), Mathematics of Program Construction. Proceedings, 1989. VI, 421 pages. 1989.

Vol. 376: N.E. Gibbs (Ed.), Software Engineering Education. Proceedings, 1989. VII, 312 pages. 1989.